Deceptive Ambiguity by Police and Prosecutors

OXFORD STUDIES IN LANGUAGE AND LAW

Oxford Studies in Language and Law includes scholarly analyses and descriptions of language evidence in civil and criminal law cases as well as language issues arising in the area of statutes, statutory interpretation, courtroom discourse, jury instructions, and historical changes in legal language.

The Legal Language of Scottish Burghs: Standardization and Lexical Bundles (1380–1560)
Joanna Kopaczyk

"I'm Sorry for What I've Done": The Language of Courtroom Apologies
M. Catherine Gruber

Dueling Discourses: The Construction of Reality in Closing Arguments
Laura Felton Rosulek

Entextualizing Domestic Violence: Language Ideology and Violence Against Women in the Anglo-American Hearsay Principle
Jennifer Andrus

Speak English or What?: Codeswitching and Interpreter Use in New York City Small Claims Court
Philipp Sebastian Angermeyer

Law at Work: Studies in Legal Ethnomethods
Edited by Baudouin Dupret, Michael Lynch, and Tim Berard

Speaking of Language and Law: Conversations on the Work of Peter Tiersma
Edited by Lawrence M. Solan, Janet Ainsworth, and Roger W. Shuy

Confronting the Death Penalty: How Language Influences Jurors in Capital Cases
Robin Conley

Discursive Constructions of Consent in the Legal Process
Edited by Susan Ehrlich, Diana Eades and Janet Ainsworth

From Truth to Technique at Trial: A Discursive History of Advocacy Advice Texts
Philip Gaines

Discourse, Identity, and Social Change in the Marriage Equality Debates
Karen Tracy

Translating the Social World for Law: Linguistic Tools for a New Legal Realism
Edited by Elizabeth Mertz, William K. Ford, and Gregory Matoesian

Deceptive Ambiguity by Police and Prosecutors
Roger W. Shuy

Deceptive Ambiguity by Police and Prosecutors

Roger W. Shuy

OXFORD
UNIVERSITY PRESS

OXFORD
UNIVERSITY PRESS

Oxford University Press is a department of the University of Oxford. It furthers the University's objective of excellence in research, scholarship, and education by publishing worldwide. Oxford is a registered trade mark of Oxford University Press in the UK and certain other countries.

Published in the United States of America by Oxford University Press
198 Madison Avenue, New York, NY 10016, United States of America.

CIP data is on file at the Library of Congress
ISBN 978–0–19–066989–8

9 8 7 6 5 4 3 2 1

Printed by Sheridan Books, Inc., United States of America

CONTENTS

1. **Introduction** 1

2. **Power, Ambiguity, and Deception** 37

3. **Police Interviewers Use Deceptive Ambiguity** 67

4. **Prosecutors Use Deceptive Ambiguity** 101

5. **Undercover Agents Use Deceptive Ambiguity** 123

6. **Cooperating Witnesses Use Deceptive Ambiguity** 147

7. **Complainants Use Deceptive Ambiguity** 169

8. **Deceptive Ambiguity in Language Elements of the Inverted Pyramid** 193

9. **The Effects, Frequency, and Power of the Government's Uses of Deceptive Ambiguity in Criminal Investigations** 221

Appendix A: Deceptive Ambiguity Created by Socio-cultural Differences 241
References 249
Index 259

1

Introduction

On July 7, 2005, the badly charred body of the former chairman of the Confederated Salish and Kootenai Tribes was found in what was left of his home after it had been torched by robbers who had apparently slit his throat. The crime remained unsolved until April 28, 2010, when Clifford Oldhorn, one of the suspected murder/arsonists, was questioned by the Lake County, Montana, police. By that time Oldhorn was 21 and like far too many on his reservation he had managed to get only an eighth-grade education. Oldhorn confessed to attempted robbery and to witnessing the murder, explaining that after the victim refused to tell them where his money was hidden, his three named accomplices started to beat and stab the old man and then set the house afire. Oldhorn told the police that because he couldn't bear to see his friends beating and torturing the victim, he fled the scene as the others began their attack and later from a distance he could see the house in flames.

After Oldham confessed that he was involved in the attempted robbery, the prosecutor led him to understand that he had been given immunity for his cooperation in solving the case. Even though Oldhorn made it clear that the murder and arson took place after he had opted out of participating in it, the Lake County Attorney's Office then charged him along with the three other young men with deliberate homicide. For unclear reasons, the charges against Oldhorn's accomplices were then dismissed without prejudice, leaving him to face the murder charge alone. At that point quite predictably he decided to stop cooperating with the police.

Before his trial in 2011, Oldhorn's attorney moved to have an evidentiary hearing to try to get Oldhorn's purported confession to the murder suppressed, but the judge rejected the motion. At trial, the jury deliberated for only ninety minutes before finding Oldhorn guilty. After the judge sentenced him to 100 years in prison, his attorney appealed the judge's earlier decision to reject his request for an evidentiary hearing.

The case eventually worked its way up to the Montana Supreme Court (DA 11-0709) which subsequently ruled that the judge should have held an evidentiary hearing that could have clarified the nature of Oldhorn's confession. The original trial judge then reversed himself and ruled that the confession had not been given voluntarily and recommended a new trial. The prosecutor appealed this ruling but the Supreme Court once again ruled that Oldhorn's confession was not given voluntarily because it contained improper influence, adding, that any direct or implied promise, however slight, may be involuntary. The Lake County Attorney objected, saying that before the trial took place, he had offered Oldhorn two alternatives in writing: (1) that if he wasn't involved in the homicide he would not be prosecuted for collateral crimes, and (2) if he was involved in the murder, his cooperation would be viewed favorably in any subsequent proceedings. Concerning the prosecutor's offer the Supreme Court ruling said that the state's interpretation of the letter would have required Oldhorn, who was 21years old and had an eighth-grade education, to discern between the terms, *collateral crimes* and *acts which would constitute accountability* in the context of a felony murder case, where Oldhorn's participation in an attempted robbery formed the basis for a deliberate homicide charge, calling this "a distinction not readily apparent even to those trained in the law."

This last clause is significant because the court recognized the use of the prosecutor's institutional power of using deceptively ambiguous language with a layperson. This finding may seem a bit unusual because power reigns supreme in the legal arena and it can be difficult for courts to admit when that power is abused. At the same time, however, when interacting with lay subjects, representatives of the law also have both the power to be clear and unambiguous as well as the power to be obscure and incomprehensible. The question is whether this power is accompanied by the intention, willingness, and skills needed to be clear and unambiguous. The State Supreme Court in the *Oldhorn* case found that the prosecution had used its institutional power to deceive the suspect, and although it did not directly accuse the prosecutor of using ambiguity in a deceptive manner, it left the door wide open for that interpretation.

The legal arena is a type of temple where its high priests often use language in ways that are foreign and incomprehensible to their subjects. The fields of medicine, economics, religion, education, and the academic world (regrettably, linguistics is also on this list) are equally capable of inflicting ambiguous language upon outsiders. What may seem unusual about the ultimate decision in the *Oldhorn* case is that the Montana Supreme Court recognized this as an important issue.

Clifford Oldhorn's case illustrates several problems that can take place in the intersection of language and law. One problem stems from the inherent power of representatives of law to use ambiguous and potentially deceptive language as they communicate with their powerless and unsophisticated suspects, in this case a relatively uneducated member of a minority population. Another problem is found in the procedural power of the lower court to reject the defense attorney's effort to have an evidentiary hearing in which he could express his need to clarify the language used by both the police interviewer and prosecutor. It was fortunate for Oldhorn that the Montana Supreme Court finally was able to uncover these problems and do what it could to provide a remedy. But this solution led to another problem. By that time Oldhorn had remained in prison for four years of his young life and still had to face one more trial in which it would be possible for the deceptive ambiguity to be recognized and repaired.

It is difficult to challenge the accusation that suspects and defendants sometimes are deceptive, untruthful, and able to distort the facts when they appear before police and prosecutors. When they deal with the legal institution, their oppositional interactions can lead to threatening, accusatory, and otherwise unpleasant situations that heighten their need to be defensive, even to the extent of using deception. But their deception is not the only deception that takes place. Relatively little has been said about the ways that deceptive ambiguity is used by police interview suspects, and by prosecutors as they question defendants, and undercover agents as they covertly tape-record their conversations with targets during sting operations.

Intentionality

Deception is widely understood as speakers' intentional efforts to cause their receivers to misperceive something that is not the truth (Coleman and Kay 1981; Zuckerman et al. 1981, Robinson 1996). Galasinski (2000: 19) takes issue with this definition of deception, pointing out that there are many deceptive utterances to which the criterion of truth or falsity do not apply, citing passive deception (Handel 1982), deception by omission or secrecy (Bok 1982), and deception by silence (Hopper and Bell 1984).

Galasinski concludes, correctly I believe, that neither falseness of the message nor omission and silence adequately define deception. He argues that deception can be the product of a subset of compliance-gaining strategies that manipulate hearers to achieve a preferred version of reality without even realizing they are doing so.

Searle (1983: 84–85) distinguishes intentions from prior intentions. He cites shifting gears while driving a car as one example of how some actions are spontaneous without a previously formed intention. His second example is that Oedipus intended to marry Jocasta, even though when he married her he did not have the intention of marrying his mother, which is what happened (101). Searle's third example was that of a dentist. A dentist knows that drilling a patient's teeth will cause pain, but he does not have the intention of causing pain and if the patient experiences no pain, the dentist does not apologize or feel that he somehow has failed. Searle adds that there is not a close connection between intention and responsibility. For example, we hold people responsible for acts that they did not intend, such as reckless driving that causes accidents.

I propose that the act of deceiving can be viewed in a similar way. There are times when deception is intentionally created and times when it is unintentional. In either case speakers are responsible for that deception. This book explores examples of both types of deception created by ambiguity, some which were very clearly intended and others in which the speaker's ambiguous language may not have intended deception but nevertheless had the same effect on suspects, defendants, and undercover targets.

Ambiguity

It is also widely understood that expressions conveying more than one possible meaning are ambiguous. That is, listeners may perceive meanings that the speakers did not intend to convey. The speakers may not have intended for the receivers to perceive the wrong message, but that's what can result. This is particularly true of ambiguous language that deceives their receivers whether or not the senders intended them to be deceived.

Police, prosecutors, or undercover agents are warned to not deceive or coerce their suspects, defendants, and targets, for if they are shown to have used such deception, it can disfavor the government's case and favor the case of those who were deceived or coerced. Sometimes, however, even though representatives of the government may avoid outright lying or any other obvious means of deception, they can manage to find other more subtle and less noticeable ways to capture their subjects planning a crime or admitting to having committed one in the past. To accomplish this they can make use of ambiguous statements or questions that cause their subjects to interpret those ambiguities in ways that the representatives of law can then use against them. This can only mean that they used ambiguity deceptively, whether intentionally or not.

I take the position that deception is created in two ways. In the first way, speakers can create deception intentionally by applying the common definition of deception, including lying, camouflage, secrecy, or omission. In the second way, speakers can produce the impression that they themselves are not being deceptive, but rather it is merely the speakers' language that causes their hearers to misperceive through no fault of the speakers. The fact that ambiguity is so common in everyday uses of language helps speakers argue that they did not create it intentionally. Somewhat similarly, it is not uncommon for disputants to hide their differences behind the expression, "it's just a matter of semantics" in the effort to remove intentionality as the cause of a problem and replace it by blaming that familiar villain called language.

As noted previously, deception is commonly considered intentional while ambiguities are often excused as mere unintentional mistakes, gaffes, or performance errors (Buller and Burgoon 1996). Perhaps an overreliance on Grice's cooperative principle of conversation (1975) leads people to believe that ambiguity is simply an unintentional speech performance error. The cooperative principle outlines four maxims, simplified here as:

- be truthful; do not say what is false or lacking in evidence
- be as informative as required, but not more than is required
- be relevant
- be brief and orderly while avoiding obscurity and ambiguity

The cooperative principle leads to powerful and unconsciously held assumptions that can cause participants to believe that their conversations are mutually beneficial and cooperative even when they are not.

In contrast, the implicit value of the cooperative principle is not often in force during police interviews, prosecutorial examinations, and undercover operations, where representatives of the law can define cooperation of their subjects as agreement to their guilt. The oppositional, adversarial, inherently noncooperative interactions of police interviews, courtroom exchanges, and undercover stings provide an opportunity to stretch, ignore, or even violate the common perception of conversational cooperation. One important way representatives of the government encourage cooperation is by using ambiguity.

During investigations of criminal behavior it makes no difference whether the representatives of the law intentionally use ambiguity to deceive. If their ambiguous statements even suggest their subjects' illegal intentions, the unwary listeners can produce responses that have the same force as admissions of guilt. In undercover investigations, the government's use of deceptive ambiguity is clearly intentional, best illustrated by covertly tape-recorded conversations in which camouflaged deception is an accepted practice that is acknowledged, encouraged, and promoted by government regulations. When prosecutors question suspects and defendants, however, they must be careful to not appear to be coercive or to elicit involuntary responses, for the use of deception is generally frowned upon by the court. They sometimes are able to do this, however, by using various types of ambiguity that can deceive their listeners. If this effort is called to their attention by opposing lawyers or by judges, they can use the excuse that it was merely their language that deceived their listeners. The question of responsibility for such deception can therefore be shifted from the speakers' intentional or unintentional deception to that of the mere careless ambiguity of the expressions they happened to use. Representatives of the government can claim that it was not their fault that listeners did not understand their ambiguities. This book describes fifteen interactions showing how the police, prosecutors, and undercover agents used ambiguity, whether intentionally or not, to deceive their listeners.

Solan (2012), who addresses the use of insincerity by lawyers (including prosecutors) provides an important exception to the paucity of attention given to deception used by representatives of the law. Solan points out that even though lawyers are not allowed to lie, they "are given special license to be insincere to the extent that would ordinarily violate social norms" (488). Lawyers are trained to be simultaneously truthful and insincere, largely because their role as advocates for their clients sometimes causes them to frame their points insincerely in ways that cause their listeners to let down their guard and forget that they are dealing with an advocate. This suggests that it can be important to describe what *sincerity* means. Standard desk dictionaries define *sincere* with words such as "free of dissimulation and adulteration, marked by genuineness, honest, true, and unfeigned." In his discussion of speech acts Searle (1983: 9) explains that we express certain illocutionary states with intentional propositional content that includes a sincerity condition that corresponds with that intentional state. The exception to this is when speakers dissociate themselves from their speech acts, such as uttering the proposition on someone else's behalf. His example is "it is my duty to inform you of X" when the speaker doesn't really want the hearer to do X. Although Solan does not express it this way, it would appear that insincerity is a type of deception. However morally questionable this may seem, it is the standard and apparently sanctioned product of our advocacy system. If lawyers have the special license to deceptively use insincerity that would ordinarily violate the social norm, we can hardly be surprised that police, prosecutors, and undercover agents may feel the same way and adopt deceptive insincerity in their interactions with their suspects, defendants, and targets.

The general public may be unaware that US police officers have permission to deceive by giving false information to their suspects as they interview them. For example, they are authorized to lie about what other witnesses and suspects have told them, about the evidence they have found, and other matters. Police can use other forms of deception as well, including ambiguous questions that lead their suspects to believe that they were responding to something that is different from what they think it to be. Police are not allowed to lie on the witness stand, although there are reports that his has happened (Cloud 1994; Slobogin 1996). During undercover operations in which the government arranges meetings with targets suspected of being willing to commit crimes such as bribery or soliciting murder, the agents representing the legal institution also are authorized and encouraged to deceive.

This book does not deal with outright lying used by government representatives. Instead, its focus is on the subtler type of deception used by police, prosecutors, and undercover agents—deceptive ambiguity. Motives for them to use deception appear to be their need to establish convincing evidence that the individuals with whom they talk are predisposed and motivated to commit the crime, that these individuals intended to do what they did, and that they are inculpating themselves voluntarily without coercion or other undue influence.

When testimony of believable witnesses or other reliable information that supports criminal charges provide clear and compelling evidence of a crime, suspects are usually convicted. But not all cases are that clear and simple, especially those in which the investigations rely on language evidence collected by police during their interviews, by prosecutors during trials and hearings, and by agents during their undercover operations, all of which rely heavily on an ability to elicit convincing inculpatory language from their suspects, defendants, and targets. Often this effort produces smoking gun evidence that helps their efforts bring a conviction, but sometimes the purported language evidence that provides such smoking gun evidence is ambiguous, and sometimes that ambiguity is the product of deceptive practices used by government representatives.

Interpreting Ambiguous Language

A great amount of power is justifiably accorded to society's institutions, including the institution of law, which helps its representatives use or interpret instances of language ambiguity in ways that support the government's efforts to convict. Anyone who has witnessed the participation of court interpreters at trials and hearings knows how fallible the interpretations can be between the spoken English used in the courtroom and its perception and use by those who speak second languages and those who communicate non-orally through American Sign Language. Unless care is taken to avoid ambiguity, this same fallibility exists during exchanges conducted entirely in English between representatives of the law and their suspects, defendants, and targets. Interpretations made by representatives of the legal institution can be shown to be fallible when more contextualized information exists that can clarify the ambiguity found in an individual and decontextualized smoking gun word, phrase, or utterance.

Since such interpretations are subject to rigorous analysis, an issue in some criminal law investigations is focused on whose interpretation of ambiguous expressions can most accurately reflect the language evidence represented in police interviews, trial testimony, and undercover tape-recordings. Even though it is dangerous to leave ambiguity unresolved or inferred, many law cases reach their conclusions in spite of such ambiguous evidence. If these ambiguities are not resolved, the legal process is left with a possible alternative—to allow interpretations to be made based on the understandings of a hypothetical "reasonable person" used as a legal standard (Tiersma 1999: 79; *Black's Law Dictionary* 2004: 2004; Kreedens 2015: 277). And how do reasonable people such as jurors interpret ambiguous expressions? They base their judgments on inferences that can fall short of being determinative.

Linguistic analysis of ambiguous language evidence can help replace the jury's need to make such inferences. The first step is to identify ambiguous passages upon which the jury's inferences can be made, for what may seem transparently clear to one person may be totally opaque to another. This is further complicated by the fact that such ambiguity is often not manifested merely by a word or expression used at a particular moment during the interaction. Even though much of linguistic analysis of ambiguity focuses on individual utterances such as words, phrases, or sentences, discourse analysts try to discover the patterned holistic meanings found in the ways individual words, sentences, and speech acts combine together in what Kecskes (2014: 13) represents as a "third space," which is not the isolated sum of its components but instead is a qualitatively different contextualized entity.

Most linguists agree that when language is ambiguous, the overall context of the message helps make the meaning clear. Even the US Supreme Court recognized the importance of contextual meaning in *King et al. v. Burwell, Secretary of Health and Human Services, 576 U.S. 2015*, decided June 25, 2015. The court ruled that the disputed expression in the Patient Protection and Affordable Care Act, "an exchange established by the state," must be read in its context and "with a view to its place in the overall statutory reading." The Court therefore ruled that the meaning of the expression used in this Act was clearly revealed in its overall context, and the contextual intention of the drafters of this law overrode the efforts of opponents in this case to wrench the disputed, isolated expression from that overall context.

As the fifteen cases in this book point out, determination of clarity and ambiguity begins with the speech event that participants believe (or are led to believe) they are in. The speech events of police interviews and courtroom trials have at least a surface transparency to most participants, while undercover operators intentionally and deceptively camouflage the speech event as something other than what it really is. Since camouflaged undercover operations are sanctioned law enforcement procedures, they by definition contain intentionally deceptive ambiguity. But can we also expect to find deceptive ambiguity in the transparent speech events carried out by police interviewers and prosecutors as they question defendants in court? Based on actual police interviews and prosecutors' questioning at hearings and trials, this book provides some answers to this question.

After linguists identify the speech event, the second step is to recognize how this speech event directly affects the participants' language that conveys their schemas about what is going on, ultimately causing them to say what they say. Participants bring to the speech event their own schemas, meaning whatever knowledge, attitudes, cultural background, and beliefs they have had in the past that they now believe to be relevant to the emergent, current speech event. It is rare that participants will reveal their schemas performatively, but these can be recognized by what they talk about and how they say it. The fact that conversations are by definition cooperative (Grice 1975) reduces the participants' chances of recognizing ambiguity because their own schemas lead them to understand what any ambiguity must mean even when they may begin to feel that something is odd about what is occurring. When this happens, it can be socially awkward to validate the other participant's topic with expressions like, "Oh, now I see that we're talking about," and it would be impolite to challenge the other participant's topic by saying something like, "Wait a minute, you're tricking me. I thought we were discussing something else." Participants' own schemas are often revealed by the topics they bring up, the responses they make to the other speaker's topics, and the speech acts they use.

After identifying the speech event and being aware of the participants' schemas growing out of it, the analyst then pays attention to agendas revealed by the topics the participants introduce and by their responses to topics introduced by others. It is not difficult to recognize the predictable agendas of police, prosecutors, and undercover agents, but it is crucial to identify the agendas of suspects, defendants, and targets, because these reveal important clues about their predispositions, intentions, motives, and voluntariness.

To further their own agendas, the speakers' uses of speech acts can be useful. For example, it is important to determine whether certain speech acts such as apologizing, promising, offering, requesting, and agreeing are uttered felicitously, for if they are not, they can't serve as acceptable representations of those speech acts. Such analysis can shed important light on the legal issues of intentionality and voluntariness. In some critical exchanges, the absence of certain speech acts can be as important as their presence. It is equally important to analyze the speech acts of the police, prosecutors, and undercover agents, for they can be produced ambiguously and even deceptively.

Representatives of law sometimes use conversational strategies that also can be deceptively ambiguous. The task of officers of the law predisposes them to find evidence that will persuade future triers of the fact that their suspects, defendants, and targets are guilty of the crimes charged. Persuading people to do something is perfectly acceptable language activity, but efforts to persuade can be questioned when certain conversational strategies are used under the broad umbrella of legitimate persuasion. Such strategies include using ambiguity when clarity is expected, blocking efforts of the other party to respond, asking simultaneous multiple questions, scripting the listener to give a desired response, and by otherwise contaminating the official record to make it look criminal (Shuy 2005: 13–29). The legal requirement of a subject's voluntariness can be questioned when the representatives of the law use deceptively ambiguous conversational strategies.

Most criminal law cases begin with the discovery of perceived smoking gun evidence that is usually found in the smallest discourse elements—the words, phrases, and sentences used by suspects, defendants, and targets, especially when the government representatives reinterpret, misinterpret, or wrench such words and grammatical expressions from the overall discourse context in which they occur. Since smoking gun evidence closely relates to the important legal issues of predisposition, motive, and intentionality, it is very important to analyze such language evidence within the entire discourse context in which it appears. The *Oldhorn* case mentioned earlier illustrates how the prosecutor deceptively selected isolated evidence from the entire discourse and reinterpreted it in a way that produced a conviction.

Although this book is about the way the police, prosecutors, and undercover agents use deceptively ambiguous language, this is not the way legal language conventionally has been analyzed and discussed. For one thing, a majority of the studies of legal language have focused mostly on written text rather than the spoken word and they almost always have concerned the problems that laypersons have in understanding what the legal arena communicates in writing. Secondly, studies of ambiguity for the most part have related to words and grammatical constructions rather than to the larger discourse elements such as the speech events, schemas, agendas, speech acts, and conversational strategies, where ambiguity also resides. Third, studies of deceptive ambiguity have been carried out primarily on the language used by suspects and defendants but, strangely enough, not on the way it is used by the empowered representatives of the legal institution.

The linguistic analyses in this book identify the ways representatives of the legal institution use deceptive ambiguity in three different types of settings:

(1) when the police use their transparent institutional power to interview suspects in custody;
(2) when prosecutors use their transparent institutional power to question defendants and witnesses during courtroom interactions; and
(3) when undercover agents, cooperating witnesses, and complainants camouflage their institutional power as they covertly tape-record their conversations with suspects who they believe have committed a crime or are predisposed to commit one in the future.

The motivation for powerful legal institutions to use deceptive ambiguity may not be totally clear, and it is not possible to delve into the minds of the police interviewers, prosecutors, and undercover agents to discover their explicit intentions. Their language, however, sometimes provides important clues that give reasons to suspect intentionality, especially after ambiguous language occurs and is not subsequently clarified by the most powerful participants in the exchanges who have that responsibility.

There are also occasions in which neither the powerful participant nor the less powerful individuals even recognize the resulting ambiguities. In such cases linguistic analysis can help reveal these for the benefit of later listeners such as judges and juries.

AMBIGUITY IN WRITTEN LANGUAGE

Most of the past concern about the relationship of language and law has focused on trying to make written language unambiguously clear to the non-legal community in matters of statutory language, contracts, jury instructions, and the warning labels that accompany commercial products. Mellinkoff had much to say about the problems created by written legal language in his monumental *The Language of the Law* (1963), but even before he wrote that book he had already discussed the legibility of legal contracts (1953). Since that time, Levi and Walker (1990), Solan (1993), Tiersma (1999, 2010), and many others have further demonstrated how linguistic analysis of written text is important, while Felsenfeld and Siegel (1981) among others have made practical suggestions to enable jurors to better understand the instructions that judges read to them. Charow and Charow (1979), Nieland (1979), Schwarzer (1981), Severance and Loftus (1982), Sontag (1990), Tiersma (1995a, 1999, 2001); Dumas 2000 and others have produced important research about jury instructions. In the early 1990s linguists also analyzed the lack of clarity in commercial warning labels related to product liability cases (Shuy 1990, 1993; Dumas 1992). Evidence of linguists' increasing interest in legal language has subsequently led to the formation of academic associations such as The International Association of Forensic Linguists and The Law and Society Association. Even more recently Oxford University Press has launched a scholarly book series called *Language and Law* to disseminate the increasing amount of research on this topic.

Despite this growing interest in legal language, there is some evidence that many of the semantic and syntactic differences that exist between written legal language and ordinary written language are not significant enough for them to be considered totally different languages. Tiersma made this point in his seminal article, "Some Myths About Legal Language" (2006), which he had discussed earlier in his book, *Legal Language* (1999). He found the main differences to be in law's specialized vocabulary, with some minor differences in syntax, but he concluded that these are not sufficiently adequate to consider written forms of legal language significantly different from the everyday written usage. He concluded that except for a specialized, professional lexicon, law's written language usage is similar to the ways other important social institutions communicate with outsiders, and regardless of law's priestly power, practitioners use it clearly enough on most occasions. It should be noted, however, that at the time Tiersma wrote this he did not address the issue of language comprehensibility in its larger discourse context that includes the examination of written speech events, schemas, agendas, and speech acts.

AMBIGUITY IN SPOKEN LANGUAGE

Serious problems of comprehension that distinguish institutional written texts from everyday spoken language are abundant in something other than specialized, technical vocabularies. This book is a search for that "something," and a major difference from previous studies is that this search takes place in the spoken language evidence found in selected interviews, hearings, trials, and undercover investigations carried out by police, prosecutors, and undercover agents rather than in the written language evidence found in documents such as statutes, pleadings, contracts, warning labels, and the written instructions that judges usually read aloud to juries. Spoken language races right by listeners faster than written language and therefore is in many ways more susceptible to misunderstandings created by ambiguity, whether or not it is intentionally deceptive.

The language evidence of police interviews can be located in the official records kept of them. The best evidence can be found in tape-recordings of the entire interviews. Next best are accurately written transcripts of whole interviews, not just parts of them. Without these there is no good way to assess police interviewing procedures. Police self-reports of their interviews and conversations with suspects can be questionable at best for they omit far too much linguistic information. In one of the cases discussed in this book the police provided neither a tape-recording nor a written transcript of the police interview. Another police interview was only partly tape-recorded. In another, a tape-recorded police interview was ignored at trial. In contrast, records of spoken or written language evidence of courtroom examinations and undercover operations are often preserved for later inspection and analysis. These records of verbal interactions found in recorded police interviews, prosecutorial examinations, and undercover operations allow for the discovery of possible uses of deceptively ambiguous language. And when deceptive ambiguity is discovered, this allows for the possibility that representatives of the legal institution used their power to deceive, sometimes intentionally.

Spoken legal evidence consists of the concurrently produced language interactions of lawyers, defendants, undercover agents, suspects, and targets that are located in the same context at the same time. It can reveal evidence of ambiguity by all participants as these speech events take place. The prosecutors' intelligence analysis depends heavily on their skills of discovering and unpacking any ambiguity that exists and determining the extent to which it is deceptive.

Language Power

The search for deceptive ambiguity begins by recognizing that the legal institution is endowed with great power, for in order to have and maintain an orderly society it is necessary to have powerful laws and a powerful administration of those laws. Chapter 2 briefly reviews some of the major research on power and describes how the institution of law is rightfully endowed with the power that guides and controls members of a society. This book does not suggest that this power is misplaced but, rather, that we should understand some of the ways it enables those who hold that power to use it. Much of the time this power works smoothly and efficiently to protect innocent citizens from becoming victims of crimes, but sometimes it also can be misunderstood, misdirected and misused.

The discovery of this misunderstanding and misdirection begins by understanding the power endowed to social institutions. The power held by the legal institution is similar to the power given to other institutions and those who represent them, including institutional representatives in the fields of medicine, military, government, law, and to an extent even the institutions of education and family.

Institutional power is often most evident in the discourse produced by the participants. For example, those endowed with power have the right to determine the speech events that, once identified, can influence the less powerful actors' resulting schemas. The speech event and schemas then govern the participants' agendas—introducing and sequencing topics that in turn are supported by the speech acts that are used within those topics, and help explain the more powerful participants' use of conversational strategies such as interrupting or blocking what the other speakers are trying to say and sometimes even usurping their turn-taking rights. This use of power during interactions with nonpowerful subjects also provides them with a license to create and use ambiguity without censure, whether or not it is intentionally deceptive, as well as the right to interpret the ambiguous language used by less powerful actors in whatever manner they choose. As the cases in this book demonstrate, representatives of powerful institutions begin their interactions with power to use language in these and other ways.

Language Ambiguity

As chapter 2 points out, we most easily recognize language ambiguity in its smallest forms. Words are perhaps the most common sources of ambiguity, with ambiguous grammar a close second. Even though lexicon and grammar may provide critical ways to produce conversational confusion, the ambiguity caused by the participants' perceptions of the speech events in which they find themselves has scarcely been recognized. Nor have ambiguities growing out of the participants' schemas and speech acts, which are closely associated with their conflicting perceptions of speech events. Ambiguity growing out of participants' agendas, which are made up of the topics they introduce and the responses they make to the topics of others, also has not received much attention. Nor has ambiguity been fully recognized in the ways powerful speakers' potentially deceptive conversational strategies can persuade less powerful listeners to adopt the appearance of the powerful person's points of view. The forms of language ambiguity discussed in this book are illustrated by how they are used not only in camouflaged undercover investigations where one might expect it, but also in the transparent interactions that take place in police stations and courtrooms, where law's already abundant institutional power would not seem to require it.

Language Deception

Unfortunately, the story of power doesn't end with ambiguity, for ambiguity often creates deception. Deception is widely understood as the intentional effort to cause receivers to misperceive something that is not the truth (Coleman and Kay 1981; Zuckerman et al. 1981; Robinson 1996). Galasinski (2000: 19) takes issue with this definition of deception, pointing out that there are many deceptive utterances to which the criterion of truth or falsity do not apply, citing passive deception (Handel 1982), deception by omission or secrecy (Bok 1982), and deception by silence (Hopper and Bell 1984). Galasinski concludes, correctly I believe, that neither falseness of the message nor omission and silence adequately define deception. He argues that those who deceive use natural language as a subset of compliance-gaining strategies for manipulating their hearers to achieve a preferred version of reality, often without realizing they are being deceived.

It is also widely understood that expressions conveying more than one possible meaning are ambiguous and if listeners understand meanings that were not intended by the speaker, they have perceived inaccurate meanings. The speaker may not have intended for the receiver to receive the wrong message, but that's what can happen. Whether or not that deception was intentionally created, the ambiguity in the message causes listeners to be deceived into believing something that the message did not intend them to understand. In most cases, police, prosecutors, and undercover agents are not allowed to deceive their suspects, defendants, and targets because exposure of such deception can work against the government's case and favor the position of the subjects with whom they interact. Sometimes, however, even though they may avoid outright lying or any other obvious methods of deception, representatives of the government manage to find other more subtle and less noticeable ways to capture their subjects planning a crime or admitting the intention to commit one. To do this the representatives of law can produce ambiguous statements or questions that cause their subjects to interpret the ambiguities in ways that the law can then use those misunderstandings against them. This can only mean that ambiguity is used deceptively, again whether intentionally or not. Although I make no claim that anyone has the ability to get inside peoples' minds to determine their intentions, the results can be the same.

I take the position that deception is created in two ways. The first conventionally understood way occurs when the speaker creates deception intentionally by applying the common definition of deception, including lying, secrecy, or omission. The second way is to give the impression that it is not the speakers who are being deceptive but rather it is merely their ambiguous language that creates the listeners' misperception, through no fault of the speaker. The fact that ambiguity is so common in language helps enable speakers to argue that they were not using it intentionally.

It is not clear why deception is commonly considered intentional while ambiguity appears to be excused as mere unintentional mistakes, gaffes, or performance errors (Buller and Burgoon 1996). As noted earlier, perhaps it is our overreliance on Grice's cooperative principle of conversation (1975) that leads one to believe that ambiguity is simply an unintentional speech performance error. In contrast, police interviews, prosecutorial examinations, and undercover operations are far from conducive to encouraging or producing cooperative behavior. Oppositional and noncooperative interactions like these provide speakers with a broad opportunity to stretch, ignore, or even violate the cooperative principle. Whatever the reason, during these types of investigations of criminal behavior it makes no difference whether or not the representatives of the law intentionally use ambiguity to deceive. If their ambiguous statements or questions do suggest illegal intentions and their subjects do not catch the hints, their responses can give the false appearance of an admission or confession.

In some investigations, the government's use of deceptive ambiguity is clearly intentional, which is best illustrated by the government-sanctioned deceptive ambiguity created by covertly tape-recorded conversations. In other types of criminal investigations, including police interviews and prosecutorial questioning, where deception is not sanctioned as an acceptable social norm, the government's representatives are more restricted and therefore need to be very cautious about how to elicit inculpatory information in ways that do not appear to be coercive or unfair. But they still have the opportunity to use ambiguity of various types that can deceive their listeners. They can also try to shift their responsibility for this deception to the ambiguous words they use rather than to themselves as speakers of those words, saying that it was not their fault that listeners did not understand these ambiguities. Chapter 2 briefly reprises some of the major work on deception.

As in all institutions, language is a major vehicle that leads to decision making. It introduces the characteristic features of the way people write and talk, and, in spite of human efforts to be clear and specific, ambiguity is an inherent and ever-present possibility. Sometimes the actors are ambiguous without intending to be and, being human, sometimes they also can be intentionally ambiguous. Those who hold power in the physical halls of justice may try hard to avoid ambiguity, but problems can arise when suspects are questioned by the police, when prosecutors interview defendants, and when targets are unknowingly engaged in undercover operations.

Even though the legal system proclaims justice for all, it is quite possible for its representatives to use ambiguous language to deceive and mislead their subjects. Even though by definition ambiguous language is capable of conveying more than one meaning, the interactions with suspects, defendants, and targets tends to favor the interpretations made by representatives of the powerful institutions over that of the relatively powerless suspects, defendants, and targets, for, after all, prosecutors and police officers are assumed to be open, transparent, and honest at all times, which is often an accurate perception.

Unfortunately, most of the research on deception in the legal context has been one-sided, focusing only on detecting suspects and defendants who allegedly lie to the police (Vrij and Mann, 2001; Roach 2010; Carter 2014). In their efforts to detect when suspects are deceptive, many police departments have relied heavily on commercial programs such as the Reid Technique, Scientific Content Analysis (SCAN), and Statement Analysis (Adams and Jarvis 2006). There are also many books, articles, and law enforcement training programs about how to help the police determine whether or not a suspect is deceptive. For example, MacDonald and Michaud (1992) claim that signs of untruthfulness are evident when suspects provide overly brief answers, repeat the questions, hesitate, qualify, talk about their own honesty, are overly polite, and give various other types of responses.

These programs and books depend heavily on such techniques as counting and comparing the number of words, noting the use of first- and third-person pronouns, vagueness, large quantities of verb strings, negative constructions, and the use of so-called cognitive verbs. The Reid technique claims to rely on Paul Ekman's many studies of nonverbal cues to deception and asks police interviewers to notice and mark these features on a worksheet form while they are interviewing their suspects. This unrealistic task does not take into account that the research of Ekman and his associates occurs in a lab setting where the researchers view the videotapes over and over again using highly sophisticated equipment. They find that spotting nonverbal clues of deception involves the complex task that accounts for multiple expressions over the subject's entire body from head to foot. This work, called leakage (Ekman and Friesen 1969), includes microfacial expressions, hand gestures, and body movements, none of which can be expected to be observed by law enforcement officers as they quickly interview suspects face-to-face. More recent work by Ekman and his associates demonstrates how difficult it can be to detect deception in a nonlaboratory context (Ekman, O'Sullivan and Frank 1999). Some law enforcement agencies also rely on several books containing questionable information (Rabon 1992, 1994; Rudacille 1994; Walters 1996; Hall and Pritchard 1996; Hess 1997). The curious thing about such reliance is that these commercial training programs and books focus only on the deception and ambiguity purportedly used by suspects, while relatively little if any attention has been paid to how law enforcement officers and prosecutors themselves use ambiguity that can deceive those suspects.

Shuy (1998) discusses the many problems with police training programs and books about how the police can identify deceivers. The most obvious indicators that suspects are lying, however, can be discovered when they provide contradictory factual information and especially when the speakers openly contradict their own previous statements. Vrij and Granhag (2012: 115) sensibly advocate paying less attention to detecting deception and more attention to the process that explains how it can happen.

It is important to point out here that I do not claim that all police and prosecutors intentionally use ambiguity to serve their own purposes. Admittedly, the cases that attorneys have brought to my attention are ones that may or may not reflect common practice. In other publications I have discussed cases in which the police and their undercover agents have followed the FBI guidelines (Heymann 1984) that require the police to be clear and unambiguous about the illegal nature of the enterprises that are represented. For example, the most greedy and predisposed targets in the 1980s FBI Abscam investigations, Congressmen Ozzie Myers and Richard Kelly, willingly accepted bribes in ways that provided no useful defense relating to the sometimes ambiguous representations made by the agents (Shuy 2013). The cases described in this book are very different in that they describe the ways that powerful police, prosecutors, and undercover agents used deceptive ambiguity to further their primary goals of capturing criminals.

Discourse Context

Although it is not possible to reach into speakers' minds to determine their intention to deceive, the very noncooperative and adversarial nature of police interviews, courtroom exchanges, and undercover operations suggests that it is highly possible for deception to occur in such discourse contexts. Even the criminal statutes admit the possibility of the presence of intentional deception used by suspects and defendants, although they say little or nothing about the intentional deception created by officers of the court. One likely clue to deception can be found when various forms of ambiguity are repeated within the same discourse context when it could have been a simple matter to clarify those ambiguities in clearer, less ambiguous ways. Such instances give the strong impression of being the same techniques of ambiguous trickery and deceit that occur in other areas of life.

It may be comforting to think that it is rare for police, prosecutors, and undercover agents to use intentional deceptive ambiguity and assume that it seldom occurs during the administration of justice, but unfortunately this impression can be challenged. Chapters 3 and 4 describe and analyze the deceptive ambiguity used during police interviews and in courtroom examinations and chapters 5, 6, and 7 concern the ways undercover agents, confidential informants, and complainants created deceptive ambiguity. Although this deception is not always intentional, there are times that the language used by representatives of law provides a very strong appearance of being deliberate in their discourse segments of speech events, schemas, agendas, speech acts, and conversational strategies as well as when it is used in their lexicon, grammatical referencing, presuppositions, omissions, minimization, exaggeration, and withholding of information.

We often see newspaper accounts of people explaining that their verbal gaffes were "taken out of context," usually with a less than satisfactory effect. Since much is made in this book about the importance of *context*, it may be prudent to try to define what linguists mean by this term. One place to begin is with the observation by Bakhtin (1981: 343), who said of authoritative discourse that it "permits no play with its borders." It is an entirety with overlapping and interlocking parts, all of which make important contributions to the whole. The analysis of discourse evidence used here tries to incorporate the entirety of those overlapping and interlocking discourse segments by starting with the largest element, the speech event, and then working through the descendingly smaller discourse segments growing out of it—the schemas, agendas, speech acts—before reaching the even smaller language units of lexicon and grammar.

The field of linguistics, like most disciplines, began by examining the smaller language units, which was clearly a practical and logical way for the field to originate. Sounds, word parts, and words were the dominant interest of the earliest linguistic scholars until eventually they turned their attention to the generative quality of sentences, and for several decades syntax became virtually synonymous with what most linguists did. Phonology, morphology, and syntax are indeed very important units of language, but something was still lacking. I can recall a meeting of the Linguistic Society of America during the late 1950s when a prominent linguist announced rather glumly that linguists would never be able to account for structured semantic meaning.

But this despair changed during the second half of the twentieth century when linguists began to analyze the structure of meaning, although limited to the sentence level and not utterances in contexts larger than that. Other theoretical linguists soon picked up the flag and developed the science of semantics further. During the 1960s the influence of Chomsky's generative grammar (1965) had carried the study of sentence-level syntax to new important levels, but not long afterward some of his former students questioned how realistic it was to presuppose the kinds of deep structure transformations that Chomsky proposed, suggesting other ways to account for the kinds of grammatical relationships that occur at the interface between syntax and meaning. An early effort was called generative semantics, which didn't last long and was followed by the work of present-day linguistic semanticists and logicians, whose focus still remains largely at the sentence level. Although the attention given to semantics was a step in the right direction, today's linguistic semantics does not take us very far in the study of entire units of discourse. Since it became clear to many linguists that the study of language does not stop at the level of sentence meaning, many of them were not discouraged from trying to see language structure and meaning in a context larger than sentences. The driving term was *context,* which in Bakhtin's words, permits no play at its borders, including the border of sentences.

The study of context by various academic disciplines began to come together toward the end of the twentieth century when anthropological linguists, conversation analysts, sociolinguists, social scientists, and artificial intelligence specialists began to focus their attention on segments of language that were larger than a sentence. Some conversation analysts limited their notion of context to smaller chunks of text, such as turn-taking behavior, while others expanded the idea of context to describe the entire text. By this they meant the explanatory environment of discourse, a concept that has remained difficult to define, for it includes the immediate and overall context and many other things that linguistics proper had not previously taken into consideration, including the sociocultural context, the social relationships between speakers, the organizational roles in which the language was used, and other factors (van Dijk 2008). Many utterances that might be considered ambiguous can be clarified by the context in which they are spoken. Solan expressed this effectively: "Language can be construed only in context. When the context is clear to everyone, it does not feel that it is even there. Yet it is there, and it always plays a role in the interpretation of language" (Solan 2014: 7).

One possible reason why the legal institution's power to create ambiguity and deception has not received the attention it deserves is that the majority of the analyses of legal language took place before the more recent developments of discourse analysis and have therefore focused primarily on specialized lexicon with relatively little attention paid to the role of discourse structure.

This book suggests that in order to better understand the ways that institutional power operates to create deceptive ambiguity in the legal arena, it is important to look for it in the interviews, trials, hearings, and investigations in which it seems most likely to occur. The process starts with the way law enforcement officers talk as they gather their language intelligence, the way prosecutors question defendants in the courtroom, and the way undercover agents, cooperating witnesses, and complainants interact with their targets.

Most linguistics work in the past has focused on the language used by a single speaker or writer. Even the more recent studies of pragmatics usually deal with the utterances of individuals. In contrast, discourse analysis focuses on the interactive organization of all the entire units of communication from their beginning to their end. Discourse analysts study not only spoken and written language beyond sentence boundaries but also the linkage of language behavior to social practices and systems of thought, ideologies, verbal contexts and the interactive processes and problems involving more than one participant in a communicative event. For spoken language, the preference is to analyze naturally occurring language rather than invented examples about how language can, could, or might be used. Rather than being a totally separate type of analytical process, discourse analysis includes the examination of all the elements of language from small to large, including its sounds, gestures, lexicon, morphology, syntax, semantics, style, sociolinguistic variability, schemas, speech events, pragmatics, speech acts, agendas, strategies, and social context.

Various types of discourse analysis have developed over the years, including at least three approaches. Conversational analysis (or ethnomethodolgy) provides very useful information about smaller interaction units such as turn-taking behaviors, adjacency pair organization, repair activities, conversational openings and closings, and evidence of preferred and dispreferred language use (Sacks, Schegloff and Jefferson 1974). Interactional discourse analysis focuses on language in its social context, stresses the speech event in which the interaction takes place, and is concerned with the social structure of groups and their representation through language (Gumperz and Hymes 1964, 1972). Critical discourse analysis views discourse as the primary domain for ideological struggles over power and the ways social and political domination are reproduced in text and talk (van Dijk 2008). All of these approaches to discourse share the belief that context and participants' sociocultural presuppositions play a crucial role in understanding spoken and written text (Gumperz 1982: 205).

Not all discourse analyses are alike and the one used in this book does not fall neatly into any one of the three categories noted above. The discourse analysis in this book borrows from and builds upon the work of all three types of discourse analysis, but it approaches the analysis in a somewhat different way. In my previous books (Shuy 2012, 2013, 2014, 2015) I have made use of the research on speech events (occasions that determine permissible topics and ways of talking) borrowed from anthropological linguists (Gumperz and Hymes (1964, 1972); Hymes 1972; Gumperz 1982, 1990), the findings about case grammar and frames from Fillmore (1968) and Goffman (1974), the construct of schemas (also called scripts) from psychologists like (Bartlett (1932), information about agendas (topics introduced and responses to those topics) from sociolinguistics (Chafe 1972; Keenan-Ochs and Schieffelin 1976; Kates 1980), theories about speech acts (how language is used to get things done) from philosophers of language (Austin 1962; Searle 1969), and the work on conversational strategies and styles from discourse analysts (Gumperz 1982; Tannen 2005). The approach to discourse analysis in this book integrates all of the above within the conventional work of linguistics, including phonetics, syntax, semantics, and pragmatics. Throughout this book the terms *speech events, schemas, agendas, speech acts,* and *conversational strategies* appear over and over again. Following is a brief description of them.

Speech Events

In contrast to the tendency of many modern linguists to view the major role of linguistics as the effort to discover the internalized rules of language (language competence), Hymes (1972) argued that speakers' language competence is discovered not only by their grammatical competence but also by the way they use language, which he called their *communicative competence*. This type of competence refers to a speaker's success in using language not only grammatically but also in socially feasible and appropriate ways.

Included in Hymes's several features of communicative competence is the speech event in which that competence is revealed. Gumperz (1982: 9) described speech events as recurring occasions that have "tacitly understood rules of preference, unspoken conventions as to what counts as valid information and what information may or may not be included." Gumperz identified some recognized speech events such as job interviews, committee negotiations, courtroom interactions, and formal hearings, noting that there were many other speech events as well. Anthropological linguists were quick to analyze the speech events in tribal contexts (e.g., Joel Sherzer's study of Cuna speech events, 1974) and I have more recently described the structure of various speech events that served as the central evidence in criminal court cases, including business transaction speech events, courtroom testimony speech events, solicitation to murder speech events, police interview speech events, and others (Shuy 2013, 2014). Speech events frame the broadest definition of context in communication.

Speech events also have been addressed by sociologists of language. Conversation analysts like Drew and Heritage (1992: 21) do not take the context of conversation for granted but rather treat it as a determined and inherent part of the speakers' ongoing contributions, adding that participants jointly and collaboratively "realize the occasion of their talk together with their own social roles in it as having some distinctively institutional character." The result of this collaboration is that the participants are informed of the goal orientation and constraints of their conversation. These authors go on to mention examples of institutional aspects of the reasoning, inferences, and implicatures that are developed in such occasions as job interviews, medical exchanges, and news interviews (it should be pointed out that some linguists have used the term, *speech event*, in a different way to refer to other less specific things than those discussed here, such as the smaller segments in a conversation or interview).

As the cases described in this book demonstrate, it is critical that all conversational participants realize what speech event they are actually are in. This realization is like knowing the appropriate rules of the game as we play checkers or chess. Failure to know for sure what speech event we are in creates an ambiguous trains-passing-in-the-night type of misunderstanding and confusion. As the cases described in this book show, serious problems arise when one of the participants gives evidence of being in one speech event while the other participant appears to be in a different one.

Schemas

At some time in our lives most of us have found ourselves in a conversation that didn't seem to make sense until one of us realized that the other person was talking about something very different from what we thought. This happened to me one time when a neighbor named Peg telephoned me and I rambled on to her as though she was a different Peg I knew. My neighbor listened confusedly for a while before she finally figured out that I thought I was talking to someone else. My schema about who I was talking with created embarrassment for me, but no harm was done and we had a good laugh. But in the legal context things can get serious when schemas lead participants astray.

Students of the psychology of language use a construct called *schema* that specifies what participants bring to each new encounter, including their already existing information, attitudes, ideas, values, and beliefs that help them interpret and organize any newly presented information. Bartlett (1932) argued that persons' memories of what they already knew enabled them to organize and construct a mental representation of new information that was based on knowledge derived from their known and remembered past information. He called this their *schemas*. Somewhat similarly, Goffman (1974) used the term, *frame analysis*, to refer to the study of the way people organize their past experience, which approach was somewhat similar to *case grammar* as put forth by Fillmore (1968). Scholars studying intercultural pragmatics use essentially the same procedure but refer to it as sociopragmatics (Kecskes 2014: 7), in which the hearers' meaning of a lexical expression results from the interaction of information stored in their minds along with their assumptions about the situation in which the verbal exchange takes place. Over the years, other scholars have developed this construct further, but it remains a recognized mental framework that enables conversational participants to confirm their pre-existing beliefs and presuppositions about what is going on. It is equally true that schemas also can be dangerous if and when they lead to misperceptions about the new information.

Schemas are not often produced performatively. That is, people do not tend to say, "Here's my schema about what is going on here," or "Your schema is far off base."

In the psychological sense, schemas are mental constructs, not physical things. But that is not all there is to say about them, because mental constructs can be revealed indirectly through language. Predisposition to commit a crime can be recognized through the best available window to the mind—the language that reveals evidence of it. The same can be said about intentionality and whether or not actions are carried out voluntarily. Schemas of speakers' guilt can be discovered through their language that suggests their perception of the speech event they believe they are in, the topics they choose to introduce, and the speech acts they use. Importantly, speakers' schemas of their innocence can be discovered in exactly the same way. Not surprisingly, the cases described in this book demonstrate that participants' schemas originate in the perceived speech events in which they participate.

Police and prosecutors hold the obvious and predictable schemas that their suspects and defendants are guilty. Otherwise there would be no reason to interview them. This schema is a natural one for jurors to hold as well, since the defendants already have been accused and charged by powerful representatives of the law. As linguistic experts begin to analyze the language evidence in a case, they too can be tempted to hold schemas of the individual's guilt or innocence, and as readers of this book read about the cases in chapters 3 to 7, they also are likely to begin with a schema of the subjects' guilt or innocence. In the context of criminal investigations it is only natural for people to hold a schema of a suspect's guilt from the very start. Therefore it is important for everyone involved in a case to understand the communicative effect of schemas. Whether or not the participants' assumptions, presuppositions, and interpretations that characterize schemas are accurate or inaccurate, these provide useful language evidence that can work for or against them in a legal context.

Although schemas provide a snapshot to help explain why speakers say what they say, it is important to note that it is difficult for participants and later listeners alike to overcome the enduring power of their initial schemas. When our schemas about what is going on are misguided, ambiguity and confusion are very likely to follow. This is potentially as problematic for expert witnesses as it is for law enforcement officers, lawyers, and triers of the facts.

Therefore, speech events give birth to schemas and schemas then serve as a kind of explanatory bridge between speech events (where schemas originate) and agendas (where schemas are often actualized). Speech events and schemas help explain why speakers introduce their topics and respond to the topics of others. Schemas are a helpful mediator, but they could not be born without a speech event that first sets the table for them. They are a kind of cognitive glue that guides further contributions. They are a mental state that is hard to identify unless we have language evidence for them, and fortunately we often have it if we know where to look. Linguists take into consideration where the schemas are born (speech events) and how they are expressed through agendas with the help of speech acts. Their major contribution is to provide helpful clues that point to predispositions and motives.

Agendas

Linguists conventionally search for and analyze the structure of words (morphology), the structure of sentences (syntax), but as noted above, in recent years they have also begun to study the structure of larger language units called discourse. Whereas the topic of a sentence (called its grammatical subject) is linearly organized and functions as the grammatical subject of that sentence, the discourse topic is globally organized and reflects a hierarchical organization of all of the sentences within that topic (van Dijk 1977: 59). In the same way that analysis of syntax reveals the grammatical subjects of sentences, the analysis of agendas reveals the subjects of larger discourse elements. To avoid using the label, *subject*, which has already been adopted by grammar, discourse analysts often refer to these language elements as discourse topics. The subjects of sentences link small chunks of information grammatically and linearly, while the topics of discourse organize larger chunks of information contained within the entire text. Topics are the *aboutness* of those larger chunks of discourse. They are identifiable products of what people consciously wish to talk about. Thus a major structural element of discourse consists of overall agendas composed of the topics that speakers introduce. But that is not all that indicates an agenda. The responses that speakers give to topics introduced by other participants can also reveal clues to their own agendas. In short, agendas are a combination of the topics a speaker introduces and that speaker's responses to relevant topics introduced by other participants in the conversations. Responses to the topics introduced by others can reflect listeners' own agendas as they disagree, agree, ignore, or change the other person's topic.

Conversational agendas can differ from other recognized types of agendas. For example, business meetings usually have a written agenda that precedes the actual meeting event. On it appear the topics to be discussed in that meeting. With such a written agenda in front of the attendees, the business meetings can progress in an orderly fashion. New topics may be added if necessary, but the written agenda's structure usually remains the way it had been planned in advance. In contrast, during interviews and conversations, although people may have an idea of what they intend to say, their planning ahead of time is much less structured than it is for written business agendas. Various participants in conversations and interviews may have their own internalized agendas and may introduce topics about which their hearers may not even have any interest. The agendas of conversations and interviews are less prescribed than the agendas of business meetings and for this reason participants can create their own agendas more spontaneously. This spontaneity produces a problem for later listeners as they try to keep track of the rapid changes relating to the participants' individual agendas and to keep them separate from the other participants' agendas.

Although the structure of a sentence can be defined by the grammatical relationship of the words that it contains, it's still only one sentence in a large number sentences that constitute a text that creates contextual meaning at a microlevel. Since discourse agendas are much larger than sentences, they provide a macrolevel picture of the development, progress, and flow of the content of a text. A conversation, however, is the product of a series of topics, whether or not those topics are specifically identified as topics by a speaker. Although they certainly have the option to do so, speakers are not required to say, "Hey, here comes my next topic now," which would be similar to producing a performative speech act.

Most people engage in everyday conversations and interviews because they have something to contribute either through the topics they themselves introduce or through their responses to the topics introduced by other participants. Conversations (and some interviews) usually are cooperative endeavors in which the basic principles include saying what is necessary, true, relevant, and unambiguous (Grice 1975). When the analyst identifies conversational agendas, the principle of relevance is especially important and this relevance depends heavily on noticing the speakers' perceptions of the speech event and schemas on which their agenda is based.

There is no way to get into the minds of speakers to know precisely what their intentions may be, but the topics they introduce and their responses to the topics of others paint as useful a picture of intentionality as we can get. In his sense, language is indeed a window to the mind, as many psychologists have pointed out. Careful description and organization of all the topics in a conversation introduced by the speakers and all the responses to all the topics of others can produce a linguistic snapshot that is often a very useful guide for assessing the possible intentions and predispositions of the participants.

Another clue to intentionality can be seen in persistence. When speakers recycle their own topics, their intentions and predispositions are made fairly clear (Shuy 2013, 2014). In a similar way, when prosecutors continue to fail to provide clarification to defendants who request it, this provides a subtle clue to their intention to not provide such clarification. This is discussed in the courtroom questioning of Steven Suyat and Father Joesph Sica in chapter 4.

Research on Topic Analysis

Linguistic interest in discourse topics appeared as early as 1972 in Wallace Chafe's article "Discourse structure and human knowledge." In 1976 Elinor Keenan-Ochs and Bambi Schieffelin described the importance of topic in conversations between children and adults. In 1980 Carol Kates's book, *Pragmatics and Semantics: An Empiricist Theory,* stressed even more the usefulness of analyzing topics. Like Hockett's earlier work (1958: 201) these linguists distinguished between topic and comment and focused on the idea that structure is not defined by either the grammatical relations of the words nor by their semantic structure. Kates (1980: 113) wrote:

> In general, something is treated as a topic, whether it is linguistically expressed or not, when it is taken as an intentional object or structure (invariant) of some type. A comment refers to way in which that object can or should or will be or does, etc., appear or manifest itself.

Not all linguists have agreed about the linguistic structure of agendas. One of the most extensive treatments of topic was done by Brown and Yule (1983), who explored this notion in both writing and speech. They first offer the gloomy opinion that "formal attempts to identify topics are doomed to failure" (68), followed by a list of ostensible problems with topic analysis. They claimed that the analyst "is often forced to depend on intuitive notions about where one part of a conversation ends and another begins" because "every speaker-change does not necessarily terminate a particular coherent fragment of a conversation" (69). Curiously, however, they go on to identify the markers of topics, including formulaic expressions, recognizable topic shifts, content, first person pronoun as topic introducers, and paratones (changes in loudness, stress, and pauses). Four years later Schiffrin's book on discourse markers (1987) identified discourse markers as additional potential indicators of topic changes.

Brown and Yule appear to overlook the fact that an already introduced topic can be continued contiguously by several speakers in the same conversation even though it was first introduced by only one of them. This continuation does not alter the fact that the topic was introduced by the first speaker and the comments on that topic by other speakers do not change what that topic was. Even when the responder adds information or disagrees with that topic, it is still the same topic that was first put on the table. Here Brown and Yule apparently equate speaker change with topic change, which is far from an accurate representation of topic analysis as the concept is used in this book.

Another criticism made by Brown and Yule is that the identification of a topic is a paraphrase of what was actually said, similar to the way headlines are used to characterize the content of newspaper articles and chapter titles are used to characterize the content of chapters in books. Although it may be possible to do this when analyzing written topics in those genres, it is not the appropriate way for linguists to mark topics in their analysis of spoken language interactions, especially in the context of critical criminal evidence. Topics identified in spoken conversation should be represented with the exact words used by the speakers who introduced that topic. Ellipsis may be used when it's necessary to save space as long as the crucial topic words remain and the gist is not altered, but there is no other justification for changing the exact words of a speaker's topic.

Brown and Yule also discuss "speaking topically," but this expression appears to be similar if not identical to what both Hymes and Gumperz refer to as the *speech event*, a category that I consider different from topics because speakers' agendas (as reflected by the topics the bring up) are nested within the speech events in which they occur. Terminological differences such as this can easily cause confusion.

It should be pointed out that until the decade of the 1980s, none of linguists' work on topics had dealt with actual conversations used as evidence in criminal cases, which are very different from the constructed conversations that linguists often discuss and use as examples. The agendas of agents in undercover criminal conversations are singularly dominant from the start and the major topics they introduce are thus oriented and limited to those agendas. If their targets are predisposed to agree to the topic of crime suggested by the agents, there is no significant conflict in agendas. But when the targets give evidence that they are not predisposed to criminality, their agendas (composed of their topics) are often very different from those of the agents and this difference bears directly on the outcome of the law cases. Comparison of the topics introduced by targets who give no indication of being disposed to commit a crime with the topics of the agents who are trying to elicit crimes can provide one clear indication of the targets' lack of intentionality and willingness to commit the crime. To be sure, some targets who are predisposed and willing to engage in criminal topics can appear to be coy and take the conversations in circuitous routes, but more often than not the topics of both parties are in harmony.

In response to these earlier treatments of topic, I began to refine and apply the ways to use it to criminal law cases in my articles (Shuy 1982) and books from 1982 to the present. Recently I have used topic analysis as a tool for analyzing tape-recorded conversations in cases of sexual misconduct (Shuy 2012), bribery (Shuy 2013), murder (Shuy 2014), and fraud (Shuy 2015). Earlier I also have published numerous journal articles using topic analysis, including one in which the types of responses to the speaker's topics create what I called *interactive topic flow analysis* (Shuy 1990).

By physically charting the topics of an interaction, analysts can produce macropictures of the structure of entire conversations that highlight the direction of its cognitive thrust. Such analysis makes it possible to determine who dominates the topic flow even though one speaker may dominate the amount of time spent by the other speakers. That is, instead of time on task, we have topic on task. Amount of talk is not the same thing as bringing up the topic in the first place because controlling the topic selection is a form of power and dominance that can be more important than the number and length of turns of talk within it.

Topic analysis is also useful because it can visually represent the flow of conversation in ways that may not be as clear when we simply hear a recording of that conversation as it happened or even when we read a written transcript of it. Talk exchanges speed by so fast that participants are often not aware of the importance of topic structure, including who introduced the topics and the responses to those topics. However, when a conversation is electronically recorded and transcribed, it is possible to physically and visually chart a topic analysis that later users can find useful, because people tend to remember what they see better than what they hear.

Topic analysis, therefore, provides a visible record of who brought up which critical topics in a way that can map and provide a snapshot of the overall agendas of the speakers. If the most legally significant topics in a conversation are introduced by one of the speakers but not by the other participants, this fact provides an important clue about which speakers found that topic most salient. The reverse of this is equally true, because when certain critical topics relating to the investigation are not introduced by targets, this is one pretty good clue that it was not prominent in their minds. Linguists are no better than anyone else at getting into the minds of speakers, but the topics people introduce or do not introduce are the best available clues to their spoken and unspoken thoughts or intentions. Likewise, speakers who introduce topics expect their hearers to respond to them. When hearers choose to not respond, or when speakers feel that the topic has not been satisfactorily resolved, they then have the option to recycle that same topic as many times as they wish in order to try to reach its satisfactory resolution. When speakers recycle their own topics, we can be relatively certain that this topic was very important clue to their intentions.

Visually mapping speakers' introduced and recycled topics in the form of a chart divides the entire conversation (or selected important parts of it) into meaningful units of analysis that can depict strong clues to the speakers' agendas. Their agendas also can be seen in direct relationship to their responses to the topics brought up by other participants throughout the conversation. Since their responses also can provide important clues to their intentions, it can be very informative to visually represent their responses to the critical topics introduced by other speakers. An effective way to do this is to visually map two columns, with the exact words of the topic on the left side and the exact words of the responses to that topic immediately next to them on the right side. In trial testimony I have found this side-by-side representation of the conversation to be a more effective method of representing the interaction to jurors than the more common interlinear text that takes the appearance of a play script.

Linguists identify topics by several criteria in addition to the ones identified earlier by Brown and Yule. One of them is whether the listeners' respond in ways that provide evidence that they recognize that a new or changed topic has occurred. Using their linguistic tools, linguists also can identify the introduction of a new topic in several other ways. The most obvious is when a topic is introduced that does not have the same focus as that which immediately preceded it. In such cases the topic is new rather than ongoing information.

Topic introductions are often but not always accompanied by a slight difference in intonation (what Brown and Yule refer to as *paratones*) signaling that this topic is different from the one preceding it (Sacks et al. 1974). Often there also is a very slight pause in the conversation before the speaker introduces a new topic.

Several discourse markers also are available for helping to determine when a new topic occurs. These include the discourse markers "well," "you know," "but," sometimes "or," and expressions such as "one more point," "wait a second," and "let's see, what else?" One of the clearest but more ironic topic markers of a new topic is "not to change the subject, but . . ." which serves as a veiled apology for changing the topic.

One potential difficulty in marking topic changes arises when responses to the newly introduced topic amplify or add a new direction, make emendations, or add additional content to that topic. When this happens, the previously introduced topic remains the topic of discussion until such time as the topic is changed to something very different.

Finally as noted above, relevant responses to newly introduced topics indicate that hearers recognize the existence of that new topic in the way listeners respond to it. All of these topic identifications together can mark the introduction or change of topics in a conversation.

Speech Acts

After identifying the speech events, schemas, and agendas of participants, the next step is to identify and examine the speech acts that emerge naturally as discourse elements within those agenda topics. Speech acts fall under the category of pragmatics, which is the study of how meaning is transmitted and understood not by grammar and lexicon alone but by the context created by the utterance, by the purported and perceived intent, and by other factors (Austin 1962; Searle 1969; Searle et al. 1980; Cole 1978; Gazdar 1979; Searle et al. 1980; Levinson 1983; Green 1989). But even pragmatic analysis by itself is not enough to resolve all ambiguity because it conventionally deals with an immediate sentence context rather than its contextualization within the other discourse elements, including the interactants' speech events, schemas, and agendas.

Speech acts are illocutionary acts performed by speakers who use this linguistic means to communicate purported direct meanings as well as indirect meanings that go beyond the perceived semantic and syntactic structure. Direct speech acts are identified by the illocutionary force of their intended meanings, such as asserting, giving directives, committing to future action, and expressing attitudes, or by the perlocutionary effect of accomplishing the speech act as it is uttered, as in "you're fired," or "I pronounce you man and wife" (Searle 1969). A perhaps oversimplified way of describing speech acts is that they are the way speakers get things done with language. Indirect speech acts are utterances in which a speaker says one thing while being properly understood to be saying something else that has a different illocutionary force (Searle 1979: 30–57). That is, one illocutionary act is performed indirectly by way of performing another illocutionary act. The utterance, "can you speak a little louder?" serves as both a question and a request for action (Searle 1975: 60). Since some utterances may perform several speech acts at the same time, such as asserting, congratulating, and apologizing, hearers can understand which meaning is relevant by following Grice's Cooperative Principle (Grice 1989: 22–41) and by using their own schemas about how the world works.

Each speech act has its own felicity conditions, the criteria that must be satisfied if the speech act is to achieve its intended purpose. Unless these felicity conditions are met, the intended speech act does not succeed. The lack of proper felicity conditions contained in many public apologies in the news provide good examples of this (Batistella 2014). According to Searle, a felicitous apology requires the apologizer to identify and restate the past offense act, specifically identify who was offended, and take ownership of that offensive act. I would add that the speaker also describes any action to be taken to repair the offense, including not repeating it. Other speech acts have their own felicity conditions.

The number of possible speech acts is long, but those most relevant to many criminal law cases include (but are not limited to) promising, admitting, advising, apologizing, agreeing, denying, offering, and reporting. Speech act analysis has played an important role in many civil cases (Shuy 2008, 2010) as well as criminal cases (Shuy 1998, 2011, 2012, 2013, 2014).

Conversational Strategies

Speakers use conversational strategies consciously and sometimes unconsciously in order to accomplish their purposes, often to persuade but sometimes for other less honorable reasons. Hansel and Ajirotutu (1982: 87) describe these conscious strategies as "ways of planning and negotiating the discourse structure over long stretches of conversation." Some such mental strategies include positive plans about what to say as well as how and when to say it, but other strategies can verge on trickery and deceit and are often accomplished through the use of ambiguous language. These strategies, sometimes used by representatives of the legal institution are described and illustrated in Shuy (2005), and include:

- camouflaging the meaning or intent of what the speaker says;
- blocking what defendants, witnesses, and targets appear to be trying to say;
- using the hit-and-run strategy of introducing a topic that suggests illegality and then quickly changing the topic before the hearer has a chance to reply;

- contaminating the official record with cursing or references to non-related topics that suggest illegality, thus permitting these to appear on the official record;
- isolating targets from crucial information that they might need in order to demonstrate their intent to act legally;
- asking multiple questions at the same time, creating the recency effect (Miller and Campbell 1959), which causes the listener to respond to the most recent question and ignore the earlier ones;
- lying or omitting information that hearers would need to know in order to avoid inculpating themselves;
- inaccurately restating what targets have said, allowing this inaccuracy to appear on the official record; and
- scripting the target in what to say in order for the government to bring about a conviction more easily.

Although it is primarily undercover agents who use these conversational strategies to further their own goals, the practice sometimes is also used by police interviewers and, to a lesser extent, by prosecutors during their questioning at trial.

Lexicon and Grammar

It is assumed that most readers of this book are familiar with the linguistic tools of lexicon and grammar. Police, prosecutors, and undercover agents alike often use words that have more than one meaning and interpret words with more than one meaning used by those with whom they interact. Grammatical ambiguity occurs frequently in referencing, most often by using unclear pronoun and deictic references. Unless such ambiguity is clarified immediately, the legal record of the interaction can misrepresent the actual meaning it reports. As will be seen in later chapters, it is the responsibility of the powerful participant to see to it that any residual ambiguity is clarified. Failure to do so gives the distinct impression that police interviewers, prosecutors, and undercover agents are deliberately permitting the ambiguity to exist, usually to their prosecutorial advantage.

Inverted Pyramid Analysis

While all of the foregoing mentioned discourse elements are important for understanding a given interaction, I consider it methodologically useful to examine them in an orderly, sequential manner following what I have called *The Inverted Pyramid* approach in which the primary discourse element, the speech event, should be identified first. The other nested discourse elements follow in a systematic fashion because they are embedded within the previous ones and acquire much of their meaning from this derivation. The schemas and agendas, critical for determining predisposition and intentionality, grow out of and are revealed through a speaker's topics and responses. The speech acts flow from and help identify the agendas. The conversational strategies used by the government representatives further identify and reinforce their own schemas and agendas and are an important consideration for determining the voluntariness of their targets. The final analysis is made of the elements of lexicon, grammar, and phonology that are nested within all of the other discourse elements. This analytical process can be illustrated in the general form of the Inverted Pyramid shown in Figure 1.1.

Recognizing this internalized language nesting enables the analyst to see how the increasingly smaller discourse elements derive their meaning from the way they are situated within the larger ones. I use size terms here as generalizations. The speech event is clearly the largest discourse element, for it is the entire unit. Schemas also continue throughout the discourse and are intermittently revealed. Agendas also continue throughout the discourse as the meat of the speech event. The smaller discourse units include the speech acts that are used during the expression of larger discourse elements of agendas, the relatively few conversational strategies that can occur throughout, and finally the smallest discourse elements that consist of the individual phrases, words, phrases, and sounds that are critical to the case.

In summary, the preferred approach is to start the analysis by first clearly identifying the largest element of discourse, the speech event, for it determines the schemas of the participants and forecasts the agendas that are revealed by topics and responses, the speech acts used within these topics and responses, and the conversational strategies that may occur at any point throughout.

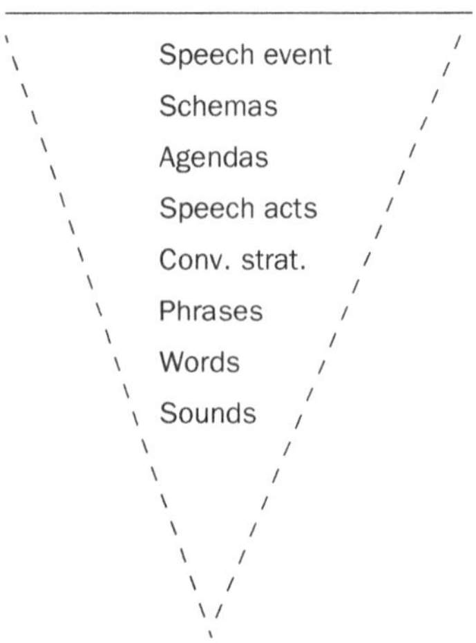

FIGURE 1.1 The Inverted Pyramid approach to analyzing discourse.

Simultaneously and intermittently within this preferred analytical sequence are the critical lexicon and grammar, the conventional elements of language that help the participants accomplish their speech events, schemas, agendas, and speech acts.

It is the nature of academics to discover the same or similar language structures and call them by different names. Kecskes's *Dynamic Model* (2014), for example, says that context comprises both prior experience and the understanding of the particular setting in which exchanges take place and that the meanings of lexicon and grammar that grow out of the information stored in the interactants' minds are based on their assumptions about the situation in which the exchanges take place. I can agree with Kecskes's analysis, but I believe the process of analyzing discourse may be better represented by *The Inverted Pyramid* approach described in this book. But Kecskes's *Dynamic Model* is similar to *The Inverted Pyramid* approach in major ways, primarily that it views discourse context as critically important to all levels of language—speech events, schemas, agendas, speech acts, conversational strategies, and lexicon/grammar. A major difference, however, is that *The Inverted Pyramid* suggests the preferred sequence in which analysis is carried out, beginning with the largest discourse element and the proceeding on down to the smallest element.

My previous work has pointed out how lawyers, prosecutors, courts, and juries have typically begun their intelligence analyses at the bottom of *The Inverted Pyramid*, focusing primarily on what is often called the smoking gun evidence that usually exists in the form of words, phrases, or sentences. Beginning an intelligence analysis at the bottom of the pyramid can prove to be unproductive because the smoking gun evidence is sometimes neutralized if not destroyed when it is contextualized within the larger discourse segments in which it is situated (Shuy 2013, 2014, 2015). When the primary focus is limited to finding the purported smoking gun evidence, it is easy to overlook the value of a holistic *Inverted Pyramid* approach. The first and most important part of the *Inverted Pyramid* is the speech event itself, for it not only gets the exchange started but also contextualizes everything that is within it and establishes the participants' resulting schemas that give evidence of their motives and predispositions. The speakers' agendas follow naturally from their perceptions of the speech event and their schemas derived from that speech event. Their agendas and speech acts not only reflect their predisposition and motives but also provide the best available evidence of their intentions. The conversational strategies used by the police, prosecutors, and undercover agents can provide evidence of ambiguities and deception created by these strategies, but they also provide important evidence about the voluntariness of what the suspects, defendants, and targets say. The smoking gun evidence is usually found in the lexicon and grammar, and even there we can sometimes find deceptive ambiguity created by representatives of law.

Comparison of Transparent and Camouflaged Language Power

After chapter 2's brief summary of current understandings of power, ambiguity, and deception, chapters 3 and 4 illustrate how these are used in government operations of police interviews and courtroom examinations where this power is transparent. The subsequent three chapters illustrate cases in which institutional power is opaque rather than transparent. All of these chapters describe and illustrate actual criminal cases in which representatives of the legal institution used their power, ambiguity, and deceptive ambiguity in critically important ways. Chapter 8 turns attention away from the fifteen investigations to a focus on those individual elements of *The Inverted Pyramid* in which deceptive ambiguity occurs—the speech events, schemas, agendas, speech acts, conversational strategies, and lexicon and grammar.

Deceptive Ambiguity in Predisposition, Intentionality, and Voluntariness

Chapter 9 offers a rough comparison of the frequency of occurrence of deceptive ambiguity found in all fifteen case examples and describes how the legal issues of predisposition, intentionality, and voluntariness are related to the linguistic elements of speech events, schemas, agendas, speech acts, conversational strategies, and lexicon and grammar. It also briefly compares the effects and power of the uses of deceptive ambiguity by representatives of the legal institution as found in the speech events, schemas, agendas, speech acts, conversational strategies, and lexicon and grammar. As can be expected, it will be shown that considerably more deceptive ambiguity is found in opaque operations than in transparent ones, but a great deal of it exists even in the transparent police interviews of suspects and the prosecutorial questioning of defendants. Although it has been suggested that the power of institutions is diminishing in Western democratic countries (Bogoch 1994), the examples presented in this book do not seem to support this hypothesis. Instead, representatives of the legal institution appear to be finding subtler ways to assert their power through the use of deceptive ambiguity.

Sociocultural Evidence of Deceptive Ambiguity

These fifteen case examples also indicated that a considerable amount of deceptive ambiguity stems from sociocultural differences between the participants. This type of difference does not fit neatly into the Inverted Pyramid analysis of the language used, but it is certainly relevant and useful to mention and is summarized in Appendix A.

Readers who are familiar with my other books may recognize some of the cases that I've described in the past, but in this book I deal with those cases through a different lens—that of power, ambiguity, and deception. I have used the real names in all of the cases except two of the undercover interactions covertly tape-recorded by complainants. In one case I changed the participants' names to Dora and Sam and in the other case I changed one of the names to Sheriff Preston and did not mention the complainant's name at all.

I either consulted or testified in all of these cases while collaborating on four of them with my colleague Robert Leonard. Leonard and I were either retained by counsel or worked pro bono in all of the cases discussed here.

2

Power, Ambiguity, and Deception

Power

Perhaps the first thing to consider about power is that it can be misused, which is certainly not a new idea. James Thurber expressed this humorously in his book, *My World and Welcome to It* (1965: 115–116):

> In the history of mankind the increase of no kind of power has, so far as I can find out, ever moved naturally and inevitably in the direction of the benign. It has, as a matter of fact, almost always tended in the direction of the malignant, don't ask me why, it just has. This tendency, it seems to me, would be especially true of the power of the mind, since it is that very power which is behind all the deviltry Man is now up to and always has been up to.

If Thurber is right, it is important to learn what we can about the various meanings of power. Fairclough disagrees with Thurber, pointing out that power is not in itself a bad thing. The power of people to do good things improves society, while illegitimate power over other people is open to criticism. Fairclough (2015: 27) points out that there is a big difference between transparent power *in* discourse and the power *behind* discourse, "where it is hidden in the sense that it is not apparent on the surface" (see also pages 73–89). This distinction will be treated throughout this book.

Teun van Dijk (2008: 41) suggests that a good way to think about power is to separate the existing studies of power, dominance, and inequality into two categories: (1) macro-level institutional analyses largely pursued by sociologists and political scientists and (2) micro-level studies of individual language use, discourse, verbal interaction, and communication that are largely carried out by linguists. He further observes that despite a great deal of research in this area, a huge gap remains between more linguistically oriented studies of text and talk that pay less attention to the macro-level concepts studied by sociologists and political scientists and the sociological and political science studies that rarely involve analyzing actual individual discourse.

Power has been studied extensively by political scientists and sociologists, among others including Mills (1956), White (1976), Wrong (1979), Therborn (1980), and Galbraith (1985), none of whom claim to provide a comprehensive definition of power. They examine power as an institutional rather than individual matter and consider social power to be indirectly operating in the minds of participants through persuasion. They treat power as a form of social control and presuppose an ideological framework. Although social scientists admittedly have not provided a completely satisfactory definition of this social power, they have described many of its salient characteristics, including control, authority, domination, reinterpretation, inequality, and persuasion.

Psychologists have found that people endowed with power are at least temporarily unable to adopt the cognitive or emotional perspective of the less powerful. Powerful agents don't attend to the powerless because they don't need them in order to get important information or resources. Such people are apparently not motivated to have empathy for the powerless and they tend to seek less diagnostic information than those with more power.

A considerable amount of linguistic work on power at the social micro level already has been carried out on parents with children, women with men, employers with employees, doctors with patients, political and media interaction, and cross-racial exchanges (van Dijk 1985; 2008: 41–54).

In the legal context there is no question about the government's institutional power at both the macro and micro levels of language and discourse. A number of excellent studies have concerned the powerful interactions of police with suspects (Rock 2007), of prosecutors with defendants (Matoesian 1993, Conley and O'Barr 1998; Ehrlich 2001; Cotterill 2003; Heffer 2005) and of general communication issues between the law and laypersons (Heffer, Rock, and Conley 2013). Although these studies are very valuable contributions, they do not focus on deceptive ambiguity and do not approach the context of the discourse interactions from the combined perspectives of speech events, schemas, agendas, speech acts, conversational strategies, and lexico-grammatical features of discourse. This book examines the institutional power of law that exists in the communicative context with non-institutional individuals (suspects, defendants, and targets). In doing this it addresses van Dijk's (2008: 41) observation that there is a gap in research connecting studies of power in macro-level institutions with studies of power found in micro-level studies of individuals.

Since the defining characteristics of power are said to include control, authority, domination, reinterpretation, inequality, and persuasion, it seems necessary to describe these in more detail.

CONTROL

Control is generally recognized as the ability of both institutions and individuals to dominate the actions of others (Fowler 1985: 61–82). Scholars generally recognize that social power involves control that is derived conventionally from access to money, status, fame, knowledge, or other scarce social resources. Crucial to the exercise of social power is that it not only provides control over content but also control of one group over other groups and their members (van Dijk 2008: 9). Certain institutions, including governments, churches, law enforcement agencies, courts, the military, and others, predetermine, control, and manage the nature of their interactions with less powerful participants. In the legal context, there is no question about the fact that police and prosecutors hold obvious control over those with whom they interact. Control becomes more complicated during undercover operations, however, when it must be managed in more subtle ways.

AUTHORITY AND DOMINATION

Power is part of a reality-creating process that conveys the authority, capacity to control, and influence of one party over others. Scholars such as Burbules (1984) view power as domination that relates to a conflict of interest. Social power is said to have two senses: (1) the authority to produce the speaker's desired effects on the listener's personal goals, and (2) the authority over others that one controls and dominates. Weber (1947: 4) combined these two senses into one definition: "Power (macht) is the probability that one actor within a social relationship will be in a position to carry out his or her own will despite resistance, regardless of the basis on which this probability exists." Fairclough (1989: ix) maintains, "An understanding of the social order is most conveniently and naturally achieved through a critical awareness of the power of language," adding that language contributes to the domination of some speakers over others. In the legal context, there is no question about the authority and domination of police, prosecutors, and undercover agents. The issue becomes how they express it.

REINTERPRETATION

Mumby and Clair (1997: 184) observe that the most effective use of power "occurs when those with power are able to get those who have less power to interpret the world from the former's point of view." Reinterpretation is a form of persuading subjects to change their opinions, values, and beliefs and sometimes even the underlying facts about them. Representatives of the powerful legal institution enjoy the great advantage of having their own opinions, values, beliefs, and interpretation of facts favored over those of suspects and defendants. This book demonstrates some of the ways they accomplished this, especially when they employ powerful conversational strategies to do so.

INEQUALITY

Conley and O'Barr (1998: 8) observe: "Power is the answer to the question of why some people get things, while others do not—why, in other words, the haves have what they do." Stated in this way, the study of power must deal with the fundamental issues of inequality in the legal institution's interactions with outsiders to that institution. In the context of statutes and case law, power is closely related to inequality, where it not only inhibits the recipient but can also produce resistance in which recipients try to defend themselves as they attempt to right the tilting ship of perceived inequality. Police and prosecutors have a distinct advantage over suspects and defendants because of the inequality of their respective status. Things can get complicated, however, when this inequality is camouflaged.

PERSUASION

These central qualities of power are strengthened and revealed by various methods of expressing them, including persuasion. The use of social power can become an effective tool of persuasion in which language power can sometimes be even more effective than logic or facts. Persuasive power normally derives from both individual identity and the social institutions in which it is constructed through discourse. Some forms of persuasion are fairer and more acceptable than others. The inequality and domination of persuasive power between the police and their suspects and between the prosecutors and their defendants is easily recognized. Less immediately apparent is how the legal institution's persuasive power is represented when it is disguised during undercover operations.

Perceptions of Power

We recognize language power best when we find ourselves amidst it. My mother held the power in my family until her older sister, my Aunt Gertie, moved in with us. My mother immediately deferred to her powerful older sister who had raised her from the time their mother died. My father, an invalid victim of what was then called sleeping sickness, had no power at all in this female-dominated home. Even as a six-year-old child I could recognize our family power asymmetry although I had no ability to analyze it. Brown and Gillman (1960: 255) describe such asymmetry as follows: "One may be said to have power over another to the degree he is able to control the behavior of the other. Power is a relationship between at least two persons, and it is non-reciprocal in the sense that both cannot have power in the same area of behavior."

Power exists all around us, whether or not we recognize it, and it is very useful to be able to know where we stand in relation to it. In some settings and situations it can be obvious, but in others it is not that clear. Institutional power is obvious when we visit a doctor, take a course in school, apply for a loan at the bank, and in many other contexts. Even when we can't specifically identify power, we can feel it. Anyone who has lived in Washington, DC, for over thirty years as I have is very aware of the way power works in that powerful city. Residents who know a member of Congress sometimes flaunt this as a symbol of their own personal power, whether real or imagined. And if they can get one of these powerful people to come to their parties, weddings, or social occasions, their perceived status can grow by bounds because being close to power can seem almost as good as having it oneself. But this perception of personal power also can have its downside. People can be tempted to magnify their own power even when their position in the power chain is considerably lower. Often there are people lower in the power chain who try to borrow the power of those them above them to assert their own will.

The transparent institutional power given to police and prosecutors is obvious, leading to the question of why they might need to supplement their already existing power by resorting to the use of deceptive ambiguity when they interview suspects and question defendants. As for undercover agents, cooperating witnesses, and complainants, perhaps they get frustrated by their lack of recognizable institutional power and therefore compensate for this by using deceptive ambiguity. Whatever the perceptions of power the police, prosecutors, and undercover operators may be, the following chapters illustrate how they enhance it by being deceptively ambiguous.

The Erosion of Institutional Power

Studies of macro-level power don't often address what some consider to be evidence of the subtle and gradual erosion of institutional power that is taking place in the institutions of churches, governments, education, and family in some parts of the world. While the power of money remains very strong, the effect of quick and easy information flow via the ubiquitous presence of electronic communication devices can now expose institutional abuses of power more easily than in the past. Some scholars believe this exposure may be responsible for the diminishing power of these institutions, especially in Western democratic countries. For example, Bogoch (1994) observes that in Israel the concepts of power, distance, and solidarity in the interactions of judicial professionals and their clients still remains authoritarian, in sharp contrast with Western judicial discourse in which the traditional authoritarian model is moving toward diminished professional dominance and control. Whether macro-level institutional power is static or eroding, the power of those who have enough control to dominate the less powerful appears to remain, largely because the way people use language is so automatic and ingrained that it doesn't easily rise to the level of conscious behavior. This is one reason the study of language power is important.

Those who study power at its individual micro level contrast it with the macro study of institutional power by using the linguistic tools of speech events, schemas, speech acts, agendas, semantics, pragmatics, and grammatical structures to study how powerful actors interact with the less powerful. Despite the obvious characteristics of control, authority, domination, inequality, persuasion, and reinterpretation found in institutional contexts, power can be often more difficult to identify in many everyday, real-world situations, largely because it is not only far more subtle than physical violence but also even more subtle than the more obvious power moves of language, such as berating, accusing, insulting, or baiting. As this book demonstrates, deceptive ambiguity effectively accomplishes this, suggesting that those who have it are simply shifting their techniques in more subtle ways.

Shifting and Equalizing Power

Tannen (1994) points out that in most everyday conversations between friends, relatives, and colleagues, the power differential is typically either absent or negotiated, depending on social conditions and relationships. Like many linguists, Tannen analyzes what van Dijk calls the micro level of language use—discourse, verbal interaction, and communication—as opposed to the macro-level analyses commonly carried out by many sociologists and political scientists. Tannen argues that that there are various types of interrelated power and that the resulting influence can have changing manifestations. In her important research on everyday, moment-to-moment conversations that take place cooperatively outside of the more oppositional legal context, she found participants shifting the power back and forth among themselves (1987: 5; 1998: 172–173).

In contrast, institutional exchanges in the innately oppositional legal context appear to be far more resistant to the equalizing of power than are everyday cooperative conversations. In legal contexts it is extremely rare to find the moment-to-moment shifting of power among the participants that Tannen observes. The cases in this book describe how some institutionally empowered participants find ways to either maintain and use their institutional power or disguise and camouflage it as they engage in what might appear to be a non-power- dominated, equalized, personal interactions with their subjects. This activity merges the study of macro-level institutional power with micro-level individual language use that often produces deceptively ambiguous results.

In contrast with studies of power in everyday conversations, the question addressed here focuses on the way representatives of legal institutions use institutional power bolstered by statutes and case law during five different types of interactions with the public. The institution of law endows judges with the highest degree of power, followed by courtroom attorneys and prosecutors, and lower still the law enforcement officers who gather the evidence for attorneys to use in the courtroom. At the very bottom of this power chain are the suspects, defendants, and witnesses. Unlike everyday conversations, there is little or no shifting of power back and forth between these relatively fixed contexts of interaction.

This book addresses institutional power in two different contexts. In the first, the institutional power is transparent to all parties in police interviews and courtroom testimony. The second context deals with institutional power that is hidden from targets during three types of undercover law enforcement operations during which law enforcement's institutional power is covertly camouflaged. In both contexts, this power is assisted by the use of deceptive ambiguity.

Transparent Institutional Power in the Courtroom

Research on language in the courtroom has demonstrated that attorneys and judges have virtually absolute power and control over defendants and witnesses (Atkinson and Drew 1979; Danet and Bogoch 1980). Philips (1998: 89–110) describes the power of judges to exert command in their courtrooms through their own speech and their control of the speech of others. Solan points out that because judges wield such enormous power, there is pressure on them to speak decisively, creating pressures that don't always operate consistently and uniformly between their judicial power and their required neutrality (1993: 2–3).

In many instances the language power of the courtroom can be subtle, routine, or benign rather than blatantly coercive. Benign uses of power also are common in many other institutions such as churches, medicine, advertising, clinical psychology, and other types of counseling. It is equally institutionally vested to parents over their children, bosses over their employees, and teachers over their students. Even most business negotiations begin with the recognition of clearly differentiated but apparently benign levels of power.

Some powerful speakers try to soften or depoliticize their influence on their hearers in order to make it more palatable to them (Ng and Bradac 1993: 7). In non-legal contexts this can even have the effect of seeming polite but, as will be demonstrated in cases described in this book, attempts made by law enforcement officers, prosecutors and undercover agents to soften their power can sometimes create a deceptive effect. In spite of those occasions when speakers express their benign or softened power, polarized discourse that expresses social inequality can result (van Dijk 2008: 5). In most non-institutional settings speakers have the ability to manifest their power through the choices they make in vocabulary, syntax, speech acts, implicatures, referencing, interrupting, and turn taking (O'Barr 1982).

As the cases described in this book will illustrate, the announced or self-evident speech event plays a critically important role as well. When the speech event is courtroom testimony, virtually all of the power resides in representatives of the law enforcement institution while defendants share little or none of it. These speech events influence the schemas that all parties bring to them. The participants' agendas are determined by that speech event, with the institutional representatives in control of which topics are brought up. Similarly, the responses made by defendants are under the powerful control of the officers and attorneys who question them. These institutional representatives also manage and control the speech acts that are elicited from non-powerful defendants. Attorneys can request, warn, threaten, complain, and give directives, but their hearers are limited to reporting their answers to the questions that the powerful speaker asks.

Attorneys are endowed with language power that makes use of a wide range of discourse roles, genres, and styles, whereas the more powerless participants have less access to the various forms of talk with which they are most familiar. Institutional power also can enable the questioners to manipulate the results of their exchanges by using various types of conversational strategies in an effort to persuade the less powerful persons to accept culpability. The power-laden speaker has the privilege of interrupting other speakers, blocking what they try to say, introducing a topic and then switching to a different topic before the other person can respond (the hit-and-run strategy), withholding information that the less powerful person might need to know, and, central to the thesis of this book, using ambiguous language to the disadvantage of the less powerful person (Shuy 2012, 2013, 2014). Combined, these are some of the language tools endowed to powerful social actors but limited or denied to the more powerless participants. Ideally, institutionally powerful speakers should not need to misuse these tools to persuade, indoctrinate, or manipulate witnesses, but the temptation is always possible and unfortunately it is sometimes realized.

Linguists have carefully researched the language of courtroom trials. Matoesian (1993) described the courtroom imbalance of power that leads to revictimization during rape trials. His subsequent book on the William Kennedy Smith rape trial described how language, culture and various forms of domination are contested and naturalized by the laws of rape (2001). Along similar lines, Cotterill's book, *Language and Power in Court* (2003) provides an analysis of the power strategies used in the famous O.J. Simpson murder trial. These books illustrate the many language mechanisms of control used by lawyers and judges in their interactions with defendants and witnesses.

Other linguists who study language power also have focused their attention on particular parts of courtroom interactions. For example, Danet and Bogoch (1980: 222–223) describe the coerciveness of lawyers' question forms, noting six features in particular: the coerciveness of falling intonation, the illocutionary ambiguity of expressions like "can you tell us," the abundant use of yes/no questions that limit responses as opposed to open-ended questions that permit answers to be more natural and informative, the lack of a question's specificity, the use of declarative questions that are geared to elicit only confirmations that the questioner wants to hear, and negative questions such as "you didn't go there, did you?" which strongly suggest the desired answer and sometimes even coerce it.

Gibbons, in his *Introduction to Forensic Linguistics* (2003) devotes an entire, detailed chapter on interaction and power in the courtroom, including topics about attorneys' use of rules of interaction, nonverbal communication, address forms, overelaboration, turn taking, coercive questions, and various pragmatic strategies.

Linguists who have studied language power in the courtroom find that lawyers seldom relinquish the floor to witnesses and discourage any long, narrative responses (Danet and Bogoch 1980; O'Barr 1982). This yields what O'Barr characterizes as the witness's "powerless style." Berk-Seligson (1990: 131) lists some the ways the powerless mode is exacerbated by English interpreters of Spanish speaking witnesses, including their use of super-politeness forms, hedges, hesitations, hypercorrections, pauses, insertions of information perceived to be underlying and assumed, un-contracted verb forms, rephrasing, and an abundance of filler expressions such as "well," "kind of," "I guess," and "you see," none of which were actually uttered by the witnesses being interpreted. As they do this, court interpreters also create the impression of the monolingual Spanish speakers' powerlessness by lengthening their turns of talk, thereby causing them to appear to have a more narrative style as opposed to the required crisp and expository style of more powerful testimony. This type of courtroom speech sharply contrasts with the assertive and definite power mode of the attorneys, who control their courtroom interactions with "yes/no" questions, interruptions, and other language devices (Shuy 1998; Berk-Seligson 2009).

Walker's (1990) study of trials involving language interpreters revealed that despite the lawyers' common and predictable approach of focusing their attention on what witnesses have to contribute, they sometimes address court interpreters directly, temporarily assigning them language power rather than speaking directly to the witnesses for whom they interpret. She also found that interpreters sometimes inaccurately report what the witnesses actually said, try to clarify the attorney's questions and witnesses's answers, and tend to prompt the witnesses and otherwise improperly manage the flow of testimony. When these things happen, the power shifts temporarily from attorneys to interpreters, in spite of the fact that their assigned role is to be virtually invisible and powerless in the courtroom (Walker 1990: 203–245).

It is reasonable to defend the asymmetry of power in the courtroom and police station. Those who defend it in the courtroom setting argue that this system is necessary in order to advance the purposes and integrity of this institution. It makes trials more orderly and shorter, saves resources, and addresses legal issues directly in ways that witnesses might not be able to appreciate. Although these arguments are no doubt accurate, it cannot be denied that the distribution of power favors the institution while at the same time professes to be operating under the banner of impartial justice. Issues of fairness further arise when that institutional power is misused with deceptive ambiguity, whether intentionally or not, in order to elicit information efficiently during courtroom testimony (Gudjonsson 1993; Shuy 1998; Leo and Offshe 2001; Leo 2008).

Transparent Institutional Power in Police Interviews

Institutional power that dominates in the courtroom is also exerted in police interviews, where suspects and witnesses are relatively powerless while police officers question them (O'Barr 1982). Many linguists have addressed the broad problems created by the power asymmetry in the social institution of police interviews (Shuy 1998; Haworth 2006: Ainsworth 2008; Rock 2014). Based on his extensive experience as an expert witness, Gibbons (2003) urges police questioners to (1) give up the false assumption that a suspect can understand many of their questions even when the questions begin with *what, where, when, why, who,* and *how* and (2) replace polar yes/no questions with ones that require a fuller, more narrative response. Other authors such as Eades (2010: 131–180), focus more narrowly on specific problems created when police interviewers communicate the required cautions to minority suspects, including second language speakers, deaf sign language users, speakers of creole languages, second dialect speakers, children, and intellectually disabled persons. Powerful language used by law enforcement officers is endemic to situations characterized by significant conflicts of interest. Conley and O'Barr (1998: 138) point out that power, domination, and bias "come vividly to light when the linguistic processes through which they are enacted are revealed."

Linguistic analysis of conflicts of interest found in police interviews and courtroom testimony grows quite naturally out of the necessarily powerful institutional framework of law. The formal, ritual, and physical attributes of exchanges in legal settings make this conflict of interest obvious and enable government representatives to use language that is heavily laden with institutional and language power. Previous work on institutional language power, however, has not focused on how that power is revealed by the way representatives of the legal institution use deceptive ambiguity.

Hidden Institutional Power in Undercover Operations

Contrasting with courtroom and police station settings in which transparent institutional power is prescribed and expected are the investigative methods used in undercover operations that are disguised to give the appearance of everyday individual, personal, and business conversations. In these settings the participants neither anticipate nor realize the existence of the hidden power differential. They also don't expect to be misled or deceived by institutional uses of ambiguity. Many conversations between friends, acquaintances, fellow workers, adult relatives, business associates, and even strangers often proceed with the expectation that the playing field of conversational power is level. Whereas in transparent courtroom exchanges and police interviews in which powerless participants are made very aware of their powerlessness, undercover police operations hide the powerful speaker's power and cause their conversational partners to be unaware of any potential deception stemming from the powerful person's use of ambiguity. Here the less powerful participants are at an even greater disadvantage because they do not assume that they are subject to conversational power restrictions found in transparent police or courtroom interviews, where they could recognize their limitations concerning turn taking, holding the floor, introducing new topics, and other linguistic features that more predictably accrue to the authority and power found in transparent institutional settings.

In reality, however, the camouflaged agents actually hold the same institutional power that is transparent in the courtroom and police station. They rely on the quite reasonable assumption that their conversational partners (targets) will not recognize this power differential in their recorded conversations. In fact, this lack of a differentiation found in transparent institutional power provides undercover agents with a significant advantage for the success of such operations. In addition, as targets engage in these conversations they don't know that their words are being recorded for use by a totally different audiences such as judges and juries. As a result of this unawareness, targets can be misled into using language less carefully than they would if they were aware of their situation.

So far we have briefly described the generally held descriptors of power—control, authority, domination, and inequality—as well as the ways it is manifested in language through reinterpretation and persuasion. The optimal procedure for analyzing deceptive ambiguity was introduced as a guide to the following analysis of fifteen criminal investigations. The chapter also discussed the more global issues of how power is perceived, whether we are witnessing an erosion of institutional power, and the question of a shifting of power that some believe is leading to an equalization in today's society. It then foreshadowed the legal institution's transparent uses of power as its representatives interact with suspects in police interviews, with defendants in the courtroom, and its camouflaged, opaque uses of power in undercover investigations of people suspected of having a predisposition and willingness to commit a crime or individuals who were suspected of having committed a crime in the past. These chapters may show that James Thurber's description of power is more than a humorous observation.

Ambiguity

I once overheard this conversation:

> "Jana told me that Ed married her."
> "Was that her first marriage before she met Roger?"

Here the speaker's failed to specify that Ed was the minister who performed wedding ceremony of Jana and Roger, but the way the speaker said it created an ambiguity that deceived the listener into thinking that Jana had been married to Ed. Ambiguity is often present in our lives and context is the common way to clarify it. Indulge me to repeat Solan's (2014: 7) apt expression: "When the context is clear to everyone, it does not feel that it is even there. Yet it is there, and it always plays a role in the interpretation of language." Sometimes ambiguity is at the heart of bad jokes, such as this very old one:

> "Please call me a taxi."
> "Okay, you're a taxi."

At other times the ambiguity stems from unintentionally omitting information as in:

> "Richard loves his wife and so does Jim."

These may be merely humorous anecdotes but when law gets involved, ambiguous language can become very serious. For example, we will see how the police stripped from context Kevin Rogers's statement to the police when he said, "I wish that it didn't happen," which the police reinterpreted as his confession that he killed the victim who was a neighbor that Kevin knew very well.

On the other hand, one of the interesting and sometimes even endearing aspects of language is its ever-present possibility to be ambiguous. Without ambiguity, jokes would not be effective, drama would be less interesting, and artistic expression would lose much of its impact. Even in our everyday conversations ambiguity fills an important communicative role, but problems can arise when ambiguity is not recognized and even more so when it creates deception.

The use of ambiguity created by police, prosecutors, and undercover agents has received considerably little attention. In order to demonstrate how their institutional power relates to their uses of ambiguity, it is important to first briefly identify what it means for language to be ambiguous. The study of ambiguity by philosophers, psychologists, sociologists, and linguists is ongoing, incomplete, and frequently controversial. It is usually agreed that ambiguity is often very useful in the areas of diplomacy, humor, and the arts, but using ambiguous language can become problematic in areas where utter clarity is expected and required, especially in legal contexts.

Ambiguity as Seen by Law

While the separate academic disciplines may have overlapping concerns and definitions of power, there appears to be a wide gap between the understandings of ambiguity by law and linguistics. Shane suggests that a Venn diagram representing the intersection of these two fields would display only a small shaded area of overlap (Shane 2006). This separation may not be the fault of either field alone, however, for most separate academic fields have a way of ignoring each other as they independently go about their own work. Complicating matters is that by far most of the attention of legal scholars is on ambiguity found in statutory interpretation and contracts, both instances of language in its written form, while for the type of ambiguity discussed in this book, the focus is on spoken language used as evidence in criminal cases.

It is well-recognized that the specialized lexicon of law produces many expressions that pose problems for laypersons to understand. Evidence of this can be found in two of the major books on the language of law, Mellinkoff's *The Language of the Law* (1963) and Tiersma's *Legal Language* (1999). Both of these scholars as well as other existing experts on this topic provide valuable information about the legal lexicon and how it developed and is used today. Tiersma even takes this subject a step further into the electronic future in his book, *Parchment Paper Pixels* (2010). Schauer points out that while law's rather technical lexicon includes such terms as *assumpsit*, *res judicta*, *interpleader*, and other words created by legal scholars, law uses many other common and ordinary words that convey a very different meanings to laypersons, such as *rights, malice, contract, speech,* and *negligence* (2015).

Despite the differences in specialized meanings, the special lexicon of law has the important advantage of managing its system from the inside. But assumptions that the specialized vocabulary of law strongly limits understanding by laypersons has been questioned by Tiersma in his article, "Some myths about legal language" (2006: 48) in which he points out that in spite of law's prolific use of archaic Latin and French-based terms, redundancy, wordiness, and dullness, legal language is much closer to ordinary English than many people think. Questions remain, however, about what happens when law's need for specialized legal language to effectively manage the legal system bumps its head with the needs of laypersons to understand what the law is trying to tell them.

The legal arena views written ambiguity as having two major senses: (1) a broad general meaning about how language is used and understood, particularly when it lacks clarity or certainty about meanings; and (2) the narrow, restricted meanings of the lexical and grammatical properties that are part of the fabric of language regardless of how people use or understand them (Shane 2006: 12). A larger problem goes beyond the specialized legal lexicon when we consider chunks of language that are larger than individual legal terms and expressions. For example, witnesses in the courtroom often run into problems when the lawyers who question them use unfamiliar syntax. Matoesian's *Reproducing Rape* (1993) illustrates the way lawyers add tags like "isn't it true" that convert their statements into questions and make use of unusually long pauses, both of which can create comprehension problems for the witnesses they question. Similarly, Ainsworth discusses the interpretation of conversational implicatures during the reading of a suspect's Miranda rights. She adds that when a suspect responds saying, "I think I would like to have a lawyer," this response has not been recognized by courts as a request for a lawyer because the speaker did not explicitly say, "I *want* a lawyer present during this interview." The case examples discussed in this book point out many of the areas in which a conflict results from the spoken ambiguities used by representatives of the legal institution and how laypersons struggle to deal with them.

Courts deal with statutory ambiguity in several ways: by referring to legislative history, by taking into account an agency's view of the statute, by applying the rule of lenity (postulating that ambiguity should be resolved in favor of the more lenient punishment), and by accounting for problems created by unclear referencing (Gundel, Hedberg, and Zacharski 1993; Farnsworth, Guzior and Malani 2010). The way legal texts are actually read and understood by people who are untrained in law is less than clear and very little empirical research exists about how ordinary readers of English interpret such unfamiliar, unclear or ambiguous legal texts.

The linguistic research about how laypersons understand pattern jury instructions provides one noteworthy exception to this gap. Important studies have been carried out on this topic by Charow and Charow (1979), Tiersma (1999, 2001, 2009), Dumas (2000), Heffer (2005), Wascher (2005), and Marder (2006, 2009). One commonly recognized problem is that judges who fear having their decisions reversed tend to read the existing written pattern instructions to jurors slowly and carefully, but often expressionless and without providing help to jurors who request clarification about what they don't understand about the judge's recitation of the instructions (Marder 2009). It is not difficult to imagine how hard it is for jurors to reach their verdicts without fully understanding the instructions the judge provides them. Heffer (2005) points out the paradox that lawyers have no trouble explaining technical terms in ordinary language during the trial, but the courts seem to forget this when it's time to give the jury instructions that are crucial for deciding the case. He refers to this as the natural tension between the power of judges' authority and their reluctance to surrender of some of that power and authority by accommodating the needs of jurors.

Tiersma's contributions to California's Blue Ribbon Commission of Jury System Improvement and Dumas's work as a member of the Tennessee Bar Association's Jury Reform Commission provide notable evidence of some recent linguistic successes concerning this knotty issue. In some states, committees appointed by the chief justice have been mandated to make jury instructions more understandable. In Arizona, for example, the jury instructions have been rewritten to be comprehensible at the sixth-grade reading level. This would appear to improve matters were it not for the fact that competent education specialists dispute the adequacy and accuracy of most reading-level measurements, especially ones that try to assign grade levels (Bailin and Grafstein 2001).

Shane illustrates the clash of the legal and linguistic approaches to ambiguity by citing the US Supreme Court case of *Frank J. Muscarello v. United States* (524 US 125) in which the lower courts had decided that the statute's expression, "carries a firearm," while committing a drug transaction crime required the mandatory five-year sentence for anyone who used or carried a firearm during that action. The lower court had ruled that the narrow meaning of *carry* included a gun that the arresting police officer found in the glove compartment of the defendant's car, even though no gun was evident during the drug sale and no gun was even visible during the transaction. The defendant appealed, claiming that *carry* conveys the meaning of having the gun on his person. The lower court, however, took the broad meaning of *carry* to include all types of transportation whether on a person's body or "somewhere currently nearby." The Supreme Court agreed with the lower court, relying on what it believed was the intention of Congress to understand *carry* in its sense of "being armed and ready for offensive or defensive action in case of conflict with another person." The Supreme Court cited dictionary definitions of *carry* as well as the way the word was used in selected passages of literature. Although both the legal and linguistic approaches to lexical ambiguity were presented in this case, the Court chose the legal interpretation of what it believed to be the intended meaning of the statute rather than the implicature that was fairly obvious in the physical context of that crime.

It is noteworthy, however, that legal approaches to ambiguity usually relate to written language where ambiguity is found in the legal community of practice, mostly in disputes over the wording of contracts, wills, and other civil matters where it is necessary to interpret the language evidence. Although much is written about how an *ordinary person* would understand the text in civil cases and statutes, the area of ambiguity found in naturally occurring language such as the conversational spoken language of *ordinary persons* during police interviews, trials, and undercover criminal investigations has received little attention.

Ambiguity as Seen by Linguistics

Most linguistic research on ambiguity has focused on language used outside the legal context. Law disputes may address lexical ambiguity or even vagueness of categorization (such as whether water is a mineral or whether cows are heifers), but they seldom deal with discourse ambiguity of the sort found in the large amounts of continuous spoken language representing police interviews, courtroom testimony, and the spoken language evidence that is tape-recorded during undercover operations. The legal arena seldom considers pragmatic ambiguity, despite the brilliant pioneering crossover work in this area by law professors who are also trained in linguistics (Tiersma 1987, 1990, 1995b, 2007; Solan 1993, 2001, 2004, 2009, 2010).

Linguists deal with three major types of ambiguity: lexical, syntactic, and pragmatic. When a word has more than one dictionary meaning, it has a potential to be ambiguous. This is not the same as vagueness, which conveys no particularly identifiable meaning. One type of lexical ambiguity stems from words that are pronounced the same way but are spelled differently (homonymic ambiguity), but this type of ambiguity usually has little importance for legal issues. Syntactic ambiguity relates to the grammatical relationships established by word order restrictions in language, often caused by ambiguous scope of modification, unclear pronoun or deictic referencing, or unclear syntactic placements of prepositional phrases. Pragmatic ambiguity stems from meanings that sentences convey in particular contexts, often with implicatures contrary to literal meanings or truth conditions.

One of the major sources of language ambiguity can be seen in the ways grammatical referencing takes place, especially with pronouns and antecedents (Chafe 1996: 37–46). Levinson (1983: 60) adds indexical references such as *this, that, these*. Some research deals with problems created when the informative quality fails to match the accessibility of the expression. Ariel (1990) found that success in communicating the reference information intended by the sender's communication depends on the accessibility of that reference to the hearer. Specifically, this is found in four areas: distance between the antecedent and the anaphor, competition created by other references, saliency of the topic in which the reference occurs, and schemas created by shared and unshared world knowledge during the interaction. When individual schemas about the distance, competition, saliency of topic, and world knowledge differ, referencing becomes ambiguous and can lead to misunderstandings and confusion. To this we can add ambiguity created by confusion about which speech event the participants believe they are in, ambiguity caused by misinterpretations created by infelicitous speech acts, and ambiguity created by certain conversational strategies.

Linguists and philosophers agree that vagueness is very different from ambiguity. An ambiguous statement offers the hearer multiple possible interpretations, while a vague description, such as "John is bald," is not ambiguous because we have a general understanding of baldness. This sentence is vague because it does not specify what "bald" refers to specifically (completely, partially in one spot, bald on his head only, permanently bald, etc.). Linguists and philosophers generally agree (*Stanford Encyclopedia of Philosophy* 2014) that ambiguity includes:

- lexical ambiguity (*duck* refers to both a noun depicting a type of fowl and also to the verb meaning to avoid something);
- syntactic ambiguity illustrated by "the chicken is ready to eat";
- quantifier and scope ambiguity illustrated by "a man dies in a car accident every five minutes";
- pronoun and deictic reference ambiguity illustrated by "it came yesterday," or "the guy was there";
- speech act ambiguity illustrated by "can you pass the potatoes" or "I'm sorry";
- presuppositional ambiguity illustrated by "Joe insulted Fred and Bill hit him";
- ellipsis ambiguity illustrated by "John loves his mother and Bill does too;" and
- inchoate ambiguity illustrated by "the vase broke."

To this we can add ambiguity created by conflicting understandings about the speech events in which the speakers participate, as well as their conflicting schemas created by their different understandings about the presumed speech events. Both of these can strongly affect the speakers' agendas as well.

An ambiguous utterance is one about which a receiver can adduce more than one semantic sense and whose senses can be pragmatically interpretable as tenable in given contexts. In contrast, a vague utterance produces uncertainty of meaning but does not provide enough information for receivers to adduce whatever sense the speaker might have intended, causing listeners to become uncertain about how to adduce the meaning of what was said (Su 1994). This difference between ambiguity and vagueness is particularly important because a vague expression often causes hearers to request clarification. In contrast, ambiguous language tends to invite listeners to apply their own ongoing schemas to the ambiguous statement and to then use these schemas to infer the meaning of what the speakers said. Their inferences, accurate or not, often relieve them of a perceived need to use the speech act of requesting clarification. Ambiguity works to the advantage of representatives of the legal institution because then they can say truthfully that they have put an important statement on the table, however ambiguous it may have been, and the respondents did not request clarification about it and therefore they must have understood the intended meaning. It often makes little difference to speakers that their listeners may not have understood the meanings conveyed through the ambiguous utterances. The damage has been done because their failure to request clarification can work against them when it is memorialized on the record of the case evidence. And it remains on that record for the prosecutor, judge, and jury to interpret this lack of request for clarification as evidence that the listeners actually understood what the speaker meant.

Cruse (1986) associates ambiguity with the appearance of its sequential location in conversations. This sequence causes hearers or readers to presuppose more than one interpretation based on their consideration of the speech event and language genre in which the interpretations occur. Hearers' initial interpretations of ambiguous statements can cause them to carry those interpretations forward throughout the interaction, even when there are later clues that it may not support them. Apparently it can be difficult to unring the bell of an original false impression.

Such possible multiple interpretations are recognized as a part of the complexity that can lead to suspending Grice's (1975) cooperative principle, the maxims of which aver that effective communication depends on people saying as much as necessary—but no more than necessary; saying that which is true; saying that which is relevant; and all the while being clear and unambiguous. Knowledge of the real-world context can sometimes help disambiguate an ambiguous expression, the lack of specificity, ellipsis, grammatical scope, indirectness, and clear referencing (especially pronoun and deictic referencing), but unless listeners recognize these disambiguators as they are happening, they can easily misunderstand the message. Everyday talk is filled with pragmatic ambiguity conveyed through various speech acts and presuppositions. Indirect speech acts, in which speakers say one thing and yet can be understood to be saying something else (Searle 1979: 30–58) also are frequent sources of ambiguity.

No language exists that can escape the possibility of ambiguity and, as Zwicky and Sadock (1975) point out, no perfect test for ambiguity has been developed. Ambiguity may be difficult to define, but it is often recognizable just the same, as former Supreme Court Justice Potter Stewart famously noted when he said of pornography that even though he couldn't define it, he knew it when he saw it (sometimes referred to as the Casablanca test). It is possible to recognize, however, when ambiguity allows for differences between sense and reference. Although lexical ambiguity can occur when the senses carry multiple meanings (such as "duck" as an action as well as "duck" as a specie of waterfowl), it often results from a lack of clarity and specificity caused by possible conflicting interpretations of presuppositional ambiguity, such as what it means to *know* something, or by hypothetical statements that are understood as unambiguous factuals, and even more commonly by multiple possible understandings that result from a speaker's unclear pronoun and deictic reference markers.

Whatever circuitous path ambiguous language takes, it is clear that it can have one of two effects on those who hear it. If they recognize the ambiguity, they have the opportunity, if they choose, to request clarification that can reveal the speaker's meaning. But if they don't recognize that the utterance contains ambiguity, they are likely to call on their schemas and perceived knowledge of the context to infer a meaning that might be different from that which the speaker intended. This alternative of inferring meaning, can have serious effects the interaction because it invites a strong risk of being wrong. When ambiguity happens, the senders' messages can be deceptive, whether or not they were intended to be. Let me be clear here. Deception is usually considered an intentional trick or ruse. Instead, I am claiming that a person can be deceived by ambiguity whether or not it was an intentional ruse or trick. This is not to say, however, that deception is always unintentional.

The exchanges described in this book illustrate the power of deceptive ambiguity that occurs in two types of interactions: (1) conversations taking place between transparent and clearly identified representatives of powerful legal institutions including local, federal, state, an international law enforcement agencies, all of which convey their clear institutional power over the persons with whom they talk, including layperson witnesses and suspects; and (2) conversations of targets with representatives of institutional power who disguise or camouflage that institutional affiliation and power. Although these power-laden speakers actually represent their legal institution in these contexts, they camouflage their institutional affiliations and converse with their targets in the presumably non-institutional guise of colleagues, fellow businesspersons, family, or friends. This provides the clearest case of intentional deceptive ambiguity. Others will be seen in the description of the fifteen cases discussed in this book.

Deception

The ballgame was scoreless in the ninth inning with nobody out. The Yankees had a runner on first base when the Red Sox pitcher summoned his catcher to the mound to talk about how to pitch to the next batter. The pitcher held his glove over his face so that the Yankees couldn't try to read his lips. The catcher kept his facemask on for the same purpose. After their conference ended, both players went back to their positions. The Yankee runner, who had taken a short lead off first base suddenly made a movement that looked like he was going to try to steal second base, but just as quickly he stopped and dashed back to the bag. The pitcher, now wary that the runner might try to steal second base, lobbed the ball to the first baseman, informing the runner that he realized what he was up to. Here we witness multiple deceptions, all part of the normal game of baseball. The players on both teams were trying to deceive each other in order to gain an advantage in the game (for many other examples of how deception is integrated into baseball, see Dickson 2003). Similar deceptive acts occur in many other team sports such as football, soccer, hockey, basketball, and rugby. Yet nobody accuses the deceivers of doing anything wrong and certainly not of committing a crime.

In spite of the fact that it is easy to see how humans commonly try to deceive each other in how they dress or use makeup to look better than they really are, deception is one of those words that we commonly relate to intentional bad acts such as cheating, trickery, double-dealing, and subterfuge, but it's a bit ironic that the same time we enjoy the intentional deception performed by magic acts, drama, movies, novels, surprise parties, and unexpected gifts. It is only when deception is deemed illegal or unethical that deceivers get in trouble by outright lying or by using the more subtle deception of being ambiguous. Even more ironically, as the case descriptions in this book illustrate, representatives of law enforcement and prosecutors are not often censured when they confront suspects and defendants deceptively through the use of ambiguity.

Deception is conventionally understood as the intentional effort to cause receivers to understand something that is not the truth. Ambiguity is conventionally understood as an expression that has more than one possible meaning. Therefore, if receivers understand a meaning that was not intended by a sender, they can perceive the wrong meaning. The sender may not have intended for the receivers to receive the wrong message, but that's what can happen. It is this ambiguity in the message that can cause them to be deceived into believing something that message did not intend them to understand, whether or not that deception was intentional.

It is widely perceived that it is not acceptable for police, prosecutors, or undercover agents to deceive their suspects, defendants, and targets because if they are shown to have used deception, the results can work against the government's cases. However, sometimes even though they may try to avoid outright lying or any other obvious methods of deception, they find another way to capture their subjects planning or admitting to commit criminal acts. One way this is achieved is by producing ambiguous statements or questions that cause their subjects to interpret that ambiguity in one way while the representatives of the law use this misunderstanding against them. Another way is for representatives of the law to infer and interpret their subjects' own amibiguity in ways that inculpate them.

Deception, Ambiguity, and the Law

Most people hold the impression that deception is always intentional. *Black's Law Dictionary* (2004) expresses this with the words *knowingly* and *recklessly*.

> **deceit,** *n.* **1:** The act of intentionally giving a false impression . . . **2:** A false statement of fact made by a person knowingly and recklessly (i.e., not caring whether it is true or false) with the intent that someone else will act upon it . . .

In contrast, *Merriam-Webster' Collegiate Dictionary (2003, 321)* stops short of using the word *intentional,* calling it an "attempt," a "device," and a "cause to accept as true," which treat it as a result of a speaker's language, whether intentional or not:

> **deceit 1:** the act or practice of deceiving: deception **2:** an attempt or device to deceive: trick **3:** the quality of being deceitful . . .

> **deceive** *vb* **1** *archaic:* ensnare **2a** *obs:* to be false to **b** *archaic:* to fail to fulfill **3** *obs:* cheat **4:** to cause to accept as true or valid what is false or invalid **5** *archaic:* to while away *vi:* to practice deceit: *also* : to give a false impression . . .

The *American Heritage Dictionary of the English Language* (2011, 469) calls deceit a practice, stratagem, trick, and falseness that causes, misleads and gives a false impression:

> **deceit** *n.* **1.** The act or practice of deceiving: deception. **2.** A stratagem; a trick. **3.** The quality of being deceitful; falseness.

> **deceive** *v.-tr.* **1.** To cause to believe what is not true; mislead. **2.** *archaic* To catch by guile; ensnare. *Intr.* **1.** To practice deceit. **2.** To give a false impression . . .

Garner's Modern American Usage (2009, 228) stops short of intentionality when it says: "To deceive is to induce someone to believe in a falsehood," adding, "the deceiver *may* know the statement to be false or reckless. To "induce" does not require intention and "may" is hardly definitive of it. He compares deception with fraud: "To defraud is to cause some kind of injury or loss by deceit. Defrauding leads a person to take action, whereas deceiving merely leads a person to a state of mind."

Since these dictionaries do not resolve the question of whether deception is always intentional, we look elsewhere, in this case to Garner's contrast of deception with fraud. Solan (2012: 493) points out that fraud includes deception that takes the form of statements that are true but misleading. He points out that lawyers are not allowed to lie but as advocates for their clients they must be both truthful and *insincere* and "whether or not those inferences reflect a fair assessment of facts or law . . . they may structure their speech to lead others into drawing inferences that will serve the lawyers' goals, whether or not those inferences reflect a fair assessment of facts or law" (487). This appears to reflect Garner's observation that defrauding leads a hearer to take action, whereas deceiving leads a person to a state of mind. As such, deception would appear to be a form of persuasion. So now the descriptors of deception are piling up: add *misleading*, *persuasion*, and *insincerity* into the mix.

If lawyers who have the privileged position of advocating for their clients by misleading, persuading, and being insincere, how different is this from outright deception? And how different is it from the equally privileged and powerful position of police during their interviews with suspects, prosecutors with their examination of defendants, and undercover agents during their efforts to capture crime as it happens?

Among the many existing statues, not one of them stands alone labeled as "deception." *Black's Law Dictionary* lists many provisions of laws that prohibit deception, using terms such as "deceptive acts," "deceptive advertising," "deceptive practice," "deceptive sales practice," and "deceptive warranty." Nevertheless, law professor Gregory Klass (2012: 449) argues that torts of deceit, negligent representation, nondisclosure, and defamation constitute what he calls "the law of deception," which characterizes the prevention of dishonesty, disinformation, artifice, coverup, trickery and other forms of false belief. Klass distinguishes three types of regulatory methods within the law of deception: (1) the interpretive laws that prohibit making untrue statements requiring interpretation of the meaning of a statement and then verifying them using everyday semantic terms; (2) the purpose-based laws, which relate to acts done with a wrong intent by concealing the truth; and (3) the causal predictive laws that use whatever tools are available from relevant disciplines to predict the deceptive and informative effects of statements. From this it would appear that the law's concern with deception depends heavily on help from academic fields such as psychology, philosophy, and linguistics, where scholars carry out both macro and micro analytical research on the nature of deceptive language behavior.

The results of efforts to try to distinguish between deception and outright lying have been murky at best. Lying is the prototypical act of deception that consists of a false statement that the speaker knows will falsely mislead the addressee (Bok, 1978; Coleman and Kay 1981; Robinson 1996). In criminal cases it is commonly accepted that suspects and defendants will lie when questioned in the police station or the courtroom. One might expect defendants to lie to protect their own interests, but the frequency with which police officers also lie is somewhat discouraging (Slobogin 1996: 1040). Lying by prosecutors at trial is noticed and caught less frequently, possibly because their performances are made publicly before judges and opposing attorneys who serve as fact-checking monitors.

It's discouraging, however, when prosecutors ask the courts to amend rulings to remove from the findings the fact that previous testimony by police officers was not completely truthful. And it's disheartening when a prosecutor tries to disqualify an expert witness with deceptive trickery. For example, in one case the linguistic expert for the defense prepared a report in which he compared the charges listed in the indictment with the tape-recorded evidence, showing line by line that the language evidence was in direct conflict with the government's specific accusations. In an evidentiary hearing the prosecutor then requested the judge to exclude the expert's analysis, saying that the prosecution did not intend to show the indictment to the jury. Based on this assertion, the judge excluded the expert. The first thing prosecutors do at trial, of course, is to outline and summarize the charges made in the indictment, and this prosecutor was no exception. The prosecutor's sleight-of-hand trickery can only be labeled as deception based on the ambiguity the he created when he said that he would not "show" the indictment to the jury. Of course he wouldn't that. Prosecutors don't do that and he did what most prosecutors do: his opening statement summarized the charges verbally. The judge became a willing participant in this deceptive ambiguity by using it as an excuse to exclude the expert. Fortunately, not all deceptive ambiguity is that blatant. The emphasis in this book is on the more subtle acts of deceptive ambiguity that are created and sometimes used by representatives of the legal institution.

Deception is generally associated with intentional trickery, fraud, double-dealing, ruse, and other forms of subterfuge closely related to the act of outright lying. Most popular dictionaries use these largely negative terms to define deception. Although certain types of deception are tolerated in human activities such as commerce, advertising, sports, the arts, and diplomacy, the institution of law has good reason to consider deception used by suspects and defendants negatively. At the same time, however, as the cases described in this book point out, this institution actually encourages and gives official blessing to the use of deceptive ambiguity during undercover operations and appears to tacitly accept its use during police interviews and courtroom questioning.

The frequency of ambiguity in the legal context raises the possibility that during their persuasive interviews and undercover conversations, government officials are using it in intentionally for the purpose of manipulating their listeners and furthering their own goals. Mellikoff (1963: 417) describes deception as "the deliberate use of language which everyone recognizes as being easily misunderstood and accepted for the sake of quick agreement." It's clear that ambiguity is not always intentional, but as far as I know, there is no known way to reach into speakers' minds to determine their intentions with any degree of accuracy. The very nature of adversarial questioning, however, allows for the possibility that ambiguity can be used in a premeditated, intentional, and deceptive manner. It is noteworthy that the terms *deception* and *ambiguity* are commonly found together in statutes describing criminal behavior. It is equally noteworthy that little is said about their uses by the government.

Courtroom exchanges and police interviews are discrete speech events in which the purported purpose is to enable the legal institution to determine the facts in a given situation such as a crime. Previous analyses of many such interviews have demonstrated that law enforcement officers and prosecutors have used ambiguity as a useful strategy for persuading their interviewees to admit or confess crimes in ways strongly suggesting that this technique was used deliberately in ways that went beyond simple fact-finding or benign persuasion (White 1979; Shuy 1998, 2013, 2014; Leo 2008). It is equally likely that the suspects and defendants use ambiguity intentionally during their efforts to avoid inculpating themselves. This might suggest that because both powerless interviewees and powerful interviewers use ambiguity deceptively, the playing field is actually level. That is, if suspects, defendants, and targets can be deceptively ambiguous, why isn't this also an acceptable practice for police, prosecutors, and undercover agents?

In 1973, The U.S. Supreme Court gave an important answer to this question concerning the appeal of the perjury conviction of Samuel Bronston (*Bronston v. United States,* 409 U.S. 352 (1973)). This is an often cited case that grew out of a previous bankruptcy hearing, during which Bronston had given an ambiguous answer to the prosecutor's ambiguous question: "Do you have any bank accounts in Swiss banks, Mr. Bronston?" Bronston truthfully answered "no, sir," apparently choosing to interpret the prosecutor's pronoun, *you*, to refer to him personally. The prosecutor's follow-up question was "Have you ever?" once again using the second person pronoun that doesn't distinguish between singular from plural. To this, Bronston responded by trying to disambiguate the prosecutor's second person pronoun, saying, "The company had an account there for about six months, in Zurich." Although in the past Bronston had indeed held a personal account in a Swiss bank, both of his answers were literally true because the prosecutor's ambiguous *you* enabled him to interpret the pronoun as a reference to his company. This literally truthful response saved Bronston from the perjury charge, leading to what has since become known as the "literal truth defense," which has caused considerable attention to be given to what *literal truth* means in the legal context (Solan and Tiersma 2005: 215–221). In the end the U.S. Supreme Court ruled that a defendant's answer must be literally true in the context of the question that the prosecutor asked.

This finding suggests that when a prosecutor's ambiguous question is capable of allowing responders to understand it in more than one way (the very definition of ambiguity), it is the responsibility of the powerful representative of the legal institution to see to it that any ambiguity becomes clarified. Regardless of whether Bronston's answers were deliberately evasive, it is apparent that the Court believes that it is the sole task of the more powerful prosecutor to clarify any ambiguities to the less powerful defendant. It is difficult to see how this conclusion about courtroom ambiguity does not also apply to ambiguous questions and answers in the context of police interviews and to the process of gathering evidence during undercover operations. In terms of the asymmetry of power between the powerful and the powerless, the pressure falls upon the powerful participant to clarify any ambiguous exchanges.

The use of power through ambiguity leads inevitably to the question of how, when, and whether ambiguity can constitute deception, whether by commission or omission. As the *Bronston* case illustrates, ambiguity can flout Grice's maxim of being clear and unambiguous, whether deliberately or not. But when such ambiguity is intentional, it can count only as a form of deception. The problem is how to know when ambiguity is used deceptively.

Research on Language and Deception

There has been a considerable amount of research about the linguistic cues to deception, including those conveyed by non-verbal body language (Ekman and Friesen 1969; Ekman et al. 1991; Ekman and O'Sullivan 1999; Leal and Vrij 2008). Research on language clues to deception includes the work on suprasegmentals (Reynolds and Rendle-Short 2010; Villar, Arciula and Paterson 2013), style (Buller and Burgoon 1966; Sip et al. 2013; Picornell 2013); self-referencing (Schober and Glick 2011), turn-taking allocation (Drew and Heritage 1992; Heydon 2005), negative emotion words (DePaulo et al. 2003), and vagueness (Burgoon et al. 2003), but virtually nothing specific has been said about the way representatives of the legal institution either intentionally or unintentionally use ambiguity to create deception.

Galasinski (2000: 17–33) argues that deception is a communicative act in which the speaker manipulates a target about truth or falsity as a way of inducing that person to hold a particular belief, adding that it is not a mere benign, persuasive, compliance-gaining technique. On the contrary he says, it is a manipulative strategy that is a way of getting hearers to agree to something without their realizing it. Galasinski addresses issues of inducing false beliefs deceptively, manipulating listeners by providing them with inaccurate pictures of the speaker's beliefs, as well as deception created by omission, half-truths, or distortions such as exaggeration, minimization, equivocation, falsification, and concealment.

Deception Used by Police, Prosecutors, and Undercover Operatives

During police interviews and courtroom questioning, suspects and defendants are subject to the following needs and concerns:

- to completely understand what is said to them before responding;
- to request clarification when they don't understand something that is ambiguous;
- to never infer or guess at meaning from unclear or ambiguous language;

- to avoid saying things that could be understood differently by their questioners; and
- to be on guard at all times about possible language tricks or traps.

The transparent power held by police who interview their suspects and by prosecutors who question their defendants provides limits on the types of persuasive tactics they can use. One limit is that their interactions are usually publicly monitored and open to review. When the police tape-record their interviews, any misuses of their power are subject to criticism by opposing attorneys and even by judges. The questioning practices of prosecutors are even more closely monitored in much the same way, especially by the court. Such monitoring can reduce the occurrence of the most egregious types of deception and coercion, but it leaves the door open to the more subtle type of questioning using deceptively ambiguity.

The very nature of undercover operations opens the door even more widely to the use of deceptive ambiguity. The targets' need to be attentive to the language spoken to them is even more critical when the real audience is not the person with whom they are talking but is, instead, a future unseen jury that targets have no reason to even imagine. To the list of concerns and needs noted above, we therefore can add:

- to know to whom you are talking.

In most (but not all) transparent speech events in the police station and the courtroom, suspects and defendants can be fairly certain about who their audience is. Depending on how linguistically, socially, and psychologically competent they are, most of the time they can also understand the relevance and importance of the topics raised, have a reasonably good idea about which speech acts to use, and, if they are alert and competent enough, try to avoid being trapped by the more powerful speaker's uses of ambiguity.

Undercover operations are different, however, for the agents of the government hide their institutional power under the guise of equal power and status. In this way the agents are more enabled to combine the triad of power, ambiguity, and deception to produce effective compliance-gaining results.

The cases described in this book demonstrate that such compliance assumes a number of conditions which, when aided by deceptive ambiguity, can lead to dispute about the results. We might expect the highest frequency of deceptive institutional practice to occur during undercover operations, when the agents hide their institutional identity from targets who cannot accurately know who their true conversational partners are and their real topics. This deceptive camouflage encourages targets to embrace schemas in which they are participating in a more familiar and predictable everyday conversation in which it does not seem important to be on guard about everything that is being said.

One can argue, as the government does, that it is more efficient to capture evidence of criminal behavior when institutionally powerful undercover agents deceptively disguise their own identity and the real topics they are talking about. The success of this type of deceptive ambiguity is no doubt the reason why the government recommends it and has its agents carry out investigations in which it is encouraged and used. At the same time, however, this practice must be recognized as one that creates intentionally deceptive scenarios that produce the strong possibility of incriminating at least some otherwise innocent people (Shuy 2005).

As the case examples in this book will show, the government's use of deceptive ambiguity frequently begins by camouflaging the speech event in which their suspects, defendants, and targets find themselves. For example, when the police interviewed a witness while claiming to be discovering facts about a suspect that did not directly implicate that witness, they created ambiguous deception about what that interview speech event really was. Their hidden intent was to discover that witness's guilt in the matter while they disguised the speech event as their concern about a different suspect. Prosecutors used the same approach with the purportedly friendly witnesses they questioned while at the same time disguising the speech event as the effort to help find out what those witnesses knew about known or suspected actual criminals. In some disguised speech events such as these, witnesses cooperating with the law are not protected by having their own lawyers present to represent and protect their interests, leaving them vulnerable to the eventual efforts by police interviewers and prosecutors to implicate them in crimes that were known to be carried out by someone else. Examples of such cases are described in later chapters.

Targets of undercover operations face even more deeply camouflaged speech events. As can be seen in the cases described in this book, what may have appeared to be an everyday speech event such as a telephone call from family member was actually a deceptively ambiguous, institutionally contrived confrontation call arranged by the police in their effort to get that target to admit his guilt. Similarly, what may seem on the surface to be a conventional business transaction speech event about the sales and purchases of goods actually was a speech event contrived by an undercover agent who tried to enmesh the target in an illegal business transaction.

The extent to which some targets eventually come to recognize that their initial perception of the speech event differs from the agent's is crucial for determining whether or not the targets inculpate themselves. Sometimes they fail to recognize the agent's speech event because their very different schemas of that speech event leads them to misperceive the agent's disguised representation of it.

Another type of deceptive ambiguity occurs in the topics that police, prosecutors, and undercover agents introduce. In courtroom questioning, prosecutors introduce only their own topics, making it difficult if not impossible for defendants to express their own agendas, predispositions, and intentions. Police interviewers are only slightly more open to hearing their suspects' agendas, for hearing their suspects' agendas does not always serve the main task of eliciting a confession. In order to satisfy their covert missions, at some point undercover agents are required to introduce and make clear the topic of the illegality of their enterprise. If they fail to make this mutually understandable, the operation faces the risk of being tainted and the judge eventually might even consider their efforts as entrapment. In many such investigations, the agents meet with their targets in perfectly legitimate settings such as business offices where they bring up topics about such things as selling a product, lobbying a politician, or checking on the progress of a product being manufactured. Since clearly and unambiguously describing their illegal intentions often causes targets to turn away, undercover agents commonly get around to introducing illegal acts slowly and subtly, often with indirectness and various hinting strategies that are often deceptively ambiguous in themselves.

In such operations the topics introduced by both parties often concern legal matters up the point at which the agent subtly hints at the illegality about what they are doing. Some targets, deeply enmeshed in the legally benign topics being discussed up to that point, miss the hints entirely and go right on talking about their products for sale, their lobbying efforts, or their manufacturing processes. Others misinterpret the indirectness about illegality and engage in some mental gymnastics in an effort to try to make these ambiguous hints fit into their ongoing legally benign schemas and agendas. Still others understand the thrust of the hints and redirect the flow of their conversation back to legality, similar to the way some people politely ignore socially inappropriate off-color jokes and go right on as though those jokes hadn't been introduced at all.

Still another type of deceptive ambiguity is accomplished through indirect speech acts, in which police, prosecutors, and undercover agents say something that their targets can understand to have a very different illocutionary force (Searle 1979: 1–57). Similar to hinting, indirectness can contain the deceptively ambiguous characteristics of omission, concealment, and minimization. This works particularly well when suspects, defendants, and targets provide clear evidence of being predisposed to commit a crime, for in such cases they understand the indirectness of the speech acts and go right on to incriminate themselves. When this happens, the government's goal of capturing crime can be considered successful. But when the targets' language indicates that they misunderstand the intent underlying the agents' indirectness and then proceed to infer something benignly different from it, their responses can still provide some potential inculpatory power, because even though their responses may not suggest guilt, the agent's indirectness has been recorded on tape and it remains there as part of the evidence for jurors to hear at trial and to make whatever inferences they wish about whether or not the target understood the agent's indirect meaning. In short, the targets can be sullied with contaminating evidence that is not of their own making.

A particularly questionable type of deception created by police, prosecutors, and undercover agents consists of the conversational strategies that they sometimes use as they try to control and influence their subjects' actions by causing them to interpret the world from the legal representative's own point of view. Even though uses of conversational strategies such as interrupting, blocking, hit-and-run, and withholding critical information are common in everyday conversation, when these strategies are used in legal settings of police interviews, courtroom questioning, and undercover operations, they can provide evidence of deceptive ambiguity.

It cannot be denied that most conversations and interviews contain some elements of unplanned and unintentional ambiguity, for there is no perfect speaker and no perfect language in which complete clarity can occur consistently. For example, some innate potential for ambiguity is built into English pronoun referencing, where the meaning of *it*, *you*, or *they* can be defined only by explicit or clearly inferred contextual references, and sometimes not perfectly even then. As mentioned above in the *Bronston* case, potential ambiguity was evident in the pronoun *you*, which from the start can refer to either one or more persons or groups of people.

But pronouns and deictic references are not the only purveyors of deceptive ambiguity. When conversational partners believe they are in separate speech events, many things they say to each other can be ambiguous. Participants' schemas about what they are talking about are heavily influenced by their perception of the speech event and can easily contrast with the contradictory schemas of the other participants. When a topic that is introduced and continued by a speaker is misperceived by the hearer as a different topic from the one the speaker had in mind, deceptive ambiguity can rear its head. And the response the hearer makes to that topic can convey similar ambiguity to the speaker that results in one of those "trains passing in the night" exchanges without either party realizing it.

Even speech acts can be deceptively ambiguous, especially when they are not produced felicitously. Warnings can be given in ways that the hearer perceives as advice or threats. Offers can be misunderstood as promises. Consent and agreement can be misunderstood when it is not clear what is consented to or agreed upon. Advice can be misconstrued as a directive, and an infelicitously uttered disagreement can be ignored.

When speakers use certain conversational strategies in the effort to persuade the other person about something, some of these can be considered benign, but those strategies that convey deceptive ambiguity have a potential for appearing to be deliberate deceptive ambiguity.

The representatives of law have an obvious institutional power advantage as they interact with suspects, defendants, and targets. With this power comes important responsibilities, including the responsibility to clarify any language ambiguities they themselves produce as well as any ambiguities produced by others, for such ambiguities create the possibility of misunderstandings not only between the participants but also for later listeners such as judges and juries. Solan refers to undetected indeterminacy in meaning as "pernicious ambiguity" (2004: 859). Deception is created by such pernicious ambiguity. Whether or not such deception is created intentionally, it causes the listener to believe it means one thing while the speaker believes it means another.

With these brief introductory comments about power, ambiguity, and deception, the following chapters describe their use as language evidence in various types of criminal law cases, including murder, sexual misconduct, bribery, perjury, fraud, and terrorism. The cases that fall into the category of transparent institutional interviewing in both the courtroom and police precinct comprise chapters 4 and 5. The cases described chapters 6, 7, and 8, illustrate a very different category of interactions in which the institutional power of law is intentionally and deceptively camouflaged. Here the targets are not in custody, have not been accused of a crime, are not aware that they are talking to institutional representatives of the law, and can't know that their conversations are being recorded for later use by prosecutors, judges, and eventually juries. Those are cases in which friends, family members, fellow workers, and business associates represent the powerful legal institution but camouflage it. The very definition of camouflage conveys intentional deception that distorts or omits the truth. However necessary such institutional camouflage may be for the purposes of law enforcement, it can be considered questionable for agents to deceptively camouflage the most critical parts of conversation—the speech events, schemas, agendas, speech acts, conversational strategies, and lexical and grammatical expressions. The emphasis of the following chapters will be on those particular linguistic features.

3

Police Interviewers Use Deceptive Ambiguity

The imposing physical settings of police stations convey the unmistakable feeling of institutional power that is plainly obvious to everyone. Average law-abiding citizens greatly value the protection that takes place within the walls of this power-laden institution where the speech event of interrogation takes place. Witnesses and suspects know that when they enter those doors they must assume a powerless role. Unfortunately, the story of power doesn't end there. The halls of justice remain the same, but the problem of ambiguity can arise when suspects and witnesses are interviewed during these police interview speech events.

As with all other institutions, language is the major vehicle that drives the decisions in this legal context. It introduces into evidence the characteristic features of the ways people write and talk and in spite of all human efforts to be clear and specific, ambiguity looms as an inherent and ever-present possibility. Sometimes the speakers are ambiguous without intending to be and, being only human, sometimes they use it intentionally. But suspects and witnesses are not the only ones who use ambiguity for their own benefit. It is unfortunate that even within a legal system that proclaims fairness and justice for all, it is quite possible for interviewees to become deceived and misled as law enforcement officers produce their own ambiguous language. Since by definition ambiguous language is capable of conveying more than one meaning, the speech event of interviewing in the legal context tends to favor the interpretations of ambiguous language made by the police over the interpretations made by relatively powerless suspects and witnesses. After all, respected officers of the law are assumed to be open, transparent, and honest at all times—as many of them are.

It may be comforting to think that deceptive ambiguity seldom occurs during the administration of justice, but unfortunately it has been known to show its face in ways other than the specialized jargon of the police. Although this deception is not always conveyed intentionally, there are times that the language used by the police offers a very strong appearance of being deliberate, especially when during their interviews they simply repeat their ambiguous grammatical references, presuppositions, omissions, distortions, minimizations, exaggerations, and concealments rather than trying to clarify or correct them.

This chapter describes some of the ways police interviewers used such ambiguity with their suspects. They usually begin their questioning by administering to suspects their *Miranda* rights, which is a separate speech event with its own structured requirements.

The *Miranda* Warning Speech Event

The initial way some law enforcement officers deceive suspects occurs when they attempt to fulfill the obligation created by the US Supreme Court's requirement that suspects must be advised about their constitutional rights. In 1966 the US Supreme Court ruling in the case of *Miranda v. Arizona* expanded the Fifth Amendment privilege against self-incrimination, which up to that time had applied mainly to courtrooms, and brought it down the legal ladder into police precincts. We begin by noting the speech acts involved in this. Despite the fact that *Miranda* is called a *warning*, the law actually requires police officers to "advise" suspects in a reasonable and clear way about their constitutional rights before starting to interview them. These well-known rights include the advice that they can remain silent, have an attorney present with them during their questioning, and have an attorney appointed for them if they can't afford one. This process of advising a suspect's rights is accompanied by a warning pointing out that whatever the suspects say to the police can be used against them at a court of law.

Since the Supreme Court didn't specify the exact wording to be used or the sequence in which this combination of advice and warnings was to be presented, various individual law enforcement agencies have printed small laminated cards to be carried by police officers at all times in order to have them handy to consult when they make arrests. It was apparently assumed by the Court that this combination of advice and warnings would be perfectly clear and unambiguous to all suspects, regardless of their age, ethnic background, maturity, intelligence, English-language competence, and emotional state. In order to be sure that the police have successfully produced the *Miranda* warning, after this recitation many law enforcement officers also ask the suspects whether they have understood what they were just told.

Almost from the beginning, the *Miranda* warning has been the subject of much dispute (White 1982). Some critics say that telling suspects "you have the right to remain silent" is hopelessly confusing, that "you have the right to have an attorney present" is ambiguous concerning when, where, and how this presence can take place, and "whatever you say may be used against you" is simply a problem for many people to understand. The notoriously lame follow-up question, "do you understand these warnings," is subject to similar criticism because this yes/no question substituting as a comprehension measure is considered the least effective way to discover what a listener has understood. In fairness, it cannot be denied that when the Supreme Court created the *Miranda* warning, it tried to ensure that police procedures would protect the constitutional rights of the citizenry, but as is often the case, the implementation these rights has been, as Tiersma described it, "a rocky road" (Tiersma 2001). Other critics use more colorful descriptions of *Miranda*, such as a "mistake" (Stuntz 2001: 975), a "spectacular failure" (Thomas 2004: 1091), and an "empty ritual" (Uviller 1996: 124). Ainsworth (2010: 112) observes that despite the constitutional constraints placed on *Miranda*, "problems in police interrogation are still a major contributor to miscarriages of justice in which the innocent are erroneously convicted of crimes."

In 1987 linguist Eugene Briere produced one of the earliest assessments of *Miranda*. The suspect was a native Thai speaker with English as his second language. The police read his *Miranda* to him in English and based on a series of relevant tests of English competence, Briere concluded that the suspect didn't possess sufficient English-language competence to understand what was being read to him. Since Briere was obviously not present at the time the rights were read to the suspect, he later administered to the defendant the best English comprehension tests available at the time and concluded that it was very unlikely that this man could have understood the *Miranda* warning that the police administered.

Since Briere's initial venture into this problem, the language of the *Miranda* warning has been severely criticized by many linguists because of its inherent assumption that second language speakers can actually understand it, even though they may compliantly tell the powerful authority figure that they did. For a summary of other case developments in the use of *Miranda* warnings with non-native English speakers, see Pavlenko (2008).

After analysts with linguistic skills examined the ambiguous aspects of the *Miranda* warning, evidence of possible comprehensibility was exposed. Linguistic research has shown that not only speakers of a second language but also native speakers of English can find these rights ambiguous and hard to understand (Berk-Seligson 1990, 2009; Shuy 1997, 2014; Roy 2000, 2014; Tiersma 2001, 2005; Solan and Tiersma 2005; Heydon 2011). Similar critiques have been made about the equivalent standardized cautions given in England and Wales (Cotterill 2000; Rock 2007) and in Australia (Gibbons 1990; Eades 2003; Heydon 2005, 2011).

Subtle and even more powerful deceptive ambiguities can be revealed during the questioning that follows the warning, when detectives use ambiguity that manipulates the evidence, misstates or misrepresents what suspects actually said, overlooks or even omits what suspects have said previously, and minimizes or conceals the detectives' own potentially questionable language strategies.

The Police Interview Speech Event

After administering suspects their rights, the conventional police interview is a speech event that is purportedly structured as follows:

1. Elicit the facts;
2. Question possible inaccuracies, deceptions, or omissions;
3. Confront the suspect with the inaccuracies, deceptions, and omissions;
4. Accuse the suspect of the crime; and
5. Elicit a confession.

The institutional power of the police interview speech event is obvious not only from the physical location in which it takes place but also from the language used during the event itself for as van Dijk points out, "activities are not independent of the language that defines it" (1985: 201). Gumperz (1990: 9) stressed the importance of speech event analysis, defining speech events as "recurring occasions that have tacitly understood rules of preference, unspoken conventions as to what counts as valid and what information may or may not be introduced." Although police interviewers are urged to follow the structure and sequence of the five-step interview speech event noted above, they often have been known to abandon the first step of eliciting facts relating to the case and begin with a step 3 confrontation or even at step 4 accusation (Shuy 2014: 61–63).

During the interview, the police also can create various deceptions that enable them to elicit admissions and confessions that prosecutors then rely upon to establish the guilt at trial, regardless of whether the targets were actually responsible for the crime for which they were charged. If the deceptive practices of the intelligence gatherers (the police) are subject to criticism, even more questionable are the practices of the intelligence analysts (the prosecutors), whose job it is to recognize any problems created in the intelligence gathered by the police, including any ambiguity or deception, and take this into consideration as they determine whether the evidence is adequate to bring and indictment and trial. Failure to recognize such problems in gathering and analyzing the evidence leaves considerable room for criticism of both the interviewer and the prosecutor. Among other things, the prosecutor's task is not only to determine whether the language evidence indicates that there was sufficient deceptive ambiguity to weaken the prosecution's case but also whether it reached the level of coercion, which, if found to be present, can create even more serious consequences for the prosecution.

Participants bring to virtually all speech events their previous knowledge, beliefs, values, and attitudes by using a psychological construct called "schema" (Bartlett 1932). Schemas are the mental plans that guide speakers' thoughts and language about what they believe is going on. In most if not all police interview speech events the interviewers begin with a schema of the suspect's guilt that typically continues throughout the interview, whereas the schemas of suspects in many cases are that they are innocent and very much want the police to believe this. These opposing schemas continue unless or until the suspects admit their guilt.

The agendas of the police interview flow naturally out of the speech event and the participants' schemas. Police interviewers introduce virtually all of the topics, manifesting their power and control during this process. They are institutionally empowered to ask all of the questions and to completely control the conversational flow. Some of their most commonly used speech acts are requesting information, denying what the suspect says, advising, accusing, warning, and complaining. They are not allowed to threaten suspects or promise them anything substantive. The powerless suspects' speech acts typically provide information, deny accusations, admit, and complain, but it is usually futile for them to request salient information or to accuse or warn their interviewers.

As the police interviewers express their agendas, they have the power to shift topics at will, in contrast with the suspects who are powerless to do this. If the interviewers choose, they can try to persuade the suspect by using indirect speech acts, hint at what they are after, omit or conceal important information, and minimize the information they give the suspect, although some of these strategies later can be subject to criticism if they are noticed by alert defense attorneys. The police can also use certain conversational strategies to further their goal, such as interrupting, blocking, and being ambiguous (Shuy 2005). These also are subject to potential criticism, as are the officers' use of certain presuppositions, words, phrases, and grammatical referencing.

Ambiguity can be located and identified in the ways the police present the speech event, including the ways suspects appear to understand it, in the ways they treat or ignore the participants' schemas, in their interview agendas, in the ways they use or do not use speech acts, in their conversational strategies, as well as in their choices of words, phrases, sentences, referencing, and other grammatical forms. The focus of this chapter is on the ways that the empowered law enforcement officers used deceptive ambiguity to accomplish their goals during police interview speech events, whether or not such use was intentional.

It is necessary to understand that unlike the practice followed in England and Wales, US police officers are permitted to use certain types of deception during their interviews. For example, they can tell suspects that the police already know things that they actually do not know, such as "we found the gun you used," "your partner has already implicated you," "we discovered your fingerprints at the scene," or "your DNA tells us that you did it." On the other hand, police interviewers are not permitted to misrepresent suspects' rights, threaten them, coerce them in any way, or offer them false assurances. In the view of some critics, the government's justification for using these clearly deceptive practices leads to the uncomfortable assumption that the only thing that really matters is that the interview will end with a confession regardless of how that confession was achieved. This method of using deception often works well for the prosecution but leaves unanswered a number of important procedural and moral questions that are apparently better recognized in England and Wales, where the police are required to focus their interviews on obtaining the highest quality of information for investigative and evidentiary purposes. Unlike the situation in the United States, their goal appears to be not simply to obtain a confession at any cost.

Although in the United States the police are allowed to create these deceptive practices, there are other types of deceptive acts that can slip by unnoticed by defense attorneys, suspects, prosecutors, and juries. One example of this is when law enforcement officers deceptively minimize the evidence by omitting the interviewer's questions in the official record of the interview. Instead, they record or report only those portions of the interview in which the suspect confessed. This deceptively manipulates the record to make it appear to be different from what may have actually taken place. In addition to this, the interviewers' deceptive strategies in creating ambiguity through choices of words, grammar, and presuppositions, whether intentional or not, can mislead suspects into believing that they are talking about something different from the interviewer's purported topic.

The following describes police interviews in three criminal cases that illustrate some of the ways the police were ambiguous and deceptive during their interviews with suspects. For more extensive analysis of the individual cases described in this section, see Shuy (1998, 2014).

Police Interviewers Use Deceptive Ambiguity with Kevin Rogers

In June 1995 the Houston police found the body of an elderly brutally murdered woman lying on the kitchen floor of her home. When the killer broke into her house, she was talking on the phone with a friend, who immediately reported the victim's screams to the police. A squad car was near the incident and an officer arrived quickly. During the next day or so the police were stymied at finding the perpetrator and in discovering any motive for the murder. Nevertheless, they publicly announced that it looked to them very much like the work of a youthful, amateur thrill killer. They found some fingerprints in the home but with no other clues to go on, they issued a call for neighborhood boys to volunteer to be interviewed, using the acceptable but possibly insincere excuse that the boys might have seen a suspicious person in or near the victim's neighborhood. Because they considered this a youthful thrill crime, they also fingerprinted the boys as they questioned them.

Kevin Rogers dutifully volunteered to be questioned and as the police talked with him they learned that he often visited the victim, sometimes did some odd jobs for her, and frequently visited her home to play with her little dog. Because his fingerprints matched those they found all over the house, Kevin became their prime suspect.

It is important to know that the police had learned from Kevin's teachers that even though he was in the eighth grade, he was severely limited intellectually and was said to function academically more like a second or third grader. This school's procedure was to pass students along to the next grade level whether or not they had mastered what was taught. His teachers and neighbors did not support the investigator's suspicion that Kevin was the killer, because all of them liked Kevin and told the police that he never caused any trouble. In spite of these positive reports, during their interview with Kevin the police quickly became convinced that he committed the crime and eventually got him to confess to it. Kevin signed this interview report, called a confession statement, which became the major evidence supporting the criminal charges brought against him.

The police didn't tape-record this interview because they claimed that their policy was to record interviews only with adult murder suspects but not with minors. Instead of tape-recording it, the police used a procedure in which the detective sat at a word processor and typed what Kevin allegedly said while he was being interviewed. Even so, the detective who did this admitted that the report was "not necessarily in Kevin's own words." This process produced fifty-one statements allegedly made by Kevin, but it failed to include any of the detective's questions that could have elicited his answers. Omitting the record of Kevin's exact words, the detective's questions, and the context and sequence of those questions constitutes a deceptive omission of evidence, whether or not it was thought to be unintentional. Even if the detectives may not have thought they were being deceptive, the result was the same because their procedure concealed at least half or more of what was said during the interview. Without such context, the evidence was minimized, one of the established characteristics of deceptive behavior. Whatever motivation the police may have had, this process could be considered an institutionally sanctioned concealment of the facts in the case. Even more problematic, by omitting the interviewer's questions, there was no way for the defense to verify that Kevin's reported answers in his confession statement directly related to the immediate questions. By following this procedure, the police violated the first criterion of transparency—that of making available all the evidence relevant to the case.

Despite the absence of Kevin's criminal motivation and with no witnesses to the crime, the prosecutor reviewed Kevin's signed confession statement and decided that the information in it was adequate to charge Kevin with capital murder as an adult. Some critics may find it inconsistent for the police to adhere to the policy of not tape-recording interviews with minors while then charging those minors as adults.

To his court-appointed attorney, Kevin vehemently denied that he had murdered the elderly lady. The problem was why then would Kevin have admitted the crime to the police and signed the confession statement. He admitted that he signed it, but did he actually know what he signed? One of the prosecution's major points was that Kevin's confession was very apparent when at the very end of the interview he apologized for his actions. Without a tape-recording of this purported apology, the police wrote down his last two statements as follows:

50. I am sorry for what I did.
51. I wish that it didn't happen.

Even if Kevin's "I am sorry for what I did" were his own words, it does not qualify as a felicitous speech act apologizing. A felicitous apology should include words specific to the event for which the alleged apology was made (Searle 1969; Battistella 2014). The ambiguity conveyed by Kevin's words "what I did" and "it" in 50 and 51 suggests that even if these words were reported accurately, exactly what they referred to was not clear. For example, they could have referred to Kevin's earlier statement that the victim had once hollered at him for shooting birds with his BB gun, which the police subsequently tried to establish as his motivation for killing the elderly woman.

Reprising the definition of ambiguity cited in chapter 1, "what I did" qualifies as ambiguous because it does not specify what Kevin did and was therefore subject to inference by the police. Note also that the US Supreme Court ruled that it is the responsibility of the powerful participant to seek and obtain clarification of ambiguous utterances (*Bronston v. United States*, 409 U.S., 1973, 358). If the police actually tried to clarify Kevin's "what I did," they provided no record of this in their own evidence. Therefore, the triers of the facts were also left to infer that Kevin was sorry for having murdered the lady. The detective's failure to clarify this ambiguity may not have constituted intentional deception but it certainly deceived the jury that convicted him of first-degree murder.

Kevin's statement 51, "I wish that it didn't happen," is also decontextualized. If the detective recorded Kevin accurately, this statement can fit the speech act of condolence better than the speech act of an apology. His "it" is non-specific and his wish that "it" didn't happen is consistent with his sorrow of losing a friendly neighbor lady and inconsistent with an event in which Kevin had killed the victim. If Kevin had said "I wish I didn't kill her" the case might be very different. But that's not what the police reported that he said. Instead, they again ignored the ambiguity residing in their un-taped record of what Kevin told them.

The police also considered the confession statement damaging because it included Kevin's knowledge of the details that the police believed could only be known by the perpetrator of the crime. The known facts were that the victim was raped, her blouse was opened, she was stabbed in the neck, a small amount of money was taken, and her underpants were found off to the side of her body. The police reasoned that if Kevin was not the killer, how could he have known some of these essential facts? They apparently overlooked that these facts could have come from three possible sources: specific knowledge that only the killer possessed, second-hand knowledge that the killer could have learned from some other source, and general knowledge that anyone might have.

Because Kevin had visited the victim's house many times, he had general knowledge about some facts, including the victim's dog, having played with it often. He had observed the victim's telephone many times and reported that he sometimes saw her talking on it. He had been in her kitchen and had seen her knife rack. In his confession, Kevin admitted that he knew these things, even though he was wrong about other things such as the color of her pants.

Kevin also had second-hand knowledge of the murder that the police treated as firsthand knowledge. The following explains how he obtained this second-hand information. When the patrol officer arrived at the crime scene, he reported that he didn't want to disturb any latent fingerprints on the victim's telephone, so he went to the house next door to call in the information to his superiors. One of Kevin's classmates lived in that house and admitted that he overheard what the policeman said. This information included that the victim was stabbed in the neck, what she was wearing, and how her body was placed, which were things that the detective asked Kevin about the following day. On that day, before the detective had a chance to pull Kevin out of class and interview him, the neighbor boy had told his classmates, including Kevin, what he heard the officer say on the phone. Kevin clearly possessed second-hand information that the detective misperceived as first-hand evidence of his guilt. But that wasn't all. The night of the murder, the local television station news program had reported this same information as well as details of her clothing and the theft of money. Kevin told the police that he had watched that program. Specific information that Kevin had about the crime was derived, therefore, from what the initial investigating patrolman conveyed while he was in the home of Kevin's classmate next door and from the local television news program. The interviewers had hopelessly confused specific knowledge with general and second-hand knowledge.

Since I was curious about the accuracy of Kevin's language as it was written in his confession transcript, I asked his attorney to tape-record an hour or so of conversation with Kevin to use as a comparison. On that tape, which was not admitted at trial, his defense attorney asked Kevin why he confessed to the murder. His response was that he didn't even know what *confession* means. Kevin told his attorney that when the detective started hollering at him, he asked for his mama but the detective told him if he'd hurry up and confess, his mama would pick him up. At that point Kevin agreed to sign the statement, believing that he was going to get to go home after seven long hours of questioning. Kevin also related to his attorney how he told the detective that he had seen a knife on the kitchen table many times. In the confession statement he told the police that he "grabbed" it, but even so the time sequence about whether he grabbed it then or at some past time was not clear, which is not surprising from a boy whose language skills were far from well-developed. Although there is no record of the questions the detective asked Kevin, the confession statement indicates that he saw the dog, saw the victim talking on the phone, and grabbed the knife on the kitchen table and used it to kill her. To his own attorney Kevin denied that he told the police that he even saw the knife that day. It remains unclear what time period his confession statement referred to and how the questions were asked to produce the admission that he stabbed the woman with a knife.

In summary, the institutionally created ambiguity in this case includes the following found in the next few sections.

AMBIGUITY PRODUCED BY THE SPEECH EVENT

Although the police did not make a tape or transcript of the interrogation, they reported that since they didn't know who the killer was, they interviewed Kevin along with other boys who lived in the area. If this explanation of the procedure is accurate, the police identified their interview to Kevin as an information-gathering speech event. It apparently turned into an accusation speech event at some point during the interview. In that Kevin cooperated with the police when they asked him what he might have seen at the time and place of the murder, his perception of the speech event was that of information gathering. Kevin volunteered to help the police concerning anything he might know about the victim and whether he had seen anything that might look suspicious. The police had no reason to suspect Kevin and they apparently did not at first indicate their suspicion to him, but then they turned this benign information-gathering speech event an into accusation speech event. Since this appears to be accepted police strategy, we may not want to blame the law enforcement officers for doing so. Nevertheless, the strategy must count as the use of ambiguous deception used by a powerful institution with a powerless, intellectually and socially challenged juvenile.

AMBIGUITY PRODUCED BY SCHEMAS

Schemas grow naturally out of the speech event. The evidence of only the signed confession statement is not sufficient for a careful analysis of Kevin's schema, but if the detective's trial testimony is accurate, at the start of the interview Kevin's schema was most likely that he was that he was trying to be helpful to the police. His schema was equally likely to have changed once it became clear to him that he was being accused of the murder. From the beginning, the police likely inferred that Kevin was the killer, but making inferences is often a dicey matter. Inferences grow naturally out of the speech event, which in this case was a police interview in which the schemas of the officers must have strayed from their purported purpose of neutrally and objectively discovering the facts.

AMBIGUITY PRODUCED BY AGENDAS

Based on Kevin's written and signed confession statement, the police interviewer had the only agenda. There is no way to retrieve a clear picture of the officer's topics and his questions, because the police did not tape-record the interview, make a transcript of it, or produce any notes about it. Based solely on a confession statement that contained only Kevin's purported answers, his lone role in the interview appeared to be to respond to the detective's topics and questions.

Both the police and the prosecutor relied heavily on the topic of the presence of Kevin's fingerprints inside the victim's home, even though, as noted earlier, there was a perfectly benign reason for their presence. Convincing suspects that their fingerprint evidence is proof of their guilt may be an appropriate and acceptable persuasive strategy to use on many suspects, but it was especially deceptive to use it on a mentally retarded fifteen-year-old boy who had little or no capacity to understand that the police were probably uncertain about the significance of this fingerprint evidence. It was equally deceptive for the prosecutor to have relied on that fingerprint evidence, for even though he undoubtedly learned that it had a high potential for being benign, he was still willing to present it to jurors who would not be likely to understand that this was the prosecutor's deceptive ploy.

In their search for Kevin's motive, the police inferred and then promoted as motive that at one time in the past he had been shooting at birds with his pellet gun. The victim disapproved of this and took Kevin's gun away from him and kept it in her house. The detective promoted this topic as Kevin's motive despite the fact that the police found that same gun in plain sight in the house exactly where the victim had kept it. The detective tried to convert this inconsistency into a motive by eliciting from Kevin that he forgot to take it.

AMBIGUITY PRODUCED BY SPEECH ACTS

With no way to verify the speech acts actually used by the police, we are left only with what the confession statement reports about Kevin's statements. Most likely, the police used the speech acts of asking questions, accusing Kevin of the murder, and accusing him of lying. Equally clearly, the confession statement indicates that Kevin's speech acts were reporting what he did and saw, denying that he had anything to do with the murder, and saying he was sorry about two things: he wished the victim had not been killed and he was sorry about what he did, although it is unclear even from his statements what he had done to be sorry about. These alleged apologies were infelicitous speech acts.

Ambiguous deception is evident in the lack of contextual information provided by the fifty-one statements that Kevin purportedly made. These statements apparently were given in response to the detective's unreported and therefore unknown speech acts of questioning, creating the inference that when Kevin allegedly told the detective about what he had done, he was referring to the day of the murder. For example, Kevin reported that he had gone to the woman's house, he had played with her puppy, he heard that the TV was on, he had accepted a glass of Kool-Aid from the victim, he saw a knife in the kitchen, he forgot to take the pellet gun, and then he went home. Based on this one-dimensional, baren confession statement, the ambiguous period of time period in which all of this happened had to be inferred, along with the missing questions that had elicited this information.

The police finally inferred that they got what they needed after Kevin allegedly admitted that he stabbed the victim "about three times in her chest and neck." How they elicited this admission remained for the jury to infer because the police deceptively omitted all of their own questions that might have revealed how they got Kevin to say it as well as how Kevin had acquired this information. The detective's omission of the temporal context of Kevin's statements was an important part of his deceptive ambiguity during the interview.

The detectives heard Kevin's speech act of reporting second-hand information about the murder and deceptively distorted it to appear to be first-hand information that only the killer could know. It was also a simple matter for the detective to deceptively distort Kevin's ambiguous and infelicitous apology to convince the prosecutor that it was actually an admission of Kevin's guilt. This distortion was aided by the detective's manipulation of Kevin's second-hand information into purported first-hand information that only the perpetrator would know. If the prosecutor had been an alert information analyst, he might have been expected to notice this and ask more about it. He did not.

AMBIGUITY PRODUCED BY CONVERSATIONAL STRATEGIES

From this bare confession statement it was not possible to discover whatever evidence there might have been about any conversational strategies the police used to elicit it. The deception here comes from omitting in the record whatever strategies they may have used. If the police were to claim that they didn't use any, their decision not to tape-recording the interview would not support their claim. Tape-recording interviews also can serve to protect the police from charges of coercion or outrageous behavior.

AMBIGUITY PRODUCED BY LEXICON AND GRAMMAR

The detective apparently ignored Kevin's lack of knowledge of expressions common to the institutional practice of the police. When Kevin's lawyer tape-recorded an interview with him about what had taken place during the police interview, he found that Kevin had no idea about the meaning of the expressions, *consult, voluntarily, my right*, and *freely and knowingly.* Kevin said:

> I know the right to remain silence (*sic*) and I ain't say nothing and I ain't understand the others. I ain't know what they was talking about then.

Even though Kevin told his lawyer that he knew what "the right to remain silence" (*sic*) meant, he demonstrated that he really didn't know this when he then seemed to contradict it, saying, "I ain't say nothing" in spite of the fact that his confession statement indicates that he apparently answered the detective's questions with speech acts of agreement. The lexical ambiguities of the *Miranda* questions qualify very nicely as deceptive trickery to many suspects, but particularly so to a mentally and socially challenged juvenile like Kevin. Even from the prosecution's evidence it is not difficult to see that ambiguity was possible in the policeman's questions. It is equally easy to see that the detective took advantage of an inarticulate, intellectually challenged suspect to use that ambiguity to satisfy his own goals.

Even though the detective testified that the words he transcribed were "not exactly" Kevin's own, he claimed that they "represented" what Kevin said. Representing what was said contradicts the definition of a confession as "an acknowledgement in express words used by the accused" (Wigmore 1904: 308). After I examined the hour-long tape-recording of Kevin talking with his attorney, it became very clear that Kevin was an inarticulate speaker of the type of Vernacular African American English that was spoken to powerful detectives in a formal context that would require him to use his best language. His best language consistently used verb third singular verbs without the standard—s; he had no past tense -ed forms; he habitually used the nonstandard *ain't* in "I ain't did that," and "I ain't say nothin'", and many others. It was particularly ludicrous for the detective to claim that the first of Kevin's fifty-one presumed utterances represented what Kevin said:

> 1. I do not want to consult with a lawyer before I make this statement and I do not want to remain silent. And I now freely and voluntarily waive my right to a lawyer and to remain silent and I knowingly make the following voluntary statement.

From what it was possible to learn about Kevin's language skill, it is a serious stretch of credibility to imagine that he was able to say anything remotely similar to the above, even accounting for the detective's caveat that the confession was "not exactly in his own words." To achieve this response, the detective is likely to have asked at least five questions here to which Kevin allegedly agreed, regardless of what the questions may have meant to him. It would have behooved the detective to have reported both how his own questions were worded and exactly what Kevin's actual responses were. Even with these omissions, compliance could be expected from a fifteen-year-old juvenile minority speaker with severe mental limitations who cowered helplessly before a powerful authority figure like a detective.

The prosecution and conviction in the case of *Texas v. Kevin Rogers* provides an astonishing record of law enforcement's use of deceptive ambiguity in the pursuit of justice. Even sadder is that if the police had tape-recorded their interview with Kevin, much of the purported information in this interview could have become clear and unambiguous. Some police departments protect themselves against being accused of unfair interviewing techniques. This one chose not to do so.

Police Interviewers Use Deceptive Ambiguity with Michael Carter

In 1989 a policeman was shot dead during an attempted home burglary in Baton Rouge, Louisiana. Four inner-city African American boys rode their bicycles to a wealthy part of town to find houses where they could steal things. Michael Carter, the youngest of the four, was assigned the task of being the lookout for the other boys. When a motorcycle patrolman who happened to be in the area at the time saw them trying to enter a home, he gave chase on foot. After catching them, he told the boys lie down on the ground. Instead, they started to run away and the only boy who was carrying a pistol shot and killed the policeman. While running away, the shooter tossed the gun to Michael, who briefly had it in his hand before tossing it into a nearby creek while he was running. Eventually they were caught and the oldest boy, their leader, told the investigator that Michael was the shooter. Michael vehemently denied this when interviewed.

Unlike the Kevin Rogers case, the police tape-recorded part of their interview with Michael but then decided to stop the recording after forty minutes of failing to get him to admit being the shooter. They stopped because Michael was crying incoherently and became so ill that he began to vomit. While crying and retching, however, ten times he managed to deny that he was the one who shot the patrolman. After a brief break the police continued the interview but without tape-recording it and therefore we can't know or verify what was said during that period. From the recorded portion, however, we can see that the detectives used one of the sanctioned deceptions accorded to police interviews. They claimed that they knew the patrolman was shot by a left-handed person and that it had to have been Michael because he was left-handed.

Undaunted by the lack of a tape-recorded admission, a detective then produced a one-page handwritten statement signed by Michael. The detective admitted that it was in his own handwriting but he claimed that he wrote down Michael's "exact words." Even at first glance, the language of the confession statement did not look like the exact words that would characterize an inner city, African American boy.

To test the accuracy of initial observations of this kind, the standard procedure is to compare Michael's tape-recorded spoken language during the interview with that of his written confession statement. This comparison demonstrated that his sentence structure varied widely between these two sets of evidence. During his interrogation Michael produced simple sentences (Subject-Verb-Object) 80% of the time, whereas his alleged written statement contained only 32% simple sentences. In contrast, the written statement had 68% compound and complex sentences while the tape-recorded partial interview contained only 20% of these sentence constructions. Considering the possibility that this strong contrast in sentence structure could have been the result of Michael's extreme stress and illness during the interview, I decided to get a larger sample of Michael's spoken language in a non-stressful context that could reveal his more normal language patterns.

To obtain such a sample, I asked Michael's attorney to meet with him at the jail and conduct a sociolinguistic style interview in which she tape-recorded him talking about any benign topic that would provide some evidence of his more normal language ability. My hope was that he would talk at length about topics such as the sports events he enjoyed or the television programs he liked to watch. Although it is clear that the police interview is a very different speech event from the speech event of a conversation with a friendly lawyer, even during such different speech events the habitual, patterned uses of vocabulary, grammar, and syntax of a young boy with limited language skills could be expected to reveal some similarities. Indeed, the comparison showed that Michael was consistent in his language patterns during the police interview and during his conversation with his attorney, but both samples of his speech were very different from his signed confession statement that the detective testified was reported in Michael's exact words. Since the syntax of the written confession didn't match either Michael's recorded oral language during the police interview or that of his interview with his attorney, the question became: whose language was in the confession statement?

The obvious place to look for an answer was the detective's own language use. As I pointed out in *The Language of Confession, Interrogation and Deception* (1998), I then compared Michael's language with the detective's testimony reported in several of his past cases and found that the syntax of Michael's confession statement bore a strong similarity with that detective's sentence patterns.

Examining the same sentence structure patterns that differentiated Michael's interview from his written confession, I found that the detective used 38% simple sentences while interviewing Michael and 41% in his past courtroom testimony in three other cases. Similarly, the detective produced 62% compound and complex sentences when he interviewed Michael and 57% in his testimony in other cases. This showed that the detective's apparently habitual pattern of sentence structure closely matched Michael's alleged syntax in the written confession statement, but it did not come close to matching Michael's syntax either in his police interview or when his attorney talked with him in jail.

Sentence structure was not the only noticeable comparison. In his past testimony in other cases, the detective habitually used the hypercorrect form, *myself,* to identify himself in a list of people, as in "the police officers included myself and other detectives," "by several people including myself," and "at various times myself and other officers drove by." Hypercorrect forms like this are one of the signs of potential grammatical confusion commonly found in the speech of people who have become aware of the need to be grammatically correct but don't quite know how to achieve it. In contrast, Michael's level of language ability was evidenced by his "I didn't shoot nobody," and "I ain't know what happened," which did not fall into that category of person who was struggling with hypercorrections, yet his brief confession statement contained one of these that the detective claimed was Michael's own words: "Myself, my cousin Lobo, Freddie Mills and Kermit Parker . . . went over to the neighborhood off Wooddale."

In summary, the following analyses of deceptive ambiguity are notable in this case.

AMBIGUITY PRODUCED BY THE SPEECH EVENT

The police interviewer's language use made it clear that he treated this speech event as a police interrogation of an adult suspect, and Michael's language gave the appearance that he was aware that he was in that speech event. There was no ambiguity resulting from the speech event in this case.

AMBIGUITY PRODUCED BY SCHEMAS

As in most police interrogations, the interviewer's questioning made it very clear that his schema was that Michael was guilty of killing the policeman. Judged by Michael's repeated denials about doing the shooting, it would seem that his schema was that he was guilty of abetting burglary of some houses but that he was not the boy who shot the patrolman. There was also no ambiguity resulting from different schemas in this case.

AMBIGUITY PRODUCED BY AGENDAS

Michael was the last of the suspects interviewed after one of the other boys had told the police that Michael was the shooter. The agenda of the interviewer was clear from his questions in which he assumed from the beginning that Michael was the one who shot and killed the patrolman. In the tape-recorded portion of the interview, there is no evidence that Michael had any agenda other than to deny the accusations. There is no way to verify what anyone said after the tape recorder was turned off, but if Michael then changed his agenda and admitted the shooting, it had to have been in that non-recorded part of the interview. In such cases, the court would have to rely on what the detective reported and inferred, namely that Michael had indeed admitted his guilt. This might have happened if there had not been linguistic evidence showing that the detective had represented Michael's confession as though he had actually said it himself.

AMBIGUITY PRODUCED BY SPEECH ACTS

A glaring contrast exists in the comparison of Michael's frequently repeated speech act of denying shooting the patrolman in the tape-recorded portion of the interview with the written confession statement that he signed later. If Michael uttered the speech act of confessing, it cannot be verified by the taped evidence in which the two detectives' primary and frequently repeated speech act was to accuse Michael of the killing. Perhaps any residual ambiguity about the truth of what happened could have been resolved if the police had continued tape-recording the interview. It is possible that the detective could have manipulated his written confession to make it appear to the prosecutor (and to a future jury) that Michael had actually confessed. It's likely that the detective was relying on the impressive power normally accorded to a signed confession, for there is usually little hope for a suspect who signs a confession statement, in spite of how it is obtained. It is admittedly difficult to be certain whether the detective created the ambiguity between what we know that Michael said and what the detectives claim he said when the tape recorder was not operating. The result, however, created deceptive ambiguity for later listeners, such as prosecutors and juries, for which they could only infer what actually happened based on the detective's words.

AMBIGUITY PRODUCED BY CONVERSATIONAL STRATEGIES

Conversational blocking is a common characteristic of persuasion, especially during oppositional exchanges of the type found in police interviews. Without possessing the information that is blocked, jurors and other evaluators of the evidence are forced to infer information that has been blocked from them. In this case the later evaluators couldn't be certain about what happened during the period when the interview was not tape-recorded. Even though Michael signed the confession statement, the detective's decision to halt the taping before he obtained a spoken confession deceptively blocked the existence such spoken evidence. It would have been possible to wait for Michael to compose himself, but the police apparently decided not to do this. Because this information was blocked, the prosecutor, judge, and potential jury were forced to infer what the critical questions and answers were after the tape-recorder was turned off. To be sure, there was a signed confession statement, but even that was ambiguous in light of the way the evidence was gathered and presented.

The conversational strategy of blocking is also evident in way the detectives constantly interrupted Michael's efforts to deny his guilt. The major conversational strategy, however, was the creation of ambiguity resulting from the lack of tape-recording the entire interview.

At the end, the detective's claim that the confession was in Michael's own language was insufficient to support the charges against Michael. During a hearing to suppress the evidence, the prosecutor decided that since Michael's statement was not tape-recorded and since there was considerable linguistic evidence that his alleged confession was in the detective's own words rather than Michael's, he would withdraw all charges. It became clear to the prosecutor that the detective had created the ambiguity by manipulating the evidence that created the inference that Michael's spoken confession actually had taken place after the tape-recording had stopped. The prosecutor first brought the charges based on the detective's deceptive evidence but then realized his error when further information was presented at the evidentiary hearing. For this, he should be given considerable credit.

AMBIGUITY PRODUCED BY LEXICON AND GRAMMAR

Apparently the detective in this case was less than familiar with what experts in police interrogation advise officers to do when they try to elicit confessions: "No attempt should be made to improve the language used by the subject himself. It should represent his confession as he tells it, and unless he does, a judge or jury may be reluctant to believe that a defendant whose education may have ended at the third grade spoke the language of a college graduate" (Inbau, Reid, and Buckley 1986: 131). When Michael's written confession statement was compared with a sample of his speech in the jail, it became clear that he could not have written the text that comprised his confession. Comparison of Michael's lexicon and syntax with that of the detective made it clear that the language of the confession was the detective's, not Michael's. The detective created the ambiguity about whose language was actually used.

The comparison of Michael's language with that of the police interviewer demonstrated even to the prosecutor that the detective had falsely attributed his own syntax and lexicon to Michael. One example of this is the question asked on tape concerning the point at which the patrolman had caught the boys and had them lying face down on the ground.

OFFICER 1: What happened to make you shoot him?
OFFICER 2: Did you think you were fixing to get shot?
MICHAEL: Yeah I thought he was going to shoot me.

These two questions were asked in succession. Michael appeared to answer the second question, exemplifying something very common in conversation called the recency principle (Miller and Campbell 1959). When two or more questions are asked at the same time, the tendency of the responder is to answer the second, most recent one. Michael's fear that the policeman would shoot him is the causal answer to the second question, not the first one. He prefaced it with "yeah," and "yeah" fits the answer to the second question's "did you think" and it does not fit the first question's "what happened." The officer claimed that Michael's answer was actually his answer to the first one.

Even though it is rare that one word alone can be diagnostic, one such word appeared in the large sample of the detective's speech in which he used the hypercorrect reflexive pronoun over and over again, as in "Myself and Detective Jones responded to the call." This reflexive pronoun appeared once in Michael's purported confession statement but never in the large sample of his everyday language. Michael had not reached the level of language learning in which insecurity about certain usage causes more upwardly bound speakers to hypercorrect when they are uncertain about which person pronoun to use. In terms of syntax, Michael used simple sentences 80% of the time while the confession statement contained 68% compound and complex sentences, which closely matched the sentence structure of the detective.

Interviewers Use Deceptive Ambiguity with Major Dragan Jokic

No transparent institutional power could be more evident than that of the International Criminal Tribunal. The impressive setting at The Hague reeks of formality, power, and control. The Tribunal deals with many types of cases, including the atrocious genocide committed during the fighting at the end of the existence of the former Yugoslavia. Within those wheels of justice, many soldiers of the Serbian Army Republica Srpska (VRS) were justifiably convicted of killing thousands of Muslim men and boys in and around Srebrenica in July 1995. But during their investigations the International Criminal Tribunal on Yugoslavia (ICTY) interviewers sometimes used their institutional power to help produce the impression that some suspects were guilty when there were reasons to believe otherwise. VRS Major Dragan Jokic provided one such case.

After investigating the genocide for some three years, the ICTY prosecutors were still not satisfied that they had completed their work and asked anyone who may have had information about the massacre come to them voluntarily and report it. Many suspects had already been tried and convicted, but the prosecutors felt that they still needed to discover some missing details about who did what and when. Major Jokic, among others volunteered to tell the ICTY interviewers what he could remember about that terrible event.

The two meetings with Jokic on December 13, 1999, and April 1, 2000, were tape-recorded and translated into English by court-appointed translators. Jokic was aware that he was being tape-recorded but during the first meeting the interviewers assured him that he was not a suspect. It is noteworthy that these interviews were conducted by prosecutors whose typical job as intelligence analysts is to evaluate the evidence previously gathered by law enforcement officers. In this case, however, the prosecutors carried out both tasks simultaneously, perhaps in an effort to reduce the time and effort normally allotted for reviewing and analyzing the evidence gathered before suspects are indicted. For this reason I consider these meetings police interviews. The questioners are sometimes referred to as interviewers and other times as prosecutors but their primary role here was as investigators.

During his second interview, Major Jokic was accused and charged along with three other VRS officers with "murder, persecutions, and inhumane acts crimes against humanity and murder as a violation of the laws or customs of war." His indictment was based entirely on the substance of these two interviews, which produced the following information.

At the beginning of the war Major Jokic, a construction engineer by training and occupation, joined the Zvornik Brigade of the VRS in 1992 and remained in it until the fighting ended in Bosnia and Herzegovina. In July 1995, authorities discovered that thousands of Bosnian Muslim civilian men and boys had been rounded up and executed in Srebrenica after the UN Security Council had declared that city a *safe area* where civilian Muslims from the surrounding areas could find safe harbor.

Major Jokic was chief of the engineering branch of the Serbian army's First Zvornik Brigade. His job description limited him to advising his Brigade Commander about matters relating to engineering services such as defense works, mining activities, road construction, and excavation projects. The army had a system of rotating duty officers at its headquarters and on July 14, 1995, it became Major Jokic's turn to spend twenty-four hours answering the phone and relaying messages between the Superior Command and his own Zvornick Brigade commanders. It was during this one-day period when Jokic was assigned to serving as duty officer that the prosecution accused him of aiding and abetting the mass murders by "failing to take the necessary and reasonable measures to prevent such acts or to punish the perpetrators thereof."

The interviewers were aware that Major Jokic was outranked by the other three officers who were indicted along with him. One was Commander of the Light Infantry Brigade. The second was Chief of Staff and Acting Commander of the Motorized Brigade. The third was Assistant Commander for Intelligence. All three had decision-making power while Major Jokic, in contrast, had no authority to give orders or to make decisions. His job description specified that he was only to offer technical advice about how best to implement the orders given by higher-ranking officers. The twenty-four hours he served as duty officer also provided him no defined authority to make any decisions or give any commands. Despite this limitation of power, the indictment accused Major Jokic of assisting "the planning, monitoring, organizing, and carrying out the burials involved in the murder operation." More specifically, the prosecutors claimed that he "assisted in having the power to coordinate communication between VRS officers and commands involving the transportation, detention, execution and burial of Srebrenica Muslims" and that he "issued or transmitted reports and updates to superiors on the progress of the overall murder operation."

One of Jokic's defense attorneys, having learned that I had recently testified in one of the genocide trials at the International Criminal Tribunal on Rwanda (ICTR), asked me to provide her with linguistic assistance concerning the Jokic interviews. She believed that the primary issue facing Jokic revolved around whether or not he, as chief of his unit's engineering branch, was knowingly and willfully involved in the movement of the heavy equipment that was used to dig the mass burial sites for the Muslims who had been executed.

A much disputed issue concerned what Major Jokic knew, did, and said during his twenty-four-hour stint as duty officer for which he was accused of assisting "in coordinating communication." The specific issue was what Jokic knew or should have known about the mostly coded messages that were his job to relay, and that even if he could have known what the coded messages conveyed, what his level of responsibility was for them. When the ICTY prosecutors made it widely known that they were trying to obtain more information, Major Jokic volunteered to talk with them, explaining that he was sickened by the genocide at Srebrenica and that he wanted to clear his name quickly.

The subsequent interviews were replete with ambiguities. So what is the source of the ambiguity in the interactions between the prosecutor and Jokic? As noted in chapter 2, Cruse proposed three specific criteria for determining ambiguity: (1) when the senses of ambiguous words are not conditioned by their contexts; (2) when the separate senses are not independently maximizable within the current universe of discourse; (3) when the independent senses of a lexical form are antagonistic to one another (1986: 59–62). Any one or more of these criteria can apply when determining whether expressions are ambiguous. The following demonstrates that the ambiguities in this case grew out of the investigators' uses of their speech events, schemas, agendas, speech acts, conversational strategies, as well as lexicon and grammar.

AMBIGUITY PRODUCED BY THE SPEECH EVENT

The two interviews were speech events conducted by powerful interviewers. The first interview gave every appearance of being an information-gathering speech event, just as Jokic understood it to be. Even though the second interview began the same way, it suddenly changed to an accusation speech event. When the investigators called Jokic to return for that second interview, his language indicated that he thought he was still in an extention of that first information-gathering speech event until the interviewer's tone suddenly changed, at which point the speech event was ambiguous to Jokic for a while until eventually it became clear to him that it had changed into an accusation speech event. The switch from one type of speech event into another type is fraught with ambiguity until such differences become clear. For a while, however, Jokic experienced a degree of puzzled ambiguity that caused him to reorient himself to the new direction in which the changed speech event was taking him. The person being interviewed is usually emotionally and verbally placed at a disadvantage when speech events are switched in process. Jokic then needed to reassess what he had already said and adjust it to the new and apparently intended speech event, which is not an easy conversational task as it becomes critical when it is suddenly revealed as an accusation speech event. This problem created by switching speech events during a conversation is further illustrated in a bribery investigation (Shuy 2013, 52–62).

AMBIGUITY PRODUCED BY SCHEMAS

When information is gathered by prosecutors whose usual job is to assess the intelligence gathered by others to use at trial, there is reason to believe that those prosecutors' schemas are that the persons they interview are likely to be guilty. In theory (although rarely in practice) police intelligence gatherers are encouraged to first let the suspects produce their own narrative, next to probe further about what the suspects say, and finally try to elicit evidence of guilt that can lead to an indictment made by prosecutors. In this unusual investigation of Jokic it was the prosecutors who gathered the intelligence evidence, after which their remaining task was to challenge their suspects with it at trial. Prosecutors who gather their own intelligence are likely to do so with the schema of a prosecution rather than that of intelligence gathering.

During their first interview with Jokic, the team of three prosecutors gave lip service to their role as intelligence gatherers, but their challenging questions gave evidence of their more accustomed role as prosecutors. During their first interview, their questions encouraged Jokic to embrace the schema that he was being questioned only for the authorities to gain further information about details of the massacre at Srebenica. In their second interview, they eventually assumed the prosecutorial schema and role, asking challenge questions and persistently accusing Jokic. It started the same way as the first interview but quickly turned into an accusation in which the questioners' schema made very clear that Jokic was one of the guilty participants, even while Jokic maintained his schema of innocence throughout. And, like most police interviewers, the language of the questions demonstrated a schema of Major Jokic's guilt, even though they were ambiguous about this during their first information-gathering speech event interview. Throughout both interviews, however, Jokic's language indicated that his schema was to try to be helpful in unearthing the perpetrators of the murders—the people that he claimed were responsible for the terrible massacre.

AMBIGUITY PRODUCED BY AGENDAS

As can be expected in police interviews, the prosecutors controlled the agenda completely. Jokic's only role was to answer their questions. While interviewers were trying to get verification about what they had been learning from others concerning the horrible events at Srebrenica, they did not do very well at implicating Jokic about his involvement and foreknowledge of the genocide plot. Even though they must have realized that Jokic stood rather low on their list of suspects, like most effective interrogators, they needed to get as much information out of him as possible. But from the way they questioned him, it is apparent that they were primarily interested in implicating him in any crimes for which he might be guilty.

In response to their agenda, Jokic informed the interviewers that while he was assigned as duty officer at the headquarters, he was able to see a long column of buses, led by white United Nations vehicles, passing by the headquarters area. He recalled that some of the personnel accompanying the column wore white belts, the sign of military police. He explained that he was first told that the buses contained prisoners to be exchanged, but later that evening he was informed that some Srebrenican prisoners had been executed and that during his recent absence on another assignment, his engineering company's excavating machinery had been sent to dig burial trenches.

Jokic reported that before his twenty-four-hour shift as duty officer began, his commander had ordered him to go to the front lines and check to see where mines had been set or, in military terms, to "reestablish the line," where fierce fighting had been taking place. Company records verified that Jokic went to that location and remained there throughout the following day when he heard unconfirmed rumors that many male Muslims had been killed in the fighting and that a grave site was being dug some distance away.

Jokic said that on July 16 he carried out his normal task of putting the military lines together at the battle site, checking for mines at the front line, moving sandbags from one location to another, and transporting various materials. Much later he learned that most of the mass burial ("terrain restoration" in military language) was done using local civilian machines and personnel conscripted for this task because during his absence most of the engineering company's resources and personnel had already been assigned elsewhere.

Jokic answered all the interviewers' questions, telling them what he knew, and he sometimes even volunteered information. It was clear, however, even though at the beginning of the second interview they led him to understand that they did not consider him a party to the killings, they believed he was still hiding something from them:

> INTERVIEWER A: And it's very important that people who were not participants in this not be smeared with the same dirty brush. Unless people like you talk about it, the stain will never get off the people who are good. Now people like you, who say they didn't participate, have a rare opportunity to help people who are good. We know that you and your unit followed those orders. . . . You are the kind of person I believe that we can cooperate with, work with.

From this point on, even though Jokic continued to express unambiguously that he had no involvement or participation in the massacre or the burial efforts that followed, the questions became accusatory and the interviewers apparently assumed that Jokic had presented his own agenda ambiguously even when there was no evidence he had done so.

AMBIGUITY PRODUCED BY SPEECH ACTS

Jokic's speech acts consisted of reporting information about what he said he saw and knew. At one point the investigators misinterpreted his repeated insistence that his superior officer had "requested" information from him, converting this into the speech act of his being "ordered" to do various things. They also misinterpreted Jokic's speech act of giving opinions ("I think," "I assume") as his speech acts of reporting known facts.

During their second meeting, the interviewers' strategy of softening or depoliticizing their power to make things more palatable and comfortable for Jokic echoed their more conciliatory tone during the first interview in which the investigators had claimed that they were only trying to get more information about the massacre. Almost immediately after this softening, however, one of the interviewers began to accuse Jokic about this involvement and clearly accused him of not being truthful, illustrated by the following exchange:

> INRTERVIEWER A: I have a little difficulty believing that you have been completely honest with me.
>
> JOKIC: I told you what I've heard.
>
> INTERVIEWER A: What you've heard is remarkably bereft of detail; void, barren, doesn't have much detail. We know that you are not being truthful. And with each additional untruth, you become further and further away. See if we can get the co-operation and the truth back on track, okay?

So what caused the interviewers to change their approach into believing Jokic was withholding information or outright lying? One reason appears to be the conflict between their speech act of requesting information about what Jokic *knew* and what Jokic (or anyone else) might think they meant by this verb. This is discussed below in the section on ambiguity produced by lexicon and grammar.

AMBIGUITY PRODUCED BY CONVERSATIONAL STRATEGIES

Although the government's authorized translation into English may have missed some of the conversational strategies used in the original language, there appeared to be no instances of them in the translation of these interviews. There was no evidence that the interviewers tried to block Jokic's efforts to talk or used a hit-and-run style of questioning or any of the other common conversational strategies found in police interviews, although since the Tribunal was conducted in English, these may have been lost in the translation process.

AMBIGUITY PRODUCED BY LEXICON AND GRAMMAR

By far the most ambiguity in these two interviews related to the words, phrases, and grammatical structures used by the questioners. The following describes six major lexical and grammatical ambiguities created by the investigators: their misinterpretation of the lexical meanings of *knowing* and *passing on information*, and their grammatical misinterpretations of Jokic's hypothetical, conditionals, referencing, and causal expressions.

"Knowing": The Ambiguity Produced by Misinterpreting Jocik's Use of the Verb Phrases, *Hearing About, Learning Of,* and *Assuming,* as His *Knowing* About Various Events

The manner in which the interviewers treated the potentially ambiguous verb, *know,* illustrates one way they used their institutional power as they tried to implicate Jokic in the genocide. The three questioners were specific about the dates about which they were concerned—July 11 through July 18, 1995. The record is clear that during the events immediately preceding the Srebrenica killings on July 11, 12, and 13, Jokic's superior officers had sent him on an assignment to pick cherries and gather wood at a distant location. While Jokic was so tasked, a high-level Brigade Commander from another company ordered Jokic's subordinate officer, Major Jevtic, who had replaced Jokic while he was tasked away from the engineering branch, to send the company's two excavating machines to dig a trench where the recently murdered Muslim prisoners were to be buried. Jokic returned from his wood gathering and cherry picking assignment on the evening of the 13th, but before resuming his normal role as chief of engineering it was his regularly scheduled turn to fulfill the responsibility of duty officer for the following twenty-four hours.

Since the interviewers suspected that Jokic had a great deal more to do with the mass burial than he was willing to admit, on December 13, 1999, they questioned him for a second time from nine in the morning until seven in the evening about his possible involvement in the genocide. Much of this interview was spent asking him about the VRS army's chain of command, his own job description, and what he knew and had seen of the events relating to the executions and mass burial. Their announced major agenda, however, was to discover what Jokic knew about the genocide.

The legal arena has several things to say about what *knowledge* means. *Black's Law Dictionary* (2004) defines it this way:

> Knowledge. 1. An awareness or understanding of a fact or circumstance; a state of mind in which a person has no substantial doubt about the existence of a fact.

Black's then goes on to distinguish *actual knowledge* (clear and direct), from *constructive knowledge* (the knowledge that a person using reasonable care or diligence should have), *imputed knowledge* (knowledge attributed because of a person's legal responsibility for another's conduct), and *personal knowledge* (gained through first-hand observation or experience, as opposed to belief based on what someone else said). Garner's *A Dictionary of Modern Legal Usage* further points out that *knowledge* requires awareness of a fact or condition, while *notice* merely requires a reason to *know of* a fact or condition.

In both interviews, Jokic provided only his actual and personal knowledge of things that apparently were not germane enough for the prosecution to indict him. He reported that he had been given *notice* about (see Garner's earlier definition) some facts, but the interviewers apparently believed Jokic had *imputed* or *constructive knowledge* to the extent that he should have known about the massacre, even though they had not elicited any such knowledge from him. Following Cruse's criteria for determining ambiguity, the prosecutor's sense of *know*: (1) did not take context into consideration; (2) did not independently maximize the current universe of discourse; and (3) was totally antagonistic to Jokic's use of the term.

A more susceptible suspect might have fallen into the trap of saying that he knew something that he had actually learned later, or from second-hand information that someone had told him, or from what he assumed, inferred, or guessed. Jokic did not do this. Using ambiguity or understanding ambiguity that does not exist while questioning suspects is not uncommon in law enforcement interviews, as illustrated by other cases in this book.

Major Jokic, however, was clearly smarter than the run-of-the-mill suspect. He was alert enough to perceive the danger of saying that he had knowledge of an event for which he had no evidence, even though there was a substantial probability that such an event had actually happened. Operating with his own sense of the context of the questioners' direction of the discourse, he answered many of their questions about what he "knew" with responses such as "I heard," "I was told," or "I learned," all of which were evidence of Garner's distinction between "notice of" and "direct knowledge of." Based on their own sense of the context and direction of the discourse, the questioners clearly wanted to learn what Jokic *knew*, but Jokic's answers weren't giving them anything helpful. What he "heard about" or "learned" was not good enough for them to make a case supporting his foreknowledge of the killings.

The prosecutors, however, ignored these different senses of *know* and kept on using the verb ambiguously, possibly hoping that Jokic eventually might slip. But Jokic continued to carefully distinguish what he knew and saw first-hand from the rumors that he had heard during the events, what he had been told by others, and what he subsequently had learned from the media and other sources during the four years that had elapsed between the Srebrenica massacre and his interviews.

It became clear that Jokic's careful responses eventually began to frustrate the interviewers. At times they appeared to be either losing awareness of any possible difference between "hearing about" something and "knowing" it or they intentionally used this ambiguity to their own advantage. When questioners ignore the actual words used in respondent's answers and still keep on using their own words in spite of this, there is a strong possibility that they are being intentionally deceptive.

In addition to the usual "wh-" questions (who, what, where, when, and how), the three prosecutors asked many other questions relating to specific times relating to Jokic's knowledge, including the following examples: "Do you know what the excavators went to do?" "Do you know who had to move on the ground?" "Do you know who those people who came by are?" "Do you know what happened to the dam?" and many others. Note the inherent ambiguity in these questions. All of them ignored the time context and current universe of discourse as they asked Jokic what he knew at the present time of the interview, not what he knew before or during the time of the genocide. Four years had passed since the massacre and like everyone else who reads newspapers, Jokic had many opportunities to "know" what had happened from the media, from others, and even from the information revealed in some of the prosecutors' own questions. There is no way that anyone can get into the minds of the prosecutors to determine their exact intentions, but one thing is clear: it would not have been difficult for the prosecutors to distinguish between Jokic's previous and current knowledge, if they tried to do so.

To the above and many other questions Jokic continued to answer, "I don't know," "I learned," or "I heard about it," which were responses that were not at all helpful for indicting him. When the prosecutors managed to ask questions about what he "knew" about events that happened *after* the July period at issue, Jokic consistently replied, "I found out" or "I've heard." When the prosecutors finally asked Jokic what he knew had happened *during* that time period in question, Jokic consistently answered, "I know" or "I knew" to 35 of their questions, but none of his "I know" responses could implicate him in the crime. It's noteworthy that even though their questions contained no referent accessibility, Jokic was careful not to be trapped by the prosecutors' questions about what he knew when apparently he didn't know the answer. His responses to such questions were either "I don't/didn't know" (forty-four times) or "I heard" and its variants, "I found out," "I learned about," and "I was told" (sixty-eight times). Jokic also responded eight times with the tentative expressions, "I think" and "I assume," which do not even convey his knowing, having heard, finding out, learning about, or being told.

In short, the prosecutors failed to get Jokic to say that he knew about events for which he claimed to have no personal knowledge. But he did know certain things, and openly said so. Jokic admitted knowing many things, such as: "Col. Obrenovic was in charge of combat activities and sent reconnaissance," "Col. Pandurevic took control over all terrain restoration," "the privately owned Komunalno Company carried out the terrain restoration," and many others.

The things Jokic said he *did not know* include the following relevant information:

- who Col. Obrenovic commanded and how
- what was happening there exactly and at what time
- what was happening in terms of combat activities
- what other measures Col. Obrenovic took from his office
- who was actually in command during the time he was away
- when the execution took place, or why
- who did the killings
- who participated in the killings

In all, Jokic's most frequent responses were "I found out," "I learned about," "I was told," "I heard," and "I think." Why would the prosecutors continue to ask these questions about what Jokic "knows" when he had very clearly distinguished what he knew from what he had heard or later learned? One likely answer is that either they were less than competent interviewers or that they knew very well what they were doing—trying to get Jokic to say that he "knew" something that he repeatedly had told them he didn't know. But the prosecution's own language evidence demonstrates that Jokic did not knuckle under during their many ambiguous uses of the verb "to know."

The Ambiguity Produced by Reinterpreting the Verb Phrase "Passed on the Information"

Three and a half months had passed before the prosecutors interviewed Jokic for the second time. This is evidence that they realized that they did not get what they wanted out of their first interview with him. Undaunted by their failure to get Jokic to say that he knew certain inculpatory things, the prosecutors then pursued different angle: that while Jokic served that one-day period as duty officer, he allegedly "passed on" the crucial orders that came in by telegraph, radio, and telephone. This time they focused only on Jokic's twenty-four-hour assignment as duty officer, apparently wanting to get Jokic to admit that he had passed along orders between commanding officers on the topic of acquiring excavating equipment for the burial. One prosecutor accused him as follows:

> You were doing your duty as a duty officer. What you did was wrong, what you did was against the law. You passed on the communication regarding the murders of prisoners, to help facilitate those murders and that's a violation, that's a crime against humanity.

In the court-authorized English translation of the following exchange, we see a verbal duel about the meaning of "asking for" and "gave you an order:"

> PROSECUTOR: So you were duty officer on the 14th, is that right?
> JOKIC: Yes.
> PROSECUTOR: And you're saying that Colonel Beara *gave you an order* regarding these machines?
> JOKIC: They were *asking for* the machines and those machines were the only ones that were there at the moment.
> PROSECUTOR: Okay, can you tell me what you remember Beara saying to you about those machines?
> JOKIC: It was only his *request.* H*e asked for* a dragging machine.
> PM: Okay, he *asked for* the digging machine, is that right?
> JOKIC: He didn't say why. I can only remember him *requesting* this and later on some of his assistants went to local industry to look for them.

It was obviously important for the interviewer to get Jokic to reveal that he had passed along this critical order. Jokic's language indicates that he considered "ask for" as the commander's request about the availability of the equipment rather than as an order to find and send it. Jokic's response also made it clear that he was not told and therefore didn't know what purpose the colonel had in mind for the machine. He didn't even admit that he passed along the request and he certainly didn't admit that Col. Beara gave him an order.

Jokic's response in this exchange was based on the topic introduced by the prosecutor: "You did not have the power to issue orders?" and more specifically, "it was your job to pass on the orders to Jevtic." Jokic answered in general terms, remaining on the introduced topic about whether or not the general procedure was for him to have the power to give orders. In contrast, the prosecutor was clearly trying to find out whether or not Jokic actually "passed on" (transmitted) a specific order to Jevtik (acting chief of engineers) at that time. If he did this, it could implicate Jokic in passing along the order for the grave-digging equipment. Jokic continued to answer with expressions such as "I couldn't," and "it's not possible that," whereas the prosecutor tried to move this from the abstract conditional to the concrete. Jokic never admitted that he actually passed along the crucial orders but his conditional verbs here apparently did not convince the prosecutors that he had denied doing so.

Grammatical Ambiguity Produced by Interpreting Hypotheticals and Conditionals as Factuals

After four years following the Srbrenica massacre, Jokic said he could not recall all of the details of those six days in June 1995. His memory problem was not unusual. When most people try to recall past events, their minds flit between what they know for sure to have happened versus what might have happened if they were able to recall the details. Jokic was no exception to this. He used the hypotheticals of "might have," "could have," and "possibly" with regularity. During law enforcement interviews, such responses are often considered the suspects' efforts to be deceptive even though it could be nothing more than their benign efforts to avoid making factual errors about critical incidents. The following exchange during the second interview is illustrative. Even though Jokic had said numerous times that his job description did not permit him the power and authority to issue orders, the prosecutors continued to ask about this anyway:

PROSECUTOR: You did not have the power to issue orders?
JOKIC: No. I had the power to pass on orders from Colonel Pandurevic or from Obrenovic. I was not in power to issue. It is possible that I could have received an order. Jevtic and me could have been given the same order by Obrevovic or Pandurevic.

Again, Jokic responded to the abstract question of his power rather than to a specific question about his power. His answer was a very clear "no." Then he elaborated about what *could* or was *possible* to happen, but he did not say that he passed along the critical order. The modal verb *could* is used primarily to express permission, reasonability, acceptability, circumstantial possibility, or potential ability (Huddleson and Pullum 2002: 197). That Jokic had permission to pass the order along does not mean that he did so. If it was acceptable, possible, or had a potential for him to pass it along also does not mean that he acted on that possibility or potentiality. The questioner must have realized this because he continued:

PROSECUTOR: But it was your job to pass on the orders to Jevtic?
JOKIC: I *could* pass it on but it was also *possible* that he gets something in written form directly from Colonel Obrenovic.
PROSECUTOR: And the same is true that when many times Colonel Obrenovic, as chief of staff, was very busy, he would not issue orders directly to Jevtic. He would rely on you to pass on the orders, right?
JOKIC: I was given orders mainly from Obrenovic. Mainly. In 90% of the cases. The engineering unit is directly under the authority of the

> Chief of Staff. The commander of the company *could be* given orders from the Chief of Staff, from Colonel Pandurevic, or from Colonel Obrenovic, and it *could be* me who passed on. I was not in power to issue an order to him (Jevtic) during the war.

Here again, the questioners confused Jokic's report about the difference between what was possible and what actually happened, and assumed that Jokic meant that he was indeed given orders to pass along relating to the massacre.

The prosecutor, apparently aware that Jokic was speaking conditionally, then tried once more to find out whether he had passed the order along to Jevtic. But Jokic stayed with his conditional verbs:

> PROSECUTOR: Okay, would it be fair to say that in the most situations, you are the one who *would have* passed the orders to the chief of engineers that you received from Obrenovic usually, or perhaps, Pandurevic?
> JOKIC: It *could have been* me. I *could* pass them on when we were both given the orders in written form.

Here the hypothetical is set by the prosecutor's question and Jokic responded in kind with a hypothetical. Next, the interviewer tried to take the issue from the hypothetical to the concrete, but Jokic stayed with the hypothetical framework established by the question sequence:

> PROSECUTOR: But it was principally you who *was* passing orders to the chief of engineers wasn't it, be they written or be they oral?
> JOKIC: In verbal, no. In writing forms it was brought by courier and he distributed it throughout the whole brigade and I *could have been* given that and Jevtic *could have been* given that order.

Jokic apparently thought he was holding his ground, speaking only about the conditions relating to procedures they normally follow. The prosecutors continued to think specifically, however, again ignoring Jokic's conditional verbs. It is unclear whether the English translation was accurate, but if so, Jokic did not help his own case by using his conditional verbs in the past perfect tense. He would have been more consistent to have continued by saying, "I could be given that" and "Jevtic could be given that," which, absent evidence from the original language, may well have been what he said in it. We can't know this, however, because the only evidence accepted at trial in this case was the English translation.

Ambiguity Produced by Unclear Referencing

Finally, the prosecutor seemed to grow tired of Jokic's conditional verbs and began to ask questions more specifically:

> PROSECUTOR: Okay. Understood. And the period between July13, 14, 15 and 16, did you pass on orders to the engineering company?

JOKIC: There were those orders that concerned alerting and covering forces on the ground. On the 13th there was an order for me to go into the woods [to chop wood and pick cherries], and it was personally Lt. Colonel Obrenovic who came.

PROSECUTOR: Did anyone pass any orders during that time period from the 13th through the 16th sending digging equipment to Petkovci, Branjero or Kozluk?

JOKIC: I think that regarding Kozluk, Colonel Pandurevic rang and said the two policemen would come. I didn't know where it wants to go, but he did say that two policemen were coming. It wasn't said where it was going to or why.

PROSECUTOR: But did you pass on *that* order to the engineering company?

JOKIC: Yes.

It should be noted here that the prosecutor introduced still another ambiguity, this one based on his grammatical reference of the deictic *that*, when he asked, "did you pass on *that* order." Jokic had just mentioned three messages that he had passed on:

- orders concerning the need to alert forces
- orders for him to go to go collect wood
- Panduric's message about two policemen coming (to pick up the digging equipment) but without saying why or where it was going.

When the prosecutor asked about "that order," he apparently believed that Jokic's response agreed that he passed on that critical order to send the digging equipment for the mass burials. But since matters were apparently less than clear about this, the prosecutor repeated his question:

PROSECUTOR: Were you involved in passing on the order to send that ULT to Petkovici?

JOKIC: No. According to my knowledge that machinery was there on the 14th already. It was taken for sure by Beara's assistants from the [local private] factories. I'm sure that it didn't go because I passed on or somebody else passed it on. I would like to explain it. When Beara's assistants came, they did not ask anyone about anything. They went about and took what they liked. I know that I didn't plan anything and that I was not included in any activities.

PROSECUTOR: Did you pass on the orders to have equipment taken up to the Branjevo farm on July 16th or 17th?

JOKIC: I think not. I can't. I think it was people from Pelemis.

Jokic's answer was an indirect "no." It would have been better for him if he had simply stopped there. But when he added a *because* clause, the prosecutors jumped on it, as the following explains.

Ambiguity Produced by Misinterpreting Causal Expressions

There is even an ambiguity within the above *because* clause. In the previously cited passage after Jokic had clearly denied passing along the order for the digging equipment, he added "I'm sure it didn't go there *because* I passed in on." With considerable stretching, this sentence is possibly capable of two meanings, based on whether *because* is interpreted as a causal or it is understood as the resultative *since:*

- I'm sure that the equipment didn't go there *because of* my action or the action of somebody else [a clear denial of causal responsibility about passing along the order];

or

- I'm sure that the equipment didn't go *since* I had already passed it on or somebody else had already passed it on [a resultative admission that he or someone else were the ones who had passed the order along].

The interviewers probably used the second interpretation, even though it makes no sense for Jokic to say that the equipment did not go there since he had already passed the message along. The prosecutors were not concerned about logic, however. They were only trying to elicit from Jokic that he passed the order along. However stretched and illogical the second interpretation might be, it was likely the way the interviewers took its meaning. Translation is the unknown factor here. Translating from one language into another language can easily obscure or lose the presuppositions and implications that carry meaning differences between causals and resultatives. The second reading, even though it was both contextually illogical and inconsistent with all that Jokic had said before, was likely the one the prosecutors used, leading them to conclude the interview as follows:

> PROSECUTOR: Mr. Jokic, you have, by your own words in the last two hours, provided us with the details of your knowledge of most of the engineering project. You've admitted passing on orders that you were very involved in this process.

It is troublesome to assign an ulterior motive to the prosecutors' use of the instances of lexical and grammatical ambiguity found in these interviews— the ambiguity of *know, pass along*, hypothetical expressions misinterpreted as factuals, conditional verbs misinterpreted as fact verbs, ambiguous references, and potentially ambiguous causal expressions. The fact that the interview contained so many repeated instances of ambiguity, however, could make a case that the prosecutors used these types of ambiguity deliberately. On January 17, 2005, the Trial Chamber of the ICTY found Jokic guilty of aiding and abetting extermination, persecution of crimes against humanity, and murder, sentencing him to nine years in prison. The sentence was affirmed on appeal, but Jokic was granted early release after serving four years of his sentence.

One prefers to believe that law enforcement officers would err on the side of caution and would be careful to disentangle ambiguities in questions and answers that could be understood in different ways. It is possible, I suppose, that the interviewers in this case were so intent on their task of following their schema of Jokic's guilt that they were unaware that their own words were actually creating a crime where there appeared to be little if any language evidence for it.

The legal system's need to question suspects is important and valuable for the purpose of capturing crime, but it cannot be denied that police interviewers can accomplish this fairly without the using deceptive ambiguity created by confusing the speech event and creating false schemas about what is happening. Creating a complete record of exactly how the interviews took place is an essential first step. Identifying the agendas and speech acts of the participants is equally important, for doing so provides both sides of the issue information that simple yes/no questions can disguise. The use of unfair conversational strategies is a deceptive way to elicit information and reinterpreting or misinterpreting specific words, such as *know*, *pass along* and others cited in this chapter constitute equally deceptive practices that are used during police interviews.

4

Prosecutors Use Deceptive Ambiguity

One of the major responsibilities of a district attorney's office is to determine the value of the physical and language evidence gathered by the law enforcement officers who have investigated the case. District attorneys don't have to accept the investigators' findings suggesting that the suspects' language demonstrates their guilt. They commonly perform an analysis of such intelligence and if they don't agree with the investigators, they can refuse to prosecute. But they often agree, probably for the same reasons that the information gatherers consider the language evidence to be clear demonstrations of the suspects' guilt.

Problems can arise, however, when that language evidence contains ambiguous statements made by the interviewer, the suspect, or both. In such cases it is the intelligence analysts' job to decide how to interpret and resolve that ambiguity. More often than not they do this in a way that favors prosecution rather than innocence. This may not seem surprising, because the schemas of investigators and prosecutors naturally tilt toward the guilt of the suspects and defendants being questioned. Often they are right, but some cases are not clear enough to produce easy decisions. It is these cases at the margin that can benefit from linguistic analysis.

Linguists and other scholars agree that ambiguous statements are capable of more than one meaning and since representatives of the law typically hold a schema that the suspects and defendants they interview are guilty, their interpretation of ambiguous expressions, whether made by defendants or by their police interviewers, makes it difficult for prosecutors to think otherwise. First of all, the police and prosecutors are on the same advocacy team. Their presuppositions support the statistical probability of guilt and aid them in creating schemas that the defendants are indeed guilty. And it is also a fact that our legal advocacy system requires both prosecutors and defense lawyers to vigorously defend their positions like debaters, even when confronted with seemingly contrary information.

These conditions make it problematic for prosecutors to interpret ambiguous language in a way that might favor defendants. It remains for defendants and their attorneys to point out realistic alternatives for understanding any ambiguous utterances in the evidence. Unfortunately, they often do not have all the requisite linguistic skills to do so.

This is precisely where linguists can either help prosecutors avoid maintaining positions that are untenable at trial or assist defense attorneys to use their analyses of ambiguous language during the process in which both sides search for accurate interpretations of the language evidence that can lead to a just conclusion of the case.

Resolution of such ambiguity is critically important in many cases. The following descriptions of three instances of courtroom questioning illustrate how prosecutors used deceptive ambiguity with defendants in two cases of perjury and one case of murder.

Prosecutor Uses Deceptive Ambiguity in the Perjury Case of Steven Suyat

In 1981 a building contractor on Hawaii's island of Maui brought charges of unfair practices against a local carpenter's union, claiming that the union had violated the National Labor Relations Board's (NLRB) rules relating to unfair picketing practices. It is acceptable for unions to picket contractors as long as those picketers do nothing but provide information. In this case, however, the contractor claimed that the picketers also were preventing non-union workers from replacing union workers at one of his construction sites. The union responded by filing affidavits and offering testimony to the NLRB that denied the contractor's claim. A subsequent NLRB hearing must have satisfied the NLRB, because the matter was not litigated.

About eighteen months later, however, the US Attorney's office began a grand jury investigation relating to the testimony of two union representatives at that NLRB hearing, charging them with perjury. This resulted in those two union representatives, William Nishibayashi and Ralph Torres, being indicted, tried, and found guilty of giving false testimony. The evidence was based on pretrial conversations that the contractor had covertly tape-recorded with these two men. On tape they had admitted to him that the intent of the picketing was to get his carpenters to join their union, a clear violation of the NLRB rules.

A third union representative, the union's business agent, Steven Suyat, had also been called to testify at the NLRB hearing. Based on his testimony the prosecutor apparently believed Suyat was untruthful, for he then separately indicted and tried Suyat for perjury.

Suyat's hearing testimony provides an example of the way the prosecutor used deceptive ambiguity that eventually led to Suyat's own trial based on seven counts of committing perjury.

His indictment made clear the relevant parts of Suyat's NLRB hearing testimony that constituted his seven counts of perjury:

Count 1

PROSECUTOR: And one of the jobs of the business agent is to organize non-union contractors, is that right?

SUYAT: No.

Count 2

PROSECUTOR: So no part of your job is to organize contractors?

SUYAT: No.

Count 3

PROSECUTOR: And no part of Mr. Nishibayashi's job is to organize contractors?

SUYAT: That's right.

Count 4

PROSECUTOR: And no part of Mr. Torres' job is to organize contractors?

SUYAT: That's right.

Count 5

PROSECUTOR: What does the word "scab" mean?

SUYAT: Pardon?

PROSECUTOR: What does the word "scab" mean?

SUYAT: I have no recollection.

Count 6

PROSECUTOR: You don't know what the word "scab" means?

SUYAT: No.

PROSECUTOR: So you don't know what you meant when you put it down here? [showing Suyat his own logbook]

SUYAT: Well, yeah---

Count 7

PROSECUTOR: Now I'll ask my question again, given the fact that this is Mr. Nishibayshi's logbook, and given your prior testimony is this statement: "Gave Ralph [Torres] and Steve [Suyat] more time for organizing non-union contractors and visiting job sites." Is that, according to your prior testimony a false statement?

SUYAT: According to what he wrote in here it depends how he put it in words.

PROSECUTOR: I'm asking you, is it true or false?

SUYAT: It's false.

One of the curious things about the seven counts of the indictment is that prosecutors can use a defendant's single statement (count 1) followed by three affirmations of that same statement (counts 2, 3, and 4) as four separate counts, thereby multiplying the alleged offense to four charges. In the same way, counts 5 and 6 were two statements of the same alleged offense and also became separate counts of perjury.

Count 7 was new and different. It grew out of the prosecutor's evidence to which Suyat previously had not been privy. The prosecutor had secured Nishibayashi's logbook and found in it some evidence that he believed was in violation of NLRB rules because it showed that the union had indeed tried to recruit non-union workers while the union was picketing a non-union job site. In this sense, count 7 also related to the first four counts.

In his brief testimony before the NLRB, Suyat's topics indicated that his agenda was to try to affirm only two things: (1) that it is *not* the proper job of union representatives to organize contractors and (2) that Nishibayashi's logbook was wrong when it said their job was to organize non-union contractors. The prosecutor interpreted Suyat's words very differently and considered his responses to constitute perjury. Analysis of Suyat's testimony upon which the aforementioned seven counts of perjury were based followed the Inverted Pyramid approach.

AMBIGUITY PRODUCED BY THE SPEECH EVENT

The speech event here is clear. It was a hearing in which the defendant was questioned and the prosecutor had all the power to ask whatever he wanted and in whatever manner he wanted to ask it. Suyat's role was to answer the prosecutor's questions with no opportunity to put forth his own agenda and with limited opportunity to request clarification if he didn't understand what was asked of him. Suyat, like most witnesses, could understand this speech event as one in which he had few if any conversational rights. His main right, a requirement in fact, was to try to answer the prosecutor's questions honestly to the best of his ability, to assume that the questions were fair, and to believe that the prosecutor's words meant the same thing that they meant to him.

An important indication of deceptive ambiguity grew out of the initial NLRB speech event in which the prosecutor brought in Suyat as a prosecution witness, presumably against his fellow union representatives Nishibayashi and Torres. Since Suyat had been called as a prosecution-friendly, fact witness during the NLRB investigation of his two union colleagues, he had no reason to think that this hearing speech event focused on his own behavior. Further, since he was not the subject of the hearing, he was not represented by a lawyer who could have objected to the ambiguity of the prosecutor's questions. Later, at Suyat's own perjury trial the prosecutor converted Suyat's previously helpful speech event role at the NLRB hearing into a very different speech event in which he became the subject of prosecution for perjury. Although this is a relatively common prosecutorial procedure, it generally goes unnoticed as a form of deceptive ambiguity used by prosecutors.

AMBIGUITY PRODUCED BY SCHEMAS

As Suyat's NLRB testimony progressed, the prosecutor's language indicated that he held a schema different from Suyat's. He did not permit Suyat to express his own agenda, and used ambiguous referencing to the point that Suyat's answers gave the appearance of being inconsistent.

Schemas of participants grow out of their perception of the speech event. Perhaps during Suyat's original friend-of-the-court testimony at the NLRB hearing, the prosecutor clearly began to hold the schema that Suyat had committed perjury, for there would be no need for his subsequent perjury trial if he thought otherwise. The language used by Suyat during the NLRB hearing demonstrated that his schema was that he was there to answer the prosecutor's questions truthfully. At his own later perjury trial Suyat's schema was that the powerful prosecutor, an intelligent man who knew things, would also know the difference between building contractors and the carpenters who worked for them. In Suyat's world, the union members were the employees and the contractors or owners of the company were the non-unionized employers and bosses of those carpenters. Therefore, when the prosecutor asked him whether the business agent's job was to "organize contractors," Suyat accurately answered "no" four times.

But why didn't Suyat try to correct the prosecutor's word here? The answer can be found in his schema growing out of this speech event. He realized that the prosecutor was an intelligent authority who held institutional power that demanded respect. Suyat was a poorly educated native speaker of Hawaiian Pidgin English who grew up on a sugar plantation in the backwoods of Molokai but had managed to better his station in life by first learning the carpentry trade and eventually becoming a union representative. For him to correct a well-educated, powerful prosecutor in this important speech event could be considered impolite, inappropriate in that context, and dangerous. To request clarification about what the prosecutor meant by *contractor* could also seem ludicrous, for Suyat's schema was that even laborers knew the simple and obvious semantic difference between contractors and the people who worked under them.

Suyat's schema of this speech event didn't encourage him to understand that the prosecutor had used *contractor* ambiguously to him. Here two schema trains passed unseen in the night. Or did they? Did the prosecutor realize his own ambiguity? The possibility that he was using this word deliberately is suggested by the fact that he continued to repeat it during four consecutive questions, getting the same answer each time. In a speech event in which the prosecutor has all the power, it behooves him to be certain that he is being understood. If that prosecutor had even a slight suspicion that Suyat's schema didn't permit him to understand what he meant, the prosecutor's follow-up questions did not even try to rephrase the critical word to provide Suyat an opportunity to clarify his answers. The Supreme Court decision in the *Bronston* case cited in chapter 2 shows that this prosecutor would be expected to provide Suyat that clarification, even though the *Bronston* decision did not address the linguistic procedures that the powerful person should use in order to ensure that any possible ambiguity was resolved. In Suyat's case, the source of the ambiguity related to the asymmetry of power in this speech event, the schemas of the participants, and Suyat's social reluctance to request clarification about the words of the powerful prosecutor. The prosecutor's repetitions of the same ambiguous or even potentially ambiguous word with no consideration of how the defendant might understand it suggests that this prosecutor was intentionally using deceptive ambiguity. Of course there is no way to get into his mind to know this for sure, but his repetition without attempting clarification is a rather strong clue to his intention.

AMBIGUITY PRODUCED BY AGENDAS

During the NLRB hearing, the prosecutor did not permit Suyat to explain his own agenda. He asked all the questions and Suyat's only role was to answer them. At trial the prosecutor then reviewed this hearing testimony and therefore could see only the words of the NLRB questions and answers without being concerned about the possibility that they could convey different meanings. To him it looked as though Suyat had indeed committed perjury. He was apparently unable to take the defendant's perspective.

During the courtroom trial questioning speech event, this same prosecutor put forth his own agenda, setting the tone for what followed. He naturally based his questions on the transcript of the NLRB hearing. Even though it is up to the skills of defense lawyers to see to it that their clients' agendas get expressed, such information can appear defensive and less strong to jurors who have already heard the prosecutors' version of the case. For various good reasons, defense lawyers seldom put their clients on the witness stand, which excludes them from being able to explain their agendas by themselves and to introduce their own topics that might shed light on the matter. Doing this limits or excludes an important language right that participants in everyday conversations are accustomed to having. After the judge decided to not allow the testimony of any expert witnesses, the only avenue left for the defense lawyer was to let Suyat try to explain his own agenda at his perjury trial.

This proved impossible, for at Suyat's trial the prosecutor controlled the agenda while Suyat's only role was to respond to whatever the prosecutor asked him. Although this standard courtroom procedure is justified for making trials orderly and avoiding wasting precious time and government expense, it furthered the possibility of unresolved ambiguity by highlighting the prosecutor's own agenda while he blocked attempts by Suyat to explain what he meant. Even when the defendant meekly tried to express his own agenda, he did not have the linguistic expertise to explain it clearly and effectively.

AMBIGUITY PRODUCED BY SPEECH ACTS

During Suyat's testimony relating to count 7, the prosecutor asked whether the words that Nishibayashi wrote in his logbook entry were true or false. In it Nishibayashi had written that a certain picketing activity would give Torres and Suyat "more time for organizing non-union contractors and visiting job sites." When prosecutors demand simple true or false answers, such all-or-nothing questions and answers often can create their own ambiguity. Here, Suyat could answer that it is apparently true that Nishibayashi wrote it, or he could answer that what Nishibayashi wrote contained false information.

So how could Suyat answer this ambiguously deceptive all-or-nothing question? He appeared to be alert to this problem by cautiously and rather indirectly using the speech act of requesting clarification in an effort to get the prosecutor to explain what his question meant. Suyat awkwardly responded, "according to what he wrote in here it depends on how he put it in words." This was not an explicit or literal speech act of requesting clarification, but it could certainly be understood as Suyat's uncertainty about the question if the prosecutor had tried to understand it that way. Instead, he chose to ignore it as a request for clarification and proceeded to exert his institutional power by demanding that Suyat answer whether that the statement was either true or false. Suyat's response was that what Nishibayashi said was false. It is noteworthy that this response was consistent with his earlier responses to counts 1 through 4 when he said that it was *not* the job of union representatives to organize non-union contractors, meaning that if Nishibayashi said this, he was wrong. But the prosecutor took this response to be still more evidence of Suyat's perjury, by apparently interpreting it to mean that Suyat was consistent with his earlier alleged false answer when he said that it was not the job of the union representative to organize contractors. Here the same discourse reference was understood in two very different ways.

AMBIGUITY PRODUCED BY CONVERSATIONAL STRATEGIES

Another of Suyat's language problems is illustrated by counts 5 and 6, in which the prosecutor asked for the meaning of the word, *scab*. Suyat was heavily under the influence of his own schema in this speech event, apparently thinking that it was obvious to anyone what that word means. Suyat expressed surprise at the prosecutor's question, saying "pardon?" which is either a request for clarification or an indication that he didn't hear well. Since the tape-recording is loud and clear and Suyat's hearing ability was not likely in question, he was apparently trying, however imperfectly, to request clarification of the prosecutor's question.

Suyat's speech act of requesting clarification indicated that he wanted to know what the prosecutor was after. Was he asking him to define *scab*? If the prosecutor clearly had asked him to give his own definition of *scab*, Suyat could have answered that he was unable to do this in a way that this powerful, educated prosecutor might find satisfactory. His answer, "I have no recollection," suggested that he was trying to recollect some kind of dictionary-type definition, but being a simple union representative who found himself in this stressful situation before a powerful prosecutor, this task apparently was too difficult for him even to attempt.

Paying no attention to Suyat's surprise, the prosecutor then changed his question without clarifying it, now using the equally ambiguous word, *know*, and asked, "You don't know what the word *scab* means?" This didn't help Suyat answer the question any differently, so he stayed with his earlier response. Finally, the prosecutor showed Suyat his own logbook in which he had once used the word *scab*, himself. To this, Suyat meekly agreed, saying, "Well, yeah—." The dash at the end reflects Suyat's rising rather than falling intonation, indicating that he apparently had not finished his turn of talk and had more to say. But the prosecutor used the conversational strategy of quickly cutting him off before he could complete his answer, apparently concluding that Suyat clearly knew what it meant because he had used that word himself. The prosecutor then abruptly concluded his questioning saying, "I have no further questions, your honor," a conversational strategy that is well-known in the legal profession to block any further testimony before any unclear matters can be clarified.

This final exchange is an example of the hit-and-run conversational strategy that illustrates another form of the deceptive strategy of blocking. It is not uncommon in the courtroom for speakers to start to explain their answers but are then cut off before they have a chance to do so. The prosecutor has the supreme power to control the exchange at any point, and particularly at points when the witness may be about to go in a direction that the questioner may not want to hear. If this exchange had taken place in any context except the speech event of courtroom testimony, Suyat probably could have had the opportunity to explain his answer—that even though he knew what the word meant and had used it himself, he felt he wasn't able to define scab adequately in the context of this formal trial speech event. As far the prosecutor was concerned, Suyat's unfinished answer had successfully established the appearance of inconsistency that suggested he had committed perjury.

AMBIGUITY PRODUCED BY LEXICON AND GRAMMAR

The prosecutor and Suyat had different understandings of various potentially ambiguous words such as *know*, *organize*, *contractor*, and *scab*, all of which the prosecutor could have made clear in the context of the sentences in which they occurred.

In spite of considerable coaching by the linguist, Suyat's defense attorney was unable to get the prosecutor's deceptive ambiguity identified and clarified at trial, and Suyat was convicted of perjury. It is generally the case that the best way for attorneys to use linguistic expert witnesses is to use their analyses themselves. This was a case in which that approach did not work.

The Prosecutor Uses Deceptive Ambiguity in the Murder Trial of Larry Gentry

In both *Language Crimes* (Shuy 1998) and *The Language of Murder Cases* (Shuy 2014) I described how at a trial in Anchorage, Alaska, in 1986 the prosecutor got Larry Gentry, a gullible, working-class bar tender with limited cognitive and social abilities, to admit that he knew that another man was going to commit a murder before it happened:

prosecutor	**Gentry**
But you knew, you knew it was some sort of shooting, but nothing more specific than that?	I wasn't too sure on it even being a shooting . . . I wasn't sure, but I kind of knew and I kind of didn't know.
You kind of suspected though?	Yeah, I suspected 'cause it was just bits and pieces I was hearing and picking up, getting a hold of.
Now by then you knew that it involved a shooting, but you didn't know who the guy was.	Yeah, it went on so long that I just figured it wasn't gonna happen. You know, it was just a bunch of bullshit.
Now we're still talking before the shooting, right?	Right. By the time it was gonna happen, yeah, I knew about it. I'd done figured it out. The night it was gonna happen I'd done figured it out.
So you knew it was going to happen?	Yes.
Looking back on it now, are you willing to accept responsibility for the fact that you did knowingly assist in the shooting?	Well, I guess I have to. I'm still trying to believe I didn't assist in it.

Gentry was convicted of aiding and abetting murder even though linguistic analysis of his recorded statements demonstrated he said that he only suspected, guessed, and inferred facts about the case. No matter. The prosecutor, whether intentionally or not, misinterpreted Gentry's "I wasn't too sure" into "I knew," and after that Gentry never realized what hit him, because from the time he said these words, he was implicated in aiding and abetting the crime. The following shows how the prosecutor deceptively manipulated this ambiguity while questioning Gentry at trial:

Even though Gentry's only involvement was that the man who committed the murder purportedly used the Gentry's car without his permission, the aforementioned exchange was enough to get Gentry tried and convicted for aiding and abetting a murder.

His conviction heavily depended on the prosecutor's use of the verb *know*, aided by ignoring Gentry's less than perfect understanding that to him this verb meant that he suspected (but did not know) that a shooting was about to take place. Even sophisticated speakers commonly say "I know it will rain tomorrow" when they can have no proof that this will actually happen. In such cases *I know* conveys the meaning of *I suspect* or *I believe* or it can even mean *I guess, I fear,* or *I figure*. The public might expect institutionally powerful prosecutors to understand that defendants' answers in which they speculate, infer, or assume information do not represent their factual knowledge.

The courts distinguish several types of knowledge. *Actual knowledge* (also called *express knowledge*) is direct and clear knowledge usually achieved by witnessing something first hand. *Notice of knowledge* quite differently relates to when persons have received information from which they could infer the existence of a relevant fact (*Black's Law Dictionary*, citing the Uniform Commercial Code at §523(a)(3)). It is not unusual for questioners, including prosecutors, to rely on the ambiguity of the meaning of verbs like *know* and use it to serve their prosecutorial purposes.

Prosecutors who manipulate suspects in this way can be expected to be sophisticated enough to understand that when defendants say they *know* something they are committing to a belief that it is true, that there is good reason to believe it to be true, and that there is substantial probability that it really is true. In his trial testimony cited previously Gentry said he "knew about it," which qualifies as *notice of knowledge* rather than *actual knowledge.* That he "wasn't too sure" certainly qualifies as lack of direct or express knowledge of it. His "I done figured it out" may sound like it represents his knowledge gained before the fact but it also qualifies as his knowledge gained after the fact, which is closely related to *notice of knowledge.*

It is important to know that this ambiguity in Gentry's case did not begin with the prosecutor's question at trial. Shortly after the investigation of the murder began, Gentry voluntarily went to the police to complain that he was being harassed by an unknown young man who told him he was the driver at the shooting incident and that Gentry's former housemate, who had access to Gentry's old car, owed him $700 for his role in the murder. Since the young man (who was actually working with the police) said couldn't locate Gentry's former housemate, he came to Gentry to learn where the former housemate was. Gentry didn't know that the police had sent this young man to see him because based on a witness's description of the car used in the shooting, the police suspected that it was Gentry's and that he was somehow involved.

The police tape-recorded their initial interview when Gentry came to them voluntarily. In it he told them the visit from the young man caused him to fear for his life, he described everything he knew about his former housemate, and he explained that he had subsequently scrapped his old car because it had stopped running. The police were skeptical, telling Gentry it was very suspicious that he scrapped his car just after this murder.

Four days later Gentry voluntarily went back to the police and told them that he had not been "totally up front" with them in his earlier meeting, having omitted the fact that his boss at the bar where he worked, Junior Paoli, probably had something to do with the crime. He added that Paoli had threatened to kill him if he mentioned this to the police. Gentry also told the police that all he knew about this was that Paoli wanted Gentry's ex-housemate to do a "job" for him. It was only after the shooting that he "done figured out" what that job was.

The police then asked Gentry to wear a wire and record any future conversations he might have with Paoli and his former housemate. An Alaska state law requires a search warrant hearing to authorize cooperating witnesses to wear a body recorder, which meant that Gentry had to appear at a hearing before a judge to authorize this. The assistant district attorney, who had listened to only the last parts of Gentry's taped interview with the police but was briefed by the interviewing officer about the parts he didn't hear, took the lead in this warrant hearing.

Under questioning during this hearing Gentry admitted to the judge that he had been buying and selling cocaine and that he had his twelve-year-old car scrapped. But while Gentry was still outside the courtroom waiting to be called in, the prosecutor had summarized for the judge why Gentry came to the police in the first place, ambiguously concluding, "He has given the police a tape recorded confession to his involvement in the matter." The prosecutor left ambiguous what that "involvement" meant. Then the officer who originally had interviewed Gentry testified that Gentry had told him he had "no idea who his former housemate was going to shoot." This information was very different from that which Gentry had told that officer. On the tape-recording of that interview, which was not presented at this hearing, Gentry actually said he didn't know that the "job" he heard them mention was a shooting. The officer compounded his creative memory of the taped conversation with Gentry by inaccurately reporting that Gentry had told him that his former housemate told him that he was going to use the car and wanted to borrow Gentry's shotgun to do the job. There was nothing remotely like this on the tape-recording of their conversation. One very bad way to repair ambiguity is to represent it inaccurately, which this officer did in his testimony before the judge.

These misstatements of the evidence were enough to convince the judge that Gentry had indeed confessed to aiding and abetting the murder. Even though Gentry had admitted that he dealt cocaine and destroyed his car, he had not confessed to any role in the murder. Contributing to Gentry's problem, he could not be represented by an attorney when he appeared before the judge in this search warrant hearing. An alert attorney, if present, could have pointed out the inaccuracies reported from the police interview. This didn't happen and as a result, the prosecutor indicted Gentry for first-degree murder.

Everyday ambiguities have their consequences, but ambiguities that are converted into inaccuracies that contradict the government's own recorded evidence are even more consequential. The following summarizes the role of deceptive ambiguity in the investigation and trial of this case.

AMBIGUITY PRODUCED BY THE SPEECH EVENT

The most crucial speech event in this case was the search warrant hearing in which law enforcement requested the judge's agreement to have Gentry wear a wire to record the suspects. The detective's role was to explain to the judge why the wire was needed and who would wear it. Gentry was led to understand that this was a benign search warrant speech event, not that it was an evidentiary speech event in which he would be accused of a crime. Because the detective provided inaccurate information about Gentry's role in the police interview, the prosecutor and the judge were misled into believing that Gentry had aided and abetted the murder. This resulted in Gentry's being arrested and indicted during a hearing in which he believed he was in a cooperative speech event about how he would be helping the police capture the killer.

AMBIGUITY PRODUCED BY SCHEMAS

Gentry revealed his own schema from the time of his first voluntary meetings with the police. He suspected some things about the murder, but he did not know for sure how it was carried out or who did it. When he dutifully appeared at the search warrant hearing, his language made it clear that his schema was that he would be helping the police capture the killer. He agreed to do this because his visit from the young man, actually an undercover witness, caused him to fear for his own life. Gentry maintained this schema even during his trial.

It is difficult to determine the schema of the detective who provided the inaccurate information to the judge, but it gave every appearance that he believed Gentry played such a knowingly significant role in the killing that this subsequent inaccurate report to the judge would lead to Gentry's conviction. An alternative interpretation of this is that the detective was simply unintentionally inept when he reported to the judge that Gentry would describe "his role in the murder." The judge could then easily hold the schema that Gentry indeed had described his active participation in it. The prosecutor's schema came from the testimony of the detective, inaccurate though it was. The prosecutor is not blameless, however, because he admittedly failed to listen to the entire tape-recording made by the police. From that point on, his schema was that Gentry had played an active role in the murder. Gentry's schema of his own lack of culpability continued during his own trial, but the prosecutor would have none of it, bound as he was to his own schema of Gentry's guilt. Schemas have a way of reproducing themselves. The entire prosecutorial schema chain was initiated by the detective's inaccurate report of the meetings he had with Gentry and continued despite Gentry's inept efforts to explain his own lack of foreknowledge of the murder.

AMBIGUITY PRODUCED BY AGENDAS

Gentry's agenda, as revealed by the topics he introduced in his initial meeting with the police, was to explain what he heard and learned about the murder and then later to assist the police by tape-recording his conversations with one of the alleged accomplices.

The agenda of the prosecutor was distorted after the policeman who first interviewed Gentry inaccurately reported what Gentry had told him. The prosecutor, who had been briefed about Gentry's meeting with the police, told the judge during a search warrant hearing that would authorize Gentry to tape-record alleged participants: "he has given the police a tape recorded confession to his involvement in the matter." Since it was a search warrant hearing in which Gentry had not yet been permitted to enter the courtroom to hear what the prosecutor had said, he couldn't even hear this misrepresentation. Participants in search warrant hearings are not aided or represented by a lawyer and as a result, the judge was convinced that Gentry confessed to something he did not say, and he was subsequently indicted. The initial ambiguity created by the police agenda became the centerpiece of Gentry's problem.

AMBIGUITY PRODUCED BY SPEECH ACTS

A major problem for Gentry at trial was to try to keep straight the timing of events that prosecutor asked him about. Gentry said repeatedly that everything relevant that he knew about the murder came after it was done, not before. But his confusion about the timing of events became apparent several times during his testimony. At one point the prosecutor asked him what his former housemate told him about the driver of the car. Gentry said that he told him about a guy driving it, then added, "this was sometime before the shooting." This response might be expected to have alerted the prosecutor to the fact that Gentry had difficulty keeping straight the timing of events. Minimally the prosecutor could have asked what time period "sometime" indicated.

Directly after this exchange the prosecutor asked him what his former housemate was talking about when he told Gentry that he had a "job" to do. Gentry answered, "He was talking about this shooting here." The prosecutor took this as Gentry's admission that he had foreknowledge of the killing, for it certainly gave that appearance. What his interpretation did not take into consideration was that Gentry had consistently reported that he did not know anything about the murder plans other than that his former housemate told him only that he had a "job" to do. It was only after the murder that Gentry learned that that his ex-housemate was involved. At this point in the interview his statement, "He was talking about this shooting here," can be understood as something like "I now realize that he was talking about this shooting here." But Gentry's language skills were not always adequate for him to separate what he knew before the killing with what he learned afterward, and the prosecutor took full advantage of his inability to keep time frames straight by converting Gentry's ambiguous responses into strong motives for convicting him of aiding and abetting.

AMBIGUITY PRODUCED BY CONVERSATIONAL STRATEGIES

One technique used by prosecutors (and shared by undercover agents) is to block a defendant's answer by asking more than one question during the same turn of talk. Listeners tend to answer the last in such a series, the most recent one, called the recency principle (Miller and Campbell 1959). The prosecutor frequently asked two or more questions at the same time, for example:

> PROSECUTOR: Now by then you knew that it involved a shooting. . . . You didn't know who the guy was?
>
> GENTRY: Yeah.

By answering the second question, that he didn't know who the guy was, Gentry's "yeah" unknowingly gave the appearance of also answering the first question—that he knew that a shooting was involved. Even though in the discourse before and after this question Gentry had consistently said that he didn't *know* that a shooting was involved, here the prosecutor extracted this answer from Gentry's consistent and ongoing context and got him to give the appearance that he knew it involved a shooting.

Additional critical conversational blocking was created by the police officer who inaccurately reported that Gentry confessed to "his involvement" in the murder, as well as by the prosecutor who accepted the policeman's statement as accurate without listening to the entire tape of that conversation that could have clarified the officer's deceptive misrepresentation.

AMBIGUITY PRODUCED BY LEXICON AND GRAMMAR

To Gentry the prosecutor used the indefinite pronoun, *it*, ambiguously. Most speakers do this sometimes, but in an important setting such as a murder trial, it behooves the powerful prosecutor to be sure that Gentry understood what he meant by *it* so that Gentry could have been clear in his response. The following is only one of many examples:

> PROSECUTOR: So you knew it was going to happen?
> GENTRY: Yes, I knew about it. I'd done figured it out.

The question is what did the ambiguous *it* mean to each speaker. It could mean that Gentry was saying that his *it* referred to his knowledge that the murder was going to happen, even though what he had been saying all along was very different. About the shooting, Gentry said he was "not too sure," "kind of knew but kind of didn't know," "suspected," and "I thought maybe it was just a bunch of bullshit." In contrast, the prosecutor used this *it* reference against Gentry, claiming that it meant that he knew full well about the murder before it took place and therefore aided and abetted by letting the killer use his car. It didn't seem to matter that at the time of the murder Gentry was in Hawaii on his honeymoon or that before that housemate moved out, he had rigged Gentry's old car to start and operate without an ignition key.

Overall, however, the most critical deceptive ambiguity was produced by the semantic confusion concerning the meaning of the verb *know*, which was central to the prosecutor's questioning strategies. It was one of the most damaging aspects of Gentry's case because the participants operated with different meanings of the verb.

The Prosecutor Uses Deceptive Ambiguity in the Perjury Trial of Father Joseph Sica

In 2006, the Dauphin County, Pennsylvania, prosecutor summoned a Catholic priest, Father Joseph Sica, to be a witness at a grand jury hearing related to an ongoing investigation of Louis DeNaples, a Scranton businessman who owned a Pocono Mountains resort with a gaming casino. DeNaples was suspected of having had suspiciously close ties with a local crime figure, Russell Bufalino, who had served prison time and died eight years earlier. Father Sica's testimony at that grand jury hearing led the prosecutor to believe that the priest was lying to cover up the alleged illegal activities of his friend DeNaples.

Father Sica and DeNaples were good friends because they had grown up together and had kept in touch with each other over the years. In contrast, the priest testified that he had met Bufalino at his ordination ceremony some twenty-five years previously, but they hadn't keep up correspondence except for the one time when Bufalino asked Father Sica to give him a blessing as he lay dying in the hospital.

The prosecutor demonstrated that he believed Father Sica had continued to be very close with Bufalino up to the time of his death and that he had lied during his testimony in order to withhold giving information that would incriminate his friend, DeNaples. The prosecutor apparently also believed that all three men had a close personal relationship. To support his belief, the prosecutor discovered a thank-you note from Bufalino and an undated group photo of Father Sica with Bufalino and DeNaples, which, unknown to the prosecutor, had been taken at Father Sica's ordination ceremony decades earlier. The prosecutor needed Father Sica's own testimony to support his belief that the priest knew Bufalino very well and was covering up what he knew about him when he testified about his ongoing relationship with DeNaples.

In 2007 the prosecutor summoned Father Sica to a grand jury hearing related to charges of his alleged perjury during his previous testimony about DeNaples a year earlier. The priest was a well-educated man who was familiar with oppositional interactions with powerful people like prosecutors. He was aware that his role in the speech event of courtroom testimony was to answer questions as honestly and completely as possible. Nevertheless, in January 2008, the grand jury indicted Father Sica for perjury based on his testimony at that hearing.

Central to the prosecutor's grand jury questioning was the meaning of the expression, *close personal relationship*. He interpreted certain words in Father Sica's testimony such as *saw, met with*, and *contacted*, to indicate that his relationship with Bufalino was intimate and very close. The prosecutor's questioning began with an indirect approach:

Q: When was the last time you recall having any contact with Russell Bufalino?
A: Twenty-some years ago.
Q: You wouldn't, it was just a, you met him?
A: Yes, sir.
Q: There, you didn't have any sort of personal relationship Russell Bufalino?
A: No. When I was a deacon in Sayre [pause] do you want me to tell you how I met him?
Q: Sure.

Father Sica was obviously not sure what the prosecutor was trying to elicit and since it was unclear to him what he meant by *personal relationship*, he requested clarification, but the prosecutor ignored his request. The priest then went on to describe how he first met Mr. and Mrs. Bufalino back at the time when he was serving as a hospital chaplain. Bufalino and his wife were visiting a patient there. The prosecutor wasn't satisfied with this answer and probed further:

Q: Did you have any personal relationship beyond that with Mr. and Mrs. Bufalino?
A: No.
Q: And it was just a chance meeting?
A: Yes.
Q: Certainly you didn't have any personal relationship with Russell Bufalino?
A: No.
Q: Or any member of his family?
A: I met his wife at the hospital.
Q: Did you have any personal relationship beyond that with Mr. and Mrs. Bufalino?
A: No.

Believing he now had evidence of perjury, the prosecutor showed Father Sica a group photo of him with Bufalino, DeNaples, and a few other people along with a handwritten note Father Sica had sent to Bufalino beginning "Dear Russ" and which briefly told Bufalino that he had written a character recommendation to the governor to be used at Bufalino's sentencing hearing after he was convicted of murder. The prosecutor also presented another piece of evidence—Father Sica's thank-you note to Bufalino for his gift of a hundred dollars. The prosecutor apparently did not understand that the character recommendation letter could be considered part of a priest's commonly expected pastoral work. He considered it evidence that Father Sica had a *close personal relationship* with Bufalino and that the priest had lied about this during his testimony before the previous grand jury hearing concerning DeNaples.

Because the indictment of a priest was big news in this community, a few days before his grand jury appearance a local radio station interviewed Father Sica, who told the reporter that one time when he traveled home to visit his parents, Bufalino, who lived near his family, invited him to dinner, although he didn't say that he accepted the invitation. The prosecutor played the interview tape in court as further evidence supporting his case for perjury.

Recall that the initial grand jury hearing concerned Joseph DeNaples. In it, Father Sica openly admitted his close personal relationship with DeNaples, testifying that they had known each other for fifty years, that Mr. and Mrs. DeNaples were like family to him, and that they would visit together "consistently and frequently." In describing this relationship, Father Sica provided his own implicit definition of what he understood to be the meaning of a *close personal relationship*, using DeNaples as the example. This stood in sharp contrast with his description of his distant and infrequent relationship with Bufalino. Since the prosecutor did not define what he meant by a *close personal relationship,* Father Sica did it for him by showing that he indeed had such a relationship with DeNaples.

The prosecutor asked Father Sica many questions about events that took place over twenty years ago such as whether he attended various Italian American Civil Rights dinners and whether he ever heard DeNaples talk about Bufalino. To these questions Father Sica answered, "I don't recall," or "I have no present recollection of that." The prosecutor considered these answers evidence of perjury even though the verb, *to recollect,* means to recover something stored further back in one's mind as opposed to the verb *remember,* which means to recover something readily at hand in one's memory, as both words are defined in Garner's *Dictionary of Modern Legal Usage* (1995).

Shortly before the perjury trial began, the district attorney reviewed the prosecutor's intelligence analysis of the evidence of Father Sica's alleged perjury and was not at all certain that the State could make a convincing case. He then asked Robert Leonard and me to review the language evidence for him in which the meaning of a *close personal relationship* was the centerpiece. We did so and produced a report that supported the district attorney's doubts about the prosecution. He then dropped the perjury charges, explaining: "we engaged expert linguists, something a little different . . . but in a perjury case precision of questioning is important."

The following summarizes points about the deceptive ambiguity that disturbed the district attorney enough to call off the prosecution.

AMBIGUITY PRODUCED BY THE SPEECH EVENT

There were two separate speech events. The first was an information-gathering speech event in the form of a grand jury hearing that led the prosecutor to believe Father Sica committed perjury. The second was Father Sica's own grand jury hearing, an accusation speech event, on which the prosecutor based his claim that the priest had indeed perjured himself during the first grand jury hearing. Father Sica was well aware of these speech events and his duty and requirements in both. There was no ambiguity about the second grand jury speech event but during the first one the prosecutor converted his information-gathering speech event into a future accusation speech event by misinterpreting Father Sica's testimony to mean something that the priest's words did not say or mean.

AMBIGUITY PRODUCED BY SCHEMAS

As usual, the schemas of the participants grew naturally out of the speech events in which their language made their schemas clear. Father Sica's schema in the first grand jury hearing was to be helpful to the prosecution by explaining what he knew about Bufalino and DeNaples. His schema was much the same in the second grand jury hearing, except that he now realized that he was the target of the prosecution and his schema then caused him to try to defend himself. The prosecutor's schema was virtually the same in both grand jury hearings—that Father Sica had committed perjury. It is possible that the prosecutor's schema of the priest's guilt prevented him from understanding Father Sica's attempts to contrast his close personal relationship with DeNaples with his distant relationship with Bufalino. The prosecutor's subsequent questioning was mistakenly guided by what he perceived as Father Sica's deliberate attempt to be ambiguous but which, upon closer analysis, was not.

AMBIGUITY PRODUCED BY AGENDAS

Father Sica's language indicated that his agenda was direct and clear—to tell the prosecutor what he knew about Bufalino and DeNaples. The prosecutor's agenda, as demonstrated by his questioning, was to discover Father Sica's perjury. Again, the prosecutor's case was so affected by his schema of guilt that he had apparent difficulty processing what Father Sica actually told him.

AMBIGUITY PRODUCED BY SPEECH ACTS

During grand jury hearing speech events prosecutors hold superordinate status and power while interviewees have only subordinate, powerless status. It is the responsibility of superordinate speakers to be certain that subordinate speakers understand what is being asked of them (*Bronston v. United States*, 409 U.S. 352 (1973)). One of the speech acts allowed to witnesses in the courtroom is the right to request clarification when they don't understand. Father Sica requested clarification several times when he was unsure about what the prosecutor asked him.

Prosecutors also have the right to request clarification when they don't understand something that the witness is saying, but this is more than their right—they have the responsibility to do this. It became apparent that the prosecutor's failure to use the readily available speech act of requesting clarification when he appeared to not understand what Father Sica told him played a role in causing his superior, the district attorney, to seek the linguistic assistance that led to his eventually dropping the case. The remaining question was why the prosecutor did not request clarification. One likely answer is that getting a clear answer would not well serve his deceptive prosecutorial schema. In this case, the prosecutor became the victim of his own created ambiguity.

In Father Sica's answer to one of the prosecutor's questions he used the speech act of admitting that he was no longer able to recall whether DeNaples had even mentioned Bufalino in their conversations. The prosecutor did not accept this as a truthful answer; instead he considered it evasive or lying. Even though there are many things that people don't recall about events that happened in their distant pasts, this prosecutor interpreted the priest's response as evidence of perjury.

AMBIGUITY PRODUCED BY CONVERSATIONAL STRATEGIES

The prosecutor used two common conversational strategies with Father Sica. First, he blocked the priest from understanding what he meant in his question about whether he had a "close personal friendship" with Bufalino. Then he refused to clarify what he meant by that expression. This strategy didn't work, for Father Sica then gave him an implicit definition with a good example of what a close personal friendship meant to him, using the example of his long and close personal relationship with DeNaples.

The second conversational strategy may fall under the category of the prosecutorial tactic of withholding information until it can be used to impeach. Although it is common practice for prosecutors to do this in order to try to impeach a witness, prosecutors' institutional power to control the flow of the speech event by requesting general information early in the questioning that can be used to contradict later requested specific information can be considered a form of rhetorical trickery and deception. Here the prosecutor could have begun his questioning by unambiguously showing Father Sica the group photo and thank-you note and then asking him whether this indicated that he had a "close personal relationship" with Bufalino. If the prosecutor had chosen this sequence of questioning, Father Sica then could have explained that the photo was taken at his ordination ceremony twenty years earlier and that his polite thank-you note was for an ordination gift that is commonplace behavior in any society. He also could have explained that this came about because he had met Bufalino by chance at the hospital where Father Sica was once chaplain and that he had invited Bufalino to his upcoming ceremony as a matter of politeness. He also could have explained that it is common for priests to write support letters for people who are about to be sentenced to prison. Instead, however, the prosecutor manipulated his sequence of questions to make it appear that Father Sica lied about his close personal relationship with Bufalino and was therefore knowledgeable about the crime family's operations. Since withholding information appears to be approved as a standard courtroom practice, the prosecutor no doubt reasoned that it could give juries the deceptive impression that the speaker was caught in a lie. This ploy failed to work with Father Sica.

AMBIGUITY PRODUCED BY LEXICON AND GRAMMAR

The undefined and deceptively ambiguous expression, *close personal friendship*, was the prosecutor's major lexical weapon. References to such types of human relationships go by several terms such as *meeting, seeing,* and *knowing well*, and they are usually accompanied by descriptive modifiers such as *intimate, close, very close, frequent, regular, casual, distant*, and others. Even then, however, more clarification is needed if one is to understand what questioners want to know. In the context of grand jury hearings, questioners are expected to be precise and unambiguous so that truthful, clear, and precise answers can be obtained. Father Sica apparently knew this and tried to be as truthful, clear, and precise as possible. When the prosecutor remained imprecise about what he meant by the expression, *close personal relationship*, he used this deceptively ambiguous expression as a weapon to try to elicit from the priest an answer that might come back to haunt him. Father Sica knew better than to fall for this deceptive ambiguity and he was intelligent and wary enough to avoid the prosecutor's trap. Not all witnesses are that perceptive.

There is much to be said in favor of our adversarial courtroom system as long as deceptive ambiguity plays no role in it. The various types of deceptively ambiguous strategies used by prosecutors in the cases of Suyat, Gentry, and Father Sica required careful linguistic attention.

5

Undercover Agents Use Deceptive Ambiguity

The advent of the government's use of recorded evidence began in the early twentieth century. The first reported appellate opinion upholding the use of evidence of a phonograph came in 1906 (*Boyne City, G&A.R. Co. v. Anderson*, 146 Mich. 328, 109 N.W. 429). It was twenty-four years later before the second appellate decision was handed down when sound motion pictures were used to uphold a confession. Next, after tape-recording equipment was invented, the government began using it in undercover operations. By the decade of the 1970s and 1980s, thanks to the Organized Crime Control Act of 1970, the government began using tape-recordings as evidence in investigations of payoffs, kickbacks, racketeering, threats, solicitation to murder, and obstruction of justice from New York to Miami. Since that time undercover operations using electronic recording have flourished in police departments and government law enforcement agencies all over America but a bit less frequently throughout the rest of the world. This type of undercover law enforcement operation introduces a type of deceptive ambiguity that is less used in police interviews and prosecutorial questioning, where the institution of law is transparent to all. In contrast, law enforcement's covert operators openly and admittedly deceive their true identity and purposes.

Today in some of these operations the targeted individuals are suspected of having committed crimes in the past such as murder, bribery, or fraud. Other targets are suspected of being predisposed to commit future crimes and the operations are geared to preventing these from happening. Undercover agents try to get these targets to unwittingly admit their crimes on tape. The purpose of covert operations is to capture evidence of the targets admitting any past offenses or to stymie their plans to commit future crimes. Undercover operations rely on deceiving targeted individuals by making them believe that their interaction with the agent is about something other than it really is until such time as the targets appear to be ripe for admitting their past crimes or their willingness to commit a new one.

Undercover agents are required to have considerable patience as they interact with targets. It is common for them to begin with the strategy of hinting at illegality without being explicit about it. If targets catch the hints and go on to inculpate themselves, the government can consider the operation successful. If the targets don't bite, an alternative strategy is for agents to refer to an illegal aspect of miscellaneous past events, whether or not the target was involved in them, in an effort to get the conversation onto an illegal track. If this doesn't work, the agents may have to resort to being clear and unambiguous about the current past or future crime, waiting for the targets to either expose their culpability or reject having anything to do with it. The strategy of making a clear and unambiguous representation of the illegal nature of the enterprise is a usually a last resort, for if targets are not interested, the government's undercover effort typically fails.

This chapter describes three law enforcement investigations in which undercover agents camouflaged their institutional power in the effort to capture the criminal behavior of suspects. Central to camouflaged interactions is that by definition representatives of law enforcement hide their institutional power as well as their true purposes during their interactions with their targets. This camouflage offers the institution even more power because the targets, being unaware of the agents' power, are less likely to be on guard. This situation also causes targets to communicate in ways that may seem ambiguous to the undercover agents as well as to later listeners, including prosecutors and juries. This chapter illustrates the ways undercover agents used deceptive ambiguity in their investigations of U.S. Senator Harrison A. Williams, automobile manufacturer John Z. DeLorean, and taxpayer Vernon Sligh.

Undercover Agents Use Deceptive Ambiguity with Senator Harrison A. Williams

The 1979–1980 Abscam investigation of US Senator Harrison A. Williams of New Jersey started after Williams's personal lawyer and friend, Alex Feinberg, got the idea of buying a defunct mine in Piney River, Virginia, which he believed could be revived to make a huge amount of money. Feinberg and a few of his associates tried to secure financing to purchase the mine because they believed it was rich in the type of titanium that could be sold to commercial paint companies such as Sherwin Williams. It is unclear how they met FBI agent Anthony Amoroso, who told them that he knew of a wealthy Arab sheik who might offer them a loan that would provide the group enough capital to purchase the mine.

There was a catch to this plan, however, for the agent told them that in order to get the sheik's financial support, the group would have to figure out a way to get him asylum and eventual citizenship in the United States. That would require the help of a US congressman because it is necessary for a member of congress to sponsor the required special legislation for such requests. For this reason Alex Feinberg asked the senator to go with him to several of the planning meetings that his business associates were having. Agent Amoroso had already insinuated himself into the group and wore a body mike to secretly tape-record everything that was said.

These audiotapes show that Williams attended portions of only four of the group's meetings. He spoke very little, but when he talked he demonstrated that he was skeptical about the idea of buying the mine but was willing to listen to his friends talk about it. At one point Feinberg insisted that Williams, who was far from being a wealthy man, could join the venture and make a nice profit to ensure a prosperous retirement someday. Toward this end, one day at a train station as Williams was about to leave on a trip to a political meeting, Feinberg quickly handed Williams some freshly printed shares of stock in their still unofficial and unformed company. Since the company did not even exist and because Williams doubted that it ever would, he considered these stock shares worthless, as evidenced by the fact that he left them unattended in his gym bag on the floor of his Senate office, where the FBI eventually discovered them after they arrested him.

During one of the meetings that Williams did not attend, agent Amoroso told the group that the wealthy Arab sheik wanted to flee his country, relocate to the United States and eventually become a citizen, adding that any financial support that the sheik could bring to the area would depend on their meeting this condition. Not surprisingly, the group immediately connected this idea with Feinberg's friend, Senator Williams, which likely was what the agent wanted to happen. When Williams attended their next meeting, he described to them the proper legislative procedure to accomplish the sheik's relocation and told them he would be willing to help with this in any way he could.

Agent Amoroso's undercover investigation ran into a problem, however, because what Williams told the group did not provide him with the evidence he needed to connect the senator with a quid pro quo bribe. Therefore, the agent arranged a meeting in which Williams would meet with the alleged sheik, but he told the senator that the purported reason for this meeting was that the sheik wanted to know about any progress that the group had made toward purchasing the mine. Williams didn't know of any such progress but agreed to meet the sheik anyway, thinking that it was part of his role as a US senator to meet with foreign dignitaries of this type and explain the necessary legal process to get asylum and eventual citizenship.

This was the only Abscam case in which the FBI produced the alleged Arab sheik, who had only been mentioned in the other Abscam investigations but had made no appearance with the other congressmen targeted by the FBI. The sheik, of course, was actually an FBI agent playing that role. As described in my book, *The Language of Bribery Cases* (Shuy 2014), Williams was deferential and polite to the sheik, believing that he was a foreign dignitary who likely did not know the workings of American culture and politics. After the brief greeting formalities, agent Amoroso left the room and the sheik began talking, all the while faking problems with his English and saying stumblingly:

> SHEIK: I, er, in the near future one two months I plan to leave my country, reside in United States. People tell me, er, a senator is in position through Congress, um, bill though, uh, bill . . . if I come to the United States, er, through your assistance for me to stay. Er, is that a problem?"

Williams replied at length that it could be done but it would not be easy and that good reasons were needed for such legislation to be introduced before it could be passed into a law. He specified that the situation has to meet rigid criteria, that it is more difficult than it was five years ago, but that it was possible when such a person has a good character and would face hardship if he was forced to return to his home country. The senator concluded by saying politely, "I would welcome the chance to know you better and support this effort of yours."

Since the sheik apparently interpreted the senator's explanation of the required procedure as his agreement to sponsor the legislation, he immediately offered him a bribe:

> SHEIK: I will, for your help, uh, assistance, I would like to give you some money for, for permanent residence.
>
> WILLIAMS: No. No. No. When I work in that kind of activity, it is purely a public, not uh, no, within my position, when I deal with law and legislation, it's not within my---

As the senator tried to finish his explanation about why he couldn't accept money for this, the telephone rang, interrupting him. The sheik answered the phone and the bribery offer ended abruptly and unsuccessfully. The call was from agent Amoroso in the adjoining room, apparently advising the sheik that since the bribe offer clearly didn't go anywhere, he should drop this approach and change the scenario to focus it on getting the senator to be explicit about how he could help the sheik obtain US residency. This topic switch was a tacit admission that the sheik's bribe offer had failed. The rest of their conversation dealt with how long it might take for Williams's associates to purchase the mine and how the legislative process takes place, neither of which topics furthered the FBI's goal to get Williams to say that he would indeed sponsor the sheik and bring the matter before Congress for a vote.

When Williams was indicted and went to trial, the prosecution introduced other issues, but the two discussed previously were most central to his ultimate conviction. Much was made of the fact that he *accepted* the stock shares in a company that never existed, even though his friends forced those shares upon the senator during a hasty and unplanned encounter at an airport after which

Williams thought so little of the whole plan that he didn't bother to store the stock certificates in a safe or even logical place.

Immediately before Williams met with the Arab sheik, Mel Weinberg, a convicted con man the FBI had recruited and paid highly to work with them in the entire Abscam operation, met with Williams and scripted him about what he should say when he met the sheik. He told Williams to brag about himself and to say things like "without me there is no deal," "I'll use my influence," "I guarantee this," "I'll move this through," and "I'm the man." The taped evidence of the senator's subsequent meeting with the sheik demonstrates that Williams said none of these things, but this evidence didn't seem to matter at trial. The senator was accused of saying them anyway, possibly because when members of the jury listened to the tape they confused what Weinberg advised Williams to say with what the senator actually said. It is not unusual for jurors to be contaminated by taped evidence in this way. Later listeners tend to forget exactly who said what.

The major crime for which Williams was convicted, however, was bribery, even though the government's own evidence made it perfectly clear that he repeatedly rejected the sheik's bribery offer, paid no attention to the phony stock shares thrust upon him by Feinberg, and completely ignored Mel Weinberg's scripting about how to brag about his own power and influence. This resulted in Senator Williams suffering the shame of being only the second US senator in history to be so convicted of a crime, forced to resign from office, and end his long service in government.

The many deceptive ambiguities created by this undercover operation include the following.

AMBIGUITY PRODUCED BY THE SPEECH EVENT

Bribery speech events are structured in four major phases: proposal, negotiation, offer, and completion (Shuy 2013: 120–123). The bribery speech event is very similar to the business transaction speech event, differing only in that the business transaction discussed during a bribery speech event is illegal. One variation of the business transaction speech event is the business progress speech event (Shuy 2015: 25; Shuy 2016: 32–42), which has a three-phase structure: reporting progress, negotiating or planning next steps, and discussing how to accomplish those next steps.

Before this meeting took place Williams was led to believe that the speech event with the sheik was a business progress speech event in which it is conventional for one party to check on the progress being made by the other party. The sheik made this clear in his first statement to Williams:

> SHEIK: I'm very happy that you are here. Um, I would like, er, to, er, er, speak, speak to your first, er, regarding the um, titanium mine. Everything is okay with the money here.

After the senator explained that he knew of no progress being made toward purchase of the mine, the sheik then switched the conversation quickly to a business transaction speech event describing the problem he needed to have accomplished by the senator:

> SHEIK: I need something from you. I, er, in the near future one two month I plan to leave my country. Reside in United States. People tell me, er, a senator is in the position through Congress, um, a bill through a bill if I come to the United States, er, through your assistance for me to stay.

Williams was prepared for the business progress speech event in which he would tell the sheik that as far as he knew there was little or no progress being made toward purchasing the defunct mine and essentially they were still nowhere. Now, realizing that the sheik had shifted the speech event into business transaction speech event, Williams explained that this was not an easy thing to do and listed a number of criteria that had to be fulfilled for it to happen.

Next, without even a single follow-up question, the sheik switched the speech event to a bribery speech event, offering a quid pro quo bribe of money for Williams's legislative help:

> SHEIK: I will, for your help, uh, assistance, I would like to give you some money for, for permanent residence.

By immediately switching the business progress speech event into a bribery speech event, the sheik gave a strong indication that he was not concerned about the group's progress in buying the mine but instead he was there to offer Williams a bribe.

After the senator rejected the bribe offer, the FBI's agent who was monitoring the conversation from a nearby room telephoned the sheik, apparently telling him to change the direction of the business transaction speech event from a bribe quid pro quo to simply securing Williams's agreement to sponsor the sheik's request for permanent residence. So the senator had to deal with the rapidly shifting consecutive and different speech events rather than the one he was prepared to talk about when he came to the meeting.

Speech event switching is a clever tactic because it catches targets off guard and confuses them. In this case, however, the senator rather quickly gathered himself together and refused the sheik's bribe offer. By first falsely representing and then switching the speech event in this way, the bribe offer speech event is on tape for all later listeners to hear and to associate with the target, regardless of whether or not it was rejected. The situation of simply being in a bribery speech event, even if that is unwanted and unsuccessful, casts a shadow over targets who find themselves in such an event, even when they reject it.

Some critics ask why a target would even agree to talk with unsavory people who offer bribes. The answer in this case is that Williams did not know that the sheik was an unsavory person and met with him because he was told that it was a very different speech event that he felt he could manage. Although the government does not consider it improper or unfair to intentionally begin an investigation of a target with a perfectly legal speech event proposition and then switch it to an illegal one, it is difficult to consider this practice as anything but deceptively ambiguous.

AMBIGUITY PRODUCED BY SCHEMAS

As indicated by the language he used, Senator Williams's initial schema was that he was in a business progress speech event. This schema then had to be changed to that of a business transaction speech event in which he was asked to sponsor legislation to get the sheik into the country. Almost immediately he had to change his new schema to the business transaction speech event in which he was offered a bribe. People are used to changes of topics, but rapid changes in schemas can be dizzying and disadvantage targets by suddenly disrupting their schemas and requiring them to think quickly as they adjust to the new speech events, a deceptive strategy in itself. But Williams accomplished his schema adjustments very well under these unusual circumstances. The sheik finally revealed his own actual schema after deceptively inducing Williams to first have two inaccurate schemas.

AMBIGUITY PRODUCED BY AGENDAS

Based on the senator's schema associated with the initial speech event that he was told he would be in with the sheik, the senator's agenda was first to report that no progress had been made by the group about buying the mine and then later to describe the legal process required for the sheik to obtain permanent residence in the United States. As the sheik changed the speech events, his agenda followed suit. In spite of his initial topics about progress in the mining venture and his need for permanent residence, the sheik's major agenda was to bribe the senator for getting him permanent residence. We can be sure of this because that is the only reason why the government would have arranged this meeting. The government would gain little by finding out the progress of the mining venture and equally little by achieving the senator's willingness to help a foreign dignitary establish asylum in this country. The government's major goal was to get Williams's agreement to accept a bribe.

The government also tape-recorded the earlier group meetings in this investigation, only small parts of which included the senator. When legal evidence contains many hours of recorded conversation, it is not easy for later listeners to keep straight who actually said what to whom. As noted earlier, among the many tapes the prosecution produced was a conversation between its hired con man Mel Weinberg and the senator in which Weinberg strongly suggested that when Williams met with the sheik, if the sheik brought up the topic of his need for congressional sponsorship, the senator should brag to him about how he could manipulate the congress into agreeing to provide legislation for the sheik to achieve citizenship. Even though the immediately following tape of Williams' meeting with the sheik produced none of Weinberg's scripting, at trial the prosecution focused on his preceding exchanges with Weinberg, astoundingly claiming that Williams said things that he did not say. This is a classic example of the way later listeners, even prosecutors, can be contaminated about who said what to whom. The prosecutor's misuse of his own language evidence created deceptive ambiguity for the jury members who fell for the trick.

Another example of the confusion about who said what to whom occurred in one the earlier meetings of the group of potential investors in the mine. At one point the chairman called for a voice vote about whether or not to go ahead with their plans to buy the mine. Even though six members of the group were present, only five voices could be heard saying "aye" in this audiotaped meeting. The senator had a distinctive bass voice, but not a single bass voice was among the five heard saying "aye." Williams indicated that he did not consider himself a participant in the potential ownership group and the lack of his distinctive bass voice is a strong indication that he did not choose to vote on a procedure in which he didn't consider himself involved. Yet the government's transcript of this meeting included Williams as one of the "aye" votes and the prosecution deceptively used this transcript rather than the tape, to accuse the senator that his agenda was that same as the rest of the group. Transcription errors of this type often occur in government-produced records and it is common for these errors to be used to create deceptive ambiguity for the jurors that subsequently supports the prosecution's inaccurate transcription of the taped evidence.

AMBIGUITY PRODUCED BY SPEECH ACTS

Although Williams did not produce the speech act of agreeing to accept the bribe or to sponsor the legislation, the prosecution ignored this and indicted him for agreeing to accept a bribe. Apparently the senator's speech act of rejecting the bribe offer four consecutive times did not discourage the sheik but caused the agents to search for other areas in which they could claim bribery was the issue. To satisfy this goal, their search warrant evidence included the bogus stock shares for the nonexistent company that FBI agents found in the senator's bag on the floor of his senate office. It also apparently didn't matter that the senator did not consider the stock certificates of any value. And it didn't matter that Williams did not *accept* these stock shares. He *received* them when his friends foisted them upon him as he was about to board a train to

New York, which is not the same thing as agreeing to accept them, especially when there is no record that he had even agreed to be part of the enterprise. Just the same, during the trial the government created deceptive ambiguity by treating the stock certificates as *things of value* (part of a quid pro quo) and the jury accepted the prosecutor's misinterpretation of the evidence and found the senator of guilty of bribery.

The prosecution also claimed that Williams used the speech act of promising to sponsor legislation to bring the sheik into the country. Williams indeed made a promise at the end of the meeting, but it was not for what the government claimed:

> WILLIAMS: You can leave with my assurance that I will do those things that will bring you on for consideration of permanency. Quite frankly, I can't do that. It is a law and has to go through the whole dignified process of passing a law. I pledge I will do all that is necessary to get you to that proper decision.

As Searle (1969: 61) aptly put it, "the meaning of a sentence is entirely determined by the meaning of its elements, both lexical and syntactical." The senator's promise, as expressed by "assurance" and "pledge," was to "bring you on for *consideration* of permanency" and "do all that is necessary to get to that proper decision." This promise was not to accomplish the sheik's request but to assist him with the conditions relating to it. This made no difference to the prosecutor, who deceptively convinced the jury that it was a felicitous promise to achieve the status of permanency for the sheik. Again, the prosecutor was able to get the jury to buy into his deceptively created ambiguity based on language that was not at all ambiguous.

AMBIGUITY PRODUCED BY CONVERSATIONAL STRATEGIES

Interrupting is one of the more common conversational strategies used in undercover criminal investigations. Interrupting is a form of blocking what the targets are starting to say. After the sheik offered Williams a cash bribe, the senator said "no" four times and then started to explain why he couldn't take the money. At that point the FBI agent who was monitoring the meeting from an adjoining room interrupted the senator's effort to explain to the sheik why in America it is illegal to give or take bribes. In my analysis of many other bribery cases I have found that blocking potential exculpatory statements is a deceptive conversational strategy that is commonly practiced by undercover agents. The irony of this is that although the government defends such practice claiming that the agents are only offering targets an "opportunity" to commit a crime, they also sometimes try to block any opportunity the target might have to reject it. This can only be considered an apparently intentional deceptive practice that creates ambiguity for the jury to try to untangle.

AMBIGUITY PRODUCED BY LEXICON AND GRAMMAR

Although the sheik spoke slowly and deliberately and used no deceptive lexicon and grammar, he tried to fake his role as a less than competent speaker of English by producing compound sentences and seemed to think that using lots of pauses and hesitation markers would be enough to produce the appearance of a foreigner struggling with the language that would cause the senator to tolerate even his most egregious statements. This created ambiguity in the social context that worked to the advantage of the prosecutor, especially when he claimed at trial that the senator appeared to be so tolerant of the sheik for making a bribery offer that he didn't excoriate him for its illegality.

The agents used deceptive ambiguity during this investigation of Senator Williams by switching the speech events, encouraging inaccurate schemas, disguising their agendas, ignoring Williams's speech acts of denial, using conversational strategies that went far beyond mere persuasion, and faking the persona of a foreign dignitary whose limited English would produce the target's sympathy and forgiveness for not understanding the proper ethics required of an American senator. That the senator was convicted of bribery is no tribute to his defense lawyer, who missed many opportunities to show the flaws in the government's case.

An Undercover Agent Uses Deceptive Ambiguity with Automobile Maker John DeLorean

In 1984, automobile executive John DeLorean was the target in a famous sting operation conducted by the combined forces of the FBI, the US Drug Enforcement Agency, the US Customs Service, and two California police departments. The investigation culminated in his arrest for allegedly agreeing to put up $1.8 million of the money remaining in his rapidly sinking car company in exchange for 100 kilos of cocaine, which would purportedly return $24 million to him after the drugs were sold on the street. The government's only evidence consisted of sixty-four audio and videotapes made over six months, first by an FBI agent posing as a banker and at the very end by James Hoffman, a drug smuggler who the FBI had recently caught flying illegal narcotics into the country and then used him as a cooperating witness (Shuy 1993:68–85).

A few years earlier the British government awarded DeLorean about $400 million to build a new automobile factory in a part of Northern Ireland with the hope that the factory would relieve the high degree of unemployment in that area. The recession of 1981 and 1982 apparently led Margaret Thatcher, the new prime minister, to refuse to honor her predecessor's promise to DeLorean of an additional $50 million for marketing, distribution, and sales once the cars started coming off of the production line. Desperately needing this additional money, DeLorean then tried and failed to convince a number of banks to give him loans and by 1982 the DeLorean Motor Company was in deep financial trouble, causing DeLorean to seek investors or loans to prevent his forthcoming bankruptcy. He needed at least $20 million to stay in business.

DeLorean then met a man who claimed to be a California banker, but who was in reality an undercover FBI agent. This banker agreed to help DeLorean get a loan and also to seek additional investors in his company. The agent tape-recorded their conversations for about five months, during which time he made no progress to help DeLorean with either method that could save his company from bankruptcy. In none of these conversations could the FBI discover any evidence of DeLorean's predisposition or intention to do anything illegal.

Then suddenly the tenor of the meetings changed dramatically. The FBI agent posing as a banker told DeLorean that although he couldn't find any way for him to arrange a loan, he knew of some people who were in the drug business who could manage to get him some quick money for his company. The videotapes showed that DeLorean was surprised by this. He didn't agree but he also didn't say "no," for although the banker had shut down the possibility of a loan, he still had left the door open about continuing to help DeLorean search for investors. Since DeLorean apparently didn't want to close the door to getting possible investors, he didn't walk away from the banker.

Because DeLorean's response still didn't provide the government with any evidence to indict him, the banker took the further step of bringing in James Hoffman, a man the DEA had recently captured while he was flying illegal drugs into the country. Hoffman was assigned to meet with DeLorean as an undercover cooperating witness and try to capture on tape DeLorean's agreement to invest in Hoffman's phony drug scheme. Getting DeLorean's agreement would undoubtedly cause Hoffman to receive favorable consideration at his future sentencing hearing, a common practice followed by some law enforcement agencies. Hoffman's capture provided the government with an unexpected and fortunate advantage, because when they questioned him, he told them that years ago he and DeLorean had been neighbors during the time they were both living in San Diego. They had not communicated since that time, but their teenage sons had remained in communication over the years. This provided the FBI with a reasonable excuse for arranging for Hoffman to reconnect with DeLorean. Hoffman's sole task, however, was to sympathize with DeLorean's financial problems and get him to agree to invest his remaining resources in Hoffman's fictitious drug scheme.

The critical videotaped meeting between the two former neighbors took place at the L'Enfant Plaza in Washington, DC. At the close of this meeting DeLorean was arrested and charged with agreeing to invest in Hoffman's narcotics scheme. The alleged smoking gun evidence was disputed because the defense claimed that the recorded conversations were deceptively ambiguous and gave strong evidence of entrapment. Linguistic analysis of the videotaped L'Enfant Plaza conversation was presented at an evidentiary hearing, after which the judge agreed that indeed the defense could plead that the government had entrapped DeLorean, which led to DeLorean's eventual acquittal at trial.

AMBIGUITY PRODUCED BY THE SPEECH EVENT

There could be no confusion about the business transaction speech event DeLorean had been in with the banker for five months. The business transaction speech event has the following structural phases:

1. Discuss a business problem
2. Offer, negotiate, and respond to an offer and discuss conditions
3. Negotiate a proposal (prices, details, payment conditions)
4. Complete the transaction by agreeing or disagreeing

All of DeLorean's discussions with the banker were in phase 1. No offers, negotiations, proposals, or completions were made, which is undoubtedly why the FBI needed to bring in Hoffman to capture illegality on tape.

The FBI agent arranged DeLorean's meeting with Hoffman as a get-together with a former neighbor in San Diego whose young sons had continued to communicate with each other over the years. DeLorean was led to believe that Hoffman might have some useful information about finding investors for his ailing car company. Hoffman's only assigned mission, of course, was to dangle a financial carrot so attractive that it would convince DeLorean to agree to participate in the drug scheme. The speech event roles were now reversed. Instead of DeLorean being the subordinate participant who was seeking finances from a superordinate participant who had access to the money, Hoffman now tried to turn DeLorean into the superordinate participant who would be the buyer of his product. This didn't work, however, because DeLorean preserved his consistent and ongoing more powerless role of the subordinate seeker of funding opportunities.

The structure of this speech event satisfied phase 1 (discuss the problem), and stage 2 (Hoffman's offer). But DeLorean gave no positive response to Hoffman's offer and there was no stage 3 negotiation. The stage 4 completion consisted of DeLorean's rejection of the offer. Since the banker who set up the meeting had indicated that Hoffman had ideas about how DeLorean could get financing, there was no reason for DeLorean to believe that the speech event would be different from his many previous business speech event conversations with the banker. During his meeting with Hoffman the simultaneously different speech events of a legitimate business meeting and an illegal business transaction struggled with each other within the same conversation until DeLorean apparently realized what Hoffman was really up to. At that point he completed the speech event by rejecting the offer to be involved in a crime. He did this by telling Hoffman a whopper of a lie, saying that he didn't need Hoffman's group because he was getting money from an unnamed "Irish group." But to that point the speech event had been two trains passing in the night. Even though Hoffman's undercover strategy may be standard FBI practice, it was certainly ambiguously deceptive up to the point that DeLorean caught on to what was going on.

AMBIGUITY PRODUCED BY SCHEMAS

DeLorean's language made it clear that his schema was that both the banker and Hoffman would help him find either a loan or investors in his car company. The banker's schema was that DeLorean would ultimately succumb to criminal behavior. Hoffman's schema was that DeLorean would bite at the opportunity to get some quick money from a drug transaction, but when Hoffman made his offer clear, DeLorean's language revealed that his schema was to reject any offer that was criminal.

Until and including the very last meeting in which the government finally openly attempted to connect DeLorean to a drug transaction, DeLorean's topics and responses indicated that his schema was only to try to obtain and loan or find investors for his company. The FBI agent deceptively appeared to join with DeLorean's schema for several months until his own schema about capturing DeLorean's guilt on tape finally was revealed in that last meeting with Hoffman at the Washington, DC hotel.

AMBIGUITY PRODUCED BY AGENDAS

Curiously, the FBI agent agreed with DeLorean's perfectly legal topics and responses through the first five months of their interactions, while patiently camouflaging his own agenda by letting DeLorean believe that he was actually trying to help him. As undercover sting operations go, five months is a comparatively long time to try to discover a predisposition to commit a crime. This prolongation of a deceptively ambiguous agenda was possibly the factor that encouraged DeLorean to keep talking with him until the agent perceived it was just the right moment to seize the opportunity to invent a criminal scenario that might succeed in tempting DeLorean to bite. The fact that up to and including that last conversation with Hoffman DeLorean's topics and responses were all legally benign strongly suggests that he had no predisposition or intention to commit a crime.

This deceptive ambiguity began as part of the FBI undercover strategy of setting up DeLorean to believe that the banker/agent could find him a loan or investors. The banker/agent's apparently real purpose for this was to use an already captured drug dealer, Hoffman, at the right moment when DeLorean was so desperate that he would succumb to the temptation of making an illegal drug transaction to save his company from bankruptcy. Perhaps this kind of intentional deception falls into the category of acceptable undercover operations, but even so, the five-month effort did not produce any evidence showing that DeLorean was either predisposed or intended to commit a crime before or during the entire investigation. The government could defend this investigation by saying that it merely provided the opportunity for DeLorean to commit a crime, but it is not difficult to believe that such an opportunity might be more appropriately given to a person for whom there was some reason to expect it rather than trying to create the appearance of such predisposition after the fact. As the defense attorneys pointed out, this looked very much like a fishing operation in which the government tried to catch a big fish in a pond in which he had never swum and had no intention of getting wet.

AMBIGUITY PRODUCED BY SPEECH ACTS

Despite DeLorean's indirectness when he told Hoffman that he was getting his money from an "Irish group," this response could only be understood as an indirect speech act of disagreement, denial, or rejection, meaning that he was not going to get his money from Hoffman's drug scheme because the financing he needed was coming from another source, the fictitious "Irish group." Even Hoffman gave evidence that he understood this rejection, for he then used the speech act of warning DeLorean, "either we go ahead or end." Despite this exchange, the prosecutor chose not to recognize DeLorean's indirect speech act of rejecting the offer but instead apparently ignored it, considered it merely ambiguous, or somehow misinterpreted it as his agreement.

DeLorean's earlier evaluative comment about the dangers involved in the agent's drug operation was deceptively misinterpreted as his willingness to be a part of it. Early in the investigation the government had leaked to the media a portion of one of the videotapes in which the agent brought a suitcase full of drugs into the meeting and opened it to show how much money could be made in the drug business. When DeLorean saw the drugs he said clearly on tape, "It'll be dangerous." The media deceptively misinterpreted this as evidence of DeLorean's speech act of agreeing to continue their discussion rather than as his evaluative comment about how dangerous such drug programs really are. The interesting part about this portion of the tape is that the prosecution never used it at trial, perhaps realizing that it was not the smoking gun that they might have wished it to be. Releasing it to the media, however, created deceptive ambiguity to the public who saw that tape on television.

After DeLorean had rejected the offer by saying he was getting his needed money from the "Irish group," Hoffman still was not ready to give up, for if he failed to persuade DeLorean to buy the drugs, any positive considerations at his forthcoming sentencing hearing would likely be slim. So he backpedaled by softening his deceptive position saying, "We don't want you not comfortable; you're not compelled, if you get money somewhere else, do it." One might expect this to have ended the conversation, because it was now clear even to Hoffman that DeLorean had rejected the idea of purchasing drugs. But apparently it also led DeLorean to become curious, so he asked whether Hoffman's contacts might be interested in providing him a loan or making an equity investment in his company.

This very question indicated that DeLorean considered a loan or capital investment to be his only options because he had rejected Hoffman's option to participate in the drug operation. To this, Hoffman answered, "Their interest is in stock." DeLorean could take some comfort from this response because it seemed to indicate that Hoffman now recognized that his effort to get his target to participate a drug deal had failed. But even though DeLorean had opened the door that he might be interested in their possible purchase of his company's stock, he still showed enough concern about the dangers of a drug outfit buying stock in his company to quickly use the speech act of warning Hoffman that if the drug people had any interest in buying stock in his company, they would have to meet the legal disclosure requirements imposed on offshore trading companies. This was his speech act of warning Hoffman that any stock purchase had to be from a legitimate buyer.

AMBIGUITY PRODUCED BY CONVERSATIONAL STRATEGIES

For some five months the FBI agent used few if any conversational strategies to get DeLorean to agree to act illegally. The possible reason for this was that the banker's apparent role was to wait until DeLorean's financial situation got dire and bankruptcy was imminent, at which point Hoffman would enter the scene and provide the real opportunity to commit a crime during that final meeting.

One of the common strategies of effective salespersons is to ignore the customer's apparent rejection of their offers and go right on as though it had never happened. Hoffman used this strategy when he took his turn with DeLorean. As noted previously, he apparently had no possible response to DeLorean's warning about getting his money from an unnamed Irish group that could only be understood as a reference to the powerful Irish Republican Army, so he ignored this and returned once more to the topic of the drug deal. Hoffman was proficient in this conversational strategy.

After failing to get DeLorean's agreement, Hoffman weakly suggested that the transaction was still possible if, instead of investing money, DeLorean could give them a few of the new cars that had just come off the assembly line. Before DeLorean could reject that suggestion, Hoffman used the hit-and-run strategy of quickly changing the subject. He asked how sales were coming along and told DeLorean that the banker with whom he had begun all of this discussion now had some other banking people who still might be able to help him secure a loan. Curiously, this was the topic that DeLorean was told the meeting would concern. When investigative scenarios constantly change directions, it's a relatively sure sign that the previous deceptively ambiguous scenarios had not worked the way the investigators had hoped.

AMBIGUITY PRODUCED BY LEXICON AND GRAMMAR

After telling Hoffman that he was getting his money from the Irish group, DeLorean offered the prosecution some hope when he added his own potential ambiguity to the exchange, saying he'll "get hold of them" and "I want to do it." His pronouns, *them* and *it,* clearly tracked grammatically to his previous statement about the Irish group (them) and the needed money (it), but Hoffman, like a good salesman, chose to ignore this and immediately recycled his own agenda saying, "We'll probably move in two to four days." Note that his first person plural, *we'll,* was also deceptively ambiguous, for it could refer to either his own group alone or to DeLorean's possible involvement with his group. Hoffman then followed this with the confusing sentence, "I built the other program in because it's within my control." His use of *other* was also deceptively ambiguous. He had presented only one program to DeLorean, the drug deal offer, and his ongoing question was whether or not DeLorean might choose to invest in it. His word *other,* therefore ambiguously could refer to his own drug program or to DeLorean's program, the "Irish group," which was then the current topic on the conversational table. Just how Hoffman's program might be considered the "other program" that he built remained ambiguous.

Following this exchange came another abrupt topic switch as Hoffman asked DeLorean how long it would take to get "confirmation of the funds available." Hoffman's *confirmation of the funds* was ambiguous about whose confirmation and whose funds. Because DeLorean had just said that he needed to confirm *it* with the Irish group, he could understand Hoffman to be asking about the confirmation and funds coming from that Irish group, while Hoffman ambiguously suggested that it meant how long it would take DeLorean to confirm that he had "the funds" needed to complete the drug deal. Once again and not surprisingly, the prosecutor chose to understand these ambiguities Hoffman's way, not DeLorean's.

After explaining how much money a person could make by investing $800,000 million in his drug operation, Hoffman outlined DeLorean's possible options: "Interim financing, which is quicker, or this: buy 100 kilos to yield a return of 14 million in ten days." His expression, *interim financing,* was ambiguous here. For months DeLorean had been trying to get interim financing for his company through a loan or stock purchases. Hoffman converted DeLorean's use of *interim* into his own proposal for a smaller investment of $300 million, which would be *interim* until DeLorean could see how well it worked and then make a larger investment of $800 million. It is not difficult to see that Hoffman was ambiguously and probably intentionally playing with DeLorean's expressed need of interim financing for his company.

One of the prosecution's purportedly strongest charges against DeLorean was that he agreed to make the drug deal when at one point he agreed with Hoffman's statement, "investment is a good thing." As noted above, the word, *investment*, was used consistently by both the banker and DeLorean throughout their sixty-three recorded meetings to refer to finding someone to invest in the DeLorean Motor Company. When Hoffman now used this word with DeLorean, there was no contextual motivation for it to mean that DeLorean was now saying that it was good thing for him to invest in the drug business. The prosecution entirely missed or misinterpreted this contextual meaning, although it was pointed out at an evidentiary hearing in which the judge agreed that it was not a smoking gun.

It is difficult to attribute benign intentions to the agents' many uses of deceptive ambiguity in this case. Their quantity, repetition, and consistency, found in all aspects of the Inverted Pyramid from speech events through lexicon, suggest strongly that the government's representatives used deceptive ambiguity intentionally to further their own purposes.

An Undercover IRS Agent Uses Deceptive Ambiguity with Taxpayer Vernon Sligh

Although undercover operations are most commonly associated with the FBI, it is not the only law enforcement agency carrying out such investigations. The U.S. Drug Enforcement Agency (DEA) and the Internal Revenue Service (IRS), as well as local and state law enforcement agencies also have investigative offices that carry out in covert operations. In 1966 a taxpayer named Vernon Sligh found himself in trouble with the IRS.

Because Sligh had been struggling with how to deal with his delinquent federal taxes, he called his local IRS office to ask about that agency's guidelines that might help him either to reduce the amount of his tax debt or help him to benefit from any other possible form of relief. He complained that the IRS representative with whom he talked on the telephone gave him no useful information, leaving him to guess about whatever facts and circumstances might help him solve his problems. Eventually he met with a different IRS representative, gave her $7,000 to fix his account, and was immediately charged with bribery.

When confronted with his damaging tape-recorded conversations with this IRS representative, Sligh had no choice but to plead guilty. The judge refused his attorney's effort to hold an evidentiary hearing in which he could have argued that his client was entrapped, but during Sligh's sentencing hearing, his lawyer prudently ensured that a subsequent plea agreement would provide Sligh the opportunity to claim entrapment growing out of the tape-recorded evidence provided by the undercover IRS agent. The lawyer was armed not only with entrapment issues growing out of the recorded conversations but also with newly discovered information showing that immediately before the IRS agent's encounters with Sligh, she had taken a seminar on bribery awareness that could possibly have predisposed her to believe that Sligh was going to try to bribe her.

The IRS agent admitted at trial that during their first untaped telephone conversation Sligh had said nothing that even suggested a bribe, but she added, "a chill went down my spine because I knew at some point he was going to try to bribe me or do something." This chill down her spine prompted her to notify the IRS Internal Investigation Office who told her to covertly tape-record her future conversations with Sligh. The following are critical excerpts of their recorded conversations. The first call produced this exchange:

SLIGH: When I talked to you and asked how much power you had, as a black man it's uncomfortable for me because of different classes of race and gender.

AGENT: You asked me how much power I have. I have the power to adjust your balance due under certain criteria, but I need a reason.

SLIGH: Yes, ma'am, uh, a reason. . . . If you give me the guidelines, I can work out a reason within those guidelines.

AGENT: I'd be risking my job. . . . The tax law is generic. . . . You would have to give me something that makes reasonable cause.

SLIGH: But you're not at liberty to tell me what the guidelines are?

AGENT: No. I have to do it based on what you tell me, not me giving you the guidelines. . . . Tell me exactly what proposal you have in mind.

SLIGH: If I can pay half of it, then we talking $15,000. Whether I can borrow $15,000 or not, I don't know, but I would be willing to try to do that.

AGENT: I need a legitimate reason to cut the balance in half, unless you're asking me to do something otherwise.

SLIGH: Well I don't know what you're able to do.

AGENT: I need a reason unless you want me to deviate.

SLIGH: My reasons might not fit within your guidelines. . . . If it deviate, I don't care.

AGENT: But why would I take that risk? I'd be risking my job.

SLIGH: I don't want you to lose your job. People can decide how to use their power whether they use it to help people or they don't.

Despite her hints, the agent still had not elicited a bribe offer from Sligh, so she agreed to accept a second call from Sligh which she taped as well. Following are the critical excerpts of this conversation:

AGENT: I'd like to help you out. You're asking me to do a favor that I have to falsify. I need a reason to take such a risk.

SLIGH: Would it make you feel better if I said I was suicidal?
AGENT: No, that wouldn't be good. Do you want me to make up a reason?
SLIGH: No, ma'am. I don't want to go to jail.
AGENT: Well, I could go to jail too.
SLIGH: Ma'am anything that you would say, I would agree with.
AGENT: I just can't take that kind of risk. At this point I'd just as soon do it by the book because I don't know that it's worthwhile to risk what I've got to do that, my job.
SLIGH: I believe truthfully that God believes that it's the right thing to do.
AGENT: I don't understand what the right thing to do is.
SLIGH: It's to use your power, whatever you have, to extricate me from this situation. I just want to let you know that I'm a genuine person, a righteous person. I don't care what you decide to do. Whatever you decide, I could live with that . . . I guess it's best that I just wait until I see you.

They met two weeks later at a restaurant. The agent wore a body mike and taped the entire conversation. Sligh began by repeating his request to get his taxes burden abated. She then offered some hints about her recent personal expenses with her car and home, but since Sligh didn't pick up on them as a request for a bribe, she then became explicit about his need to bribe her:

AGENT: I kinda understand what you're saying. You're gonna give me something and you would like me to fix your account. I can adjust the penalties or adjust the tax. There's not somebody behind me checking.
SLIGH: How much would that be? I've got friends that could give me money. I'm talking between five and ten, so you pick a number.
AGENT: How about the middle? Seven. I can give you the paperwork saying this account is uncollectable.
SLIGH: And you don't have to give a reason for making it uncollectable?
AGENT: I can just make one up.

It was very clear that Sligh had finally given up trying to get the information that he requested originally and now agreed to bribe the agent to make his tax burden go away. When they met again five days later, he gave her $7,000 in cash and was arrested immediately. His lawyer's earlier provision that Sligh preserved the right to claim entrapment at the sentencing hearing was fortuitous. The Court reviewed the case and agreed that the agent indeed had used outrageous behavior that had entrapped Sligh.

Even though the case ended happily for Sligh, the agent's interviewing technique provides a model of how undercover agents can use deceptive ambiguity.

AMBIGUITY PRODUCED BY THE SPEECH EVENT

To the agent, these recorded conversations with Sligh constituted a bribery speech event. In contrast, Sligh considered these conversations to be a conventional business consultation speech event in which he might be able to get the information that he thought she should have been able to provide. Therefore, up to the time that Sligh finally reluctantly understood that his only hope for tax relief was to give the agent a bribe, their conversations were two very different speech events. The agent testified at trial that when Sligh talked with her, he made it clear that he wanted her advice, which supported Sligh's perception of the speech event they were in. She also testified that she told him she had the power to help him remove the levy from his taxes and had offered to extend the deadline for his payment.

Sligh made it very clear that he was confused about how to submit his tax returns and wanted to get help. The agent's recent seminar on bribery had prompted that chill that she claimed went down her spine. Even though there was no language evidence to support this, she believed that Sligh seemed to be suggesting the possibility that he might be willing to offer her a bribe in exchange for reducing his tax burden. These very different needs and beliefs led to conversations in which two simultaneous and conflicting speech events continued up to their final meeting, at which point Sligh apparently finally understood that he was actually involved in a bribery speech event in which the only solution to his problem was to give the agent a bribe of $7,000 in exchange for solving his problem. By that time the agent had slowly but successfully changed Sligh's initial perception of the speech event from legal to illegal.

As seen in other undercover investigations discussed in this book, the government asserts the right to provide an *opportunity* for suspects to commit crimes. This strategy may prove to be successful in many operations, but when cognitively weak and emotionally stressed targets like Sligh are trying to do something in a legitimate and legal way and later are told by powerful and trusted authorities that it is not possible to solve their problem by acting legally, they can become confused about this new *opportunity* when they discover that it's their only hope for extracting themselves from a difficult situation. There can be no defense for committing a crime, but the circumstances leading up to that crime can be very relevant. Part of such relevance is the fact that Sligh apparently didn't suspect that he was in a bribery speech event until no other avenue appeared to be open to him. Switching the speech event in the midst of conversations creates ambiguity that can only be considered deceptive.

The recorded conversations also make it clear that Sligh evidenced no predisposition to commit the crime of bribery. He did not ask that the entire amount of delinquent taxes be wiped out. He requested (and was denied) the guidelines about how to get his tax burden deferred or reduced. He suggested ways of paying what he owed, saying that he could borrow the needed money from his friends. Since he provided no evidence of a criminal predisposition, the agent tried to create his missing predisposition after the fact by giving him the opportunity to bribe her in an intentionally deceptive manner.

AMBIGUITY PRODUCED BY SCHEMAS

Sligh's language made it clear that his schema was based on his perception of the speech event, which in his case was that of a business consultation speech event in which he was the powerless participant seeking the help of powerful authorities. The IRS agent revealed that her schema from the very beginning was to convert Sligh's benign speech event into a bribery speech event although she was unable to make this clear to Sligh until she finally explained that his only available avenue was to bribe her to solve his problem. Sligh abandoned his schema of trying to get help for his tax return after he finally realized that there was nothing for him to do but offer the agent a bribe.

AMBIGUITY PRODUCED BY AGENDAS

Up to the time Sligh finally tumbled to the reality that his only way to get his taxes reduced was to bribe the agent, all of his topics and responses concerned his need for help about how to discover a way to pay the money he owed. In contrast, the IRS agent's initial topics and responses gave the deceptively ambiguous appearance that she was willing to help him. After she realized that he did not understand her ambiguous hints of illegality, she made clear to him that he'd have to bribe her, which he subsequently did. The fact that all of Sligh's previous topics were about requesting her to help him in a legal manner indicated that his intention was to act legally and that he was not predisposed to commit a crime.

AMBIGUITY PRODUCED BY SPEECH ACTS

Sligh began with repeated speech acts of requesting information about the IRA guidelines he thought he needed to complete his tax forms. The agent first advised him ambiguously that she could give him help "under certain circumstances."

She didn't identify those circumstances and then flatly refused to answer his request for help unless he gave her a "reason" for doing so, ambiguously adding the speech act of warning him that she would be "risking" her job if she did so. To Sligh's speech act of requesting clarification about what she meant by this the agent gave him a speech act directive, "you're gonna give me something" and explained, "I would have to falsify" to get it done. When the agent finally used clear and unambiguous speech acts, Sligh apparently realized that bribing her was his only solution and therefore offered her money.

AMBIGUITY PRODUCED BY CONVERSATIONAL STRATEGIES

Scripting is the name of a conversational strategy used by undercover agents who place words, usually illegal words, into the mouths of their targets (Shuy 2005). The point is to persuade the targets to say on tape what the agent has suggested or, more crucially, to put into the targets' minds that they have already said such words even if they haven't done so. At one point the agent did the latter saying: "I kinda understood what you were saying. You're gonna give me something and you would like me to fix your amount." Since Sligh never made this quid pro quo offer, the agent scripted it for him out of thin air. This scripting conveyed what the agent must have known were the necessary requirements of a bribery offer. It made little difference that Sligh was not the person who produced this quid pro quo offer. The fact that it simply existed in the government's evidence would be enough for later listeners, such as prosecutors, juries, and judges, to find it ambiguous as to who actually said them. Scripting a target about what to say can only be considered deceptively creating ambiguity in the minds of the target as well as later listeners.

AMBIGUITY PRODUCED BY LEXICON AND GRAMMAR

The agent's other ambiguities were in the lexicon that she used with Sligh, including the words and expressions, *power, reasons, deviate, risk, do the right thing*, and *favor*.

Power

Sligh used the word, *power*, during his first telephone call with the agent. The context of his use of this word makes it clear that to him *power* referred to the knowledge and authority vested in the IRS agent to help him to understand the tax requirements that might guide him in resolving his problem. Eventually during their conversations, however, the agent used Sligh's own word, *power,* to suggest that her ability to help Sligh could be actuated only if he would bribe her to use her power. Two different contextual meanings of the same word make it ambiguous, and in spite of Sligh's failure to give evidence that he understood her meaning of *power* until the very end, the agent tried hard to establish her own meaning of the term in the minds of later listeners such as jurors. In short, she took advantage of Sligh's original meaning of *power* and deceptively converted to suit her own purposes.

Reason

In their first conversation the agent told Sligh, "you need to give me a reason," apparently hinting that this would be an excuse for her to illegally abate Sligh's taxes. In contrast, Sligh's use of *reason* consistently implied or referred to his need to see the guidelines that could tell him what he could and could not do. In their second phone call the agent was clearer about her intent: "I'd like to help you out. You're asking me to do a favor that I have to falsify. I need a reason to take such a risk. . . . Do you want me to make up a reason? Sligh's answer was "No, ma'am. I don't want to go to jail." Here Sligh clearly rejected the agent's suggestion that *reason* related to falsifying his tax record. The agent finally clarified her previously ambiguous meaning in their last conversation: "You're gonna give me something and you would like me to fix your account." Even then Sligh asked her if she wouldn't have to provide the IRS with reasons for making his tax burden uncollectable. He apparently still considered her use of *reasons t*o mean reason*s* for helping him with his taxes, and not the agent's reason*s* to falsify them. The two of them used *reasons* to convey two different meanings, the very definition of ambiguity. There is good reason to suspect that she was using this ambiguity deliberately and deceptively.

Deviate

After Sligh repeated that he didn't know what the agent was able to do for him, she told him: "I need a reason unless you want me to deviate." She was still fishing for Sligh to offer her a bribe, this time using *deviate* as a prompt. It is not clear whether Sligh understood the meaning of *deviate,* but his response to her recycled his need to know what the guidelines said, adding "if it deviate, I don't care." This response might be considered his agreement for her to deviate illegally from the guidelines, but it wouldn't be possible for him to know whether he wanted her to deviate from them without knowing what her *deviations* were and by then he was desperate enough to not care whether it deviated or not. The agent's use of *deviate* was an ambiguously deceptive signal of something illegal in the context of their discussion. Agents often use such signals of criminality in the apparent effort to avoid using words that convey the stronger illegal meanings (Shuy 2012, 2013, 2014). Her usage here can only be considered intentional.

Risk and *Right Thing to Do*

In their first recorded conversation, Sligh said, "Anything that you would say, I would agree with." The agent then introduced the word *risk*, saying "I'd be risking my job" and "I just can't take that kind of risk." At this point Sligh could understand this to mean that she would risk her job by giving him the guidelines he wanted. If Sligh caught her hint of illegality at all, he gave no evidence of it in his response: "I believe truthfully that God believes that it's the right thing to do," which is consistent with Sligh's understanding that giving him the guidelines is the right thing for her to do. Apparently still not getting what she wanted to hear, the agent then asked what he meant by *the right thing to do.* Sligh responded that he wanted her to use her power "to extricate me from this situation." The benign procedural *right thing* to do contrasts with the potentially illegal *risk* that the agent might take. If Sligh understood the agent to be suggesting illegal behavior, he gave no indication of understanding her meaning of *risk* here. Rather than being clear and unambiguous, undercover agents often deceptively skirt the issue with ambiguous terms that their targets find difficult to disagree with. The agent here did not explain what this *risk* was and Sligh let it pass without providing any evidence that he recognized it as a signal of illegality.

Favor

During their second recorded telephone conversation the agent rephrased Sligh's request for information that could help him, saying: "You're asking me to do a favor that I have to falsify." There is no taped evidence that Sligh had been asking her to falsify anything. In fact, he didn't even used the word *favor.* He merely asked for information and the guidelines so that he would know what to do, thinking that she had the power and authority to help him. The agent's meaning of doing him a favor conveyed or at least implied illegality. By inserting the word *favor* here, the agent slipped another deceptively ambiguous term into their conversation.

The government agent in this case was particularly adept at using deceptive ambiguity with Sligh. Simultaneous conflicting speech events led to simultaneous conflicting schemas about what was happening. Ignoring Sligh's agenda and converting it into the agent's own agenda, ignoring Sligh's speech acts of requesting information and clarification, using the conversational strategy of scripting, and using ambiguous lexicon to her own advantage makes this case a classic example of how government representatives use deceptive ambiguity.

6

Cooperating Witnesses Use Deceptive Ambiguity

We now turn to the way law enforcement uses cooperating witnesses to gather criminal intelligence in undercover operations. These are not to be confused with complainants, who are discussed in chapter 7. Some cooperating witnesses first bring the potential crime to the attention of law enforcement but most are known offenders who are used by law enforcement because they are familiar with the type of crime being investigated and have already been caught. There are two types of cooperating witnesses: internal and external.

Internal cooperating witnesses are people who are closely connected with the alleged victims. They often are family members or close associates of the target whose motives for bringing the crime to the attention of law enforcement are not always clear. They may simply believe that their accusations are accurate or they may have a personal grudge against the target and simply desire justification. Whatever their motives, internal cooperating witnesses have immediate and logical access to their targets.

External cooperating witnesses are not as close to their targets as internal cooperating witnesses. Commonly they are in the same line of work and often they don't even know their targets. The major difference between internal and external cooperating witnesses is motivation. Many of the external cooperating witnesses commonly used by law enforcement have been caught in the same crimes as those now being investigated and they agree to be cooperating witnesses in order to gain favor at their sentencing hearings.

In the solicitation to murder investigation of T. Cullen Davis, the police used an internal informant, Davis's employee and surface friend, who functioned as a cooperating witness to record his conversations with the target. Internal cooperating witnesses can be useful because it is natural for them to talk with the targets they already know, and, as the Davis investigation illustrated, it does not take much time for them to establish the intimate level of conversation required for capturing guilt on tape.

External cooperating witnesses do not have the same advantage. They do not know the target personally and therefore require more time to achieve the level of intimacy to suggest the proposed criminality. But they tend to be involved in the same area of business, which can make meeting their targets and conducting conversations with them seem feasible. Probably most important, however, is that the government often uses external cooperating witnesses who have been caught recently in the same crime as that of the ongoing investigation. They are therefore experts in that crime in ways that law enforcement officers are not. The major motive for external cooperating witnesses to agree to work with the police is that they have much to gain, because by cooperating with the prosecutor, they hope to have their sentences reduced at their forthcoming sentencing hearings. Often the use of external cooperating witnesses is the only avenue available to law enforcement, and that was the approach the government took in the investigations of both Yochanan Cohen and Marwan El-Hindi, both of which took many months to complete.

The government's advantage in using external cooperating witnesses in such investigations is that they have the persuasive skills of con artists and fully realize the intricacies of crimes such as illegal drug transactions, soliciting murder, bribery, or, as in Cohen's case, corruption by offering kickbacks in exchange for lucrative foreign business contracts. But in other investigations external cooperating witnesses are not under current indictments and have not even been involved in the same activity or business as the target. They are known to have the skills of con artists in the past and since they are good at pretending to be beginners at something their targets want to accomplish, they try to become part of it, as illustrated in the investigation of El-Hindi. Here the cooperating witness played the external role of a recent convert to Islam who was now soliciting religious guidance while at the same time trying to convert this experience into a terrorist plot. Both types of external cooperating witnesses are usually skilled enough to provide the degree of believability that can make their undercover operations succeed.

One of the government's disadvantages in using either internal or external cooperating witnesses is that both types often are not skilled in the legal requirements for eliciting a crime and therefore they sometimes fail to produce evidence that is adequate for an indictment. Another disadvantage of using external cooperating witnesses under indictment is that their need to succeed can cause them try so hard that it creates entrapment issues for the prosecution.

An important difference between the intelligence gathering done by transparent institutional police officers and by camouflaged cooperating witnesses is that the latter are often so good in their natural roles as con artists that they sometimes frighten their targets away as they expose themselves to be the slick con men they really are. In spite of this, law enforcement tends to employ them because of their history of being so proficient at the use of deceptive ambiguity. Sometimes there is nothing quite as effective as using good con men to capture others in their same areas of business, as documented by Robert Greene's *Sting Man* (1981) and Ned Polsky's *Hustlers, Beats, and Others* (1969).

This chapter describes examples of both internal and external cooperating witnesses who carried out undercover tape-recorded operations for law enforcement.

An Internal Cooperating Witness Uses Deceptive Ambiguity with T. Cullen Davis

One of the most sensational murder cases in Texas legal history concerned the seemingly unending saga of a flamboyant Fort Worth Texas oil millionaire, T. Cullen Davis (Shuy 2014). In the mid-1970s after his marriage to his equally flamboyant wife Priscilla had disintegrated, Davis moved out of his mansion (which is still referred to as "the mansion" in Fort Worth), while Priscilla continued to live there. Shortly after he moved out, a masked man broke into the mansion and shot and killed Priscilla's new boyfriend and her teenage daughter from a previous relationship. Priscilla was also shot but the wound to her breast was relatively minor. As she was recovering, she accused Davis of being that masked intruder and not long after this he was tried for the murders. The case against Davis was weak and he was subsequently acquitted because of the lack of convincing evidence against him. That evidence consisted of Priscilla's account that even though she could not see the shooter's face because of the ski mask, the intruder had Davis's build and mannerisms. Two alleged witnesses, friends of Priscilla, also testified that they were outside the house and saw the masked man leave right after the murders and identified him as Davis. Their testimony was equally unconvincing to the jury.

Not surprisingly, after the murder trial ended Davis filed for a divorce. During this period, Davis had heard rumors that Priscilla and the judge in their divorce proceedings had become romantically intimate. Davis then asked David McCrory, one of his midlevel employees at Davis's oil equipment manufacturing company, to spy on his wife and the judge, with instructions to follow them, try to catch them in a romantic liaison, and report back to him what he found.

For reasons that remain unknown, instead of spying on the couple, McCrory went straight to the police and told them that Davis had asked him to find a hit man to kill the judge, Priscilla, and Priscilla's two friends who claimed to have seen Davis leave the scene of the earlier murders. The police then wired up McCrory with a body transmitter and sent him out to talk with Davis to try to capture evidence about locating a hit man.

The conversation that the government used to bring an indictment against Davis was both audio- and videotaped while the two men were sitting in Davis's car in a Fort Worth parking lot. The government's recording equipment was crude by today's standards and the videotape, made from a van parked across from Davis's car, provided only grainy pictures while its audio picked up only occasional words and phrases. But McCrory's body mike recorded enough of their brief conversation to convince the prosecutor that he had all the evidence he needed to indict Davis for soliciting murder.

Before the trial began in Fort Worth in 1979, the prosecution leaked to the media a partial transcript of what it considered to be the strong smoking gun evidence:

> MCCRORY: I got Judge Eidson dead for you.
> DAVIS: Good.
> MCCRORY: I'll get the rest of them dead for you. You want a bunch of people dead, right?
> DAVIS: Alright, but—

Davis's defense lawyers believed that something was not right about this transcript but they couldn't tell what. They then asked me to analyze the entire tape-recorded conversation and when I correlated the audiotape with the occasionally audible parts of the much clearer videotape taken from the van across the parking lot, I discovered that this passage was not the smoking gun the prosecutor thought it was.

Here's why I thought this. By the time McCrory made this alleged smoking gun statement, the videotape demonstrated that Davis already had gotten out of the vehicle and was moving toward the car's trunk to retrieve his sunglasses. While this was happening, the two men continued to talk simultaneously over each other. The transcript was accurate about the words spoken by McCrory and Davis, including Davis's "good" and "alright but" but these words were part of a continuous and very different topic they had been talking about before Davis got out of his car. By focusing only on this isolated portion of the conversation, the government ignored the continuous context of what they were talking about at that time.

The smoking gun transcript that the prosecution had leaked to the press also neglected to add what Davis said after his "alright but," which created their impression that his "alright" was actually an admission of agreement to solicit murder. Transcripts are not evidence, but judges usually permit them to be used during trials as a way of helping jurors keep track of what was said. But errors and omissions in transcripts can have strong effects on jurors, for even when listeners hear the tapes, they tend to hear what they see on a transcript and they tend to remember more of what they see than what they hear. An inaccurate transcript can create both ambiguity and deception, no matter whether the prosecution knowingly or unknowingly created it.

The two men's only ongoing topic to that point had been about McCrory's boss, Art, who had complained to McCrory about his missing so much time from his job lately. Art did not know that McCrory's absence was because he was doing this detective work for Davis. When the missing context of the foregoing transcript was matched with the videotape's weak audibility but relatively clear video taken from the van across the parking lot from the car, it indicated that McCrory took advantage of the physical distance between himself and Davis to utter a few damaging words while Davis was out of hearing range. McCrory's damaging words included "this fuckin' murder business is a tough son of a bitch" and "you got me into this goddamn deal," spoken while Davis, now outside the car, continued to talk about the complaint made by McCrory's boss concerning his absence from work as Davis said, "Alright, but I got to have an alibi ready for Art when the subject comes up." Note that the leaked government transcript stopped with Davis's "alright but," and omitted the rest of his sentence about the topic of having an excuse to give Art.

When Davis returned to the front seat of the car he added: "So give me some advance notice," to which McCrory replied, "I will. I gotta go." Apparently believing that he had the evidence he needed, McCrory quickly got out of the car and the conversation ended. The prosecution maintained that Davis heard McCrory's statements about the "murder business" and "this goddamn deal" and that Davis's statement, "give me some advance notice," meant that McCrory should inform him before he has the people killed instead of Davis's request that McCrory tell him when he planned to miss work so that Davis could alert Art about his absence. The prosecutor's interpretations failed, however, when their entire conversation was placed in the continuous context of Davis's ongoing and continuous topic about finding an excuse to tell McCrory's boss, Art, why McCrory was missing so much time on his job.

This cooperating witness's undercover investigation was flawed in many ways, but it is clear that the prosecutors either did not try very hard to uncover what their own audio and video evidence actually could tell them or they ignored what was actually on the tapes and tried to make McCrory's deceptively ambiguous statements appear to be unambiguous and clear. Apparently thinking the video tape was useless, they did not pay any attention to it. At any rate, Davis was acquitted after a long and heated trial.

The prosecution relied heavily on McCrory's deceptive ambiguity in the following ways.

AMBIGUITY PRODUCED BY THE SPEECH EVENT

Davis's language indicates that his idea of the speech event was that it was a report from his employee, McCrory, about the progress he was making in his task of spying on Priscilla's suspected amorous activities with the judge. McCrory's language indicates that his perception of the speech event was that he was reporting about the murder of the judge and his plans for the murder of Davis's wife and the two witnesses at his previous murder trial. Davis's language indicated that throughout the entire very brief conversation he maintained his perception that the conversation was a report of progress about the spying speech event without tumbling to McCrory's perception of the very different speech event of reporting about the progress on the murders.

AMBIGUITY PRODUCED BY SCHEMAS

As usual, the different simultaneous speech events led to very different schemas about what they were talking about. Davis's schema grew naturally out of his view of his perception of the speech event. This was clearly revealed by his discussion of the issues involved in McCrory missing work to spy on Priscilla and the judge. McCrory's schema was very different, and it encouraged the prosecutor to believe that since Davis had no love for his wife or the judge with whom she allegedly was having a romantic relationship, he had a strong predisposition to have them both killed. It is also likely that the prosecutor's disappointment at the result in Davis's recent acquittal in the previous trial for murder played a role in the prosecutor's thinking. As a result, Davis's schema that they were in the speech event of reporting progress about spying on Priscilla was very different from the prosecution's schema that Davis was soliciting murder.

AMBIGUITY PRODUCED BY AGENDAS

When prosecutions search only for smoking gun evidence, they often overlook the discourse context in which the alleged smoking guns exist. In this case, topic analysis came to Davis's rescue. Davis's only ongoing topic was an unambiguous benign one about creating an alibi for Art concerning McCrory's missing work rather than McCrory's topic that attempted to make Davis's topic look like his agreement to murder people. McCrory deceptively manipulated the evidence to further his own agenda that would assure the appearance of illegality. Davis talked only about McCrory's immediate boss, Art, who had complained about his missing so much time at work. The one and only time McCrory mentioned killing people was when Davis was out of hearing range as he continued to talk about Art's complaint about McCrory missing so much time on his job.

AMBIGUITY PRODUCED BY SPEECH ACTS

Davis's only speech acts were those of advising and requesting information. He first advised McCrory that he had told Art that McCrory should be treated like any other employee. Davis's indirect request for information about McCrory's progress in spying on Priscilla and the judge went unanswered, as did his request for McCrory to give him advance notice about when he planned to miss work so that Davis could justify this to Art.

McCrory's speech acts were reporting that he got Priscilla and the judge dead and promising to get other people dead, both spoken out of Davis's hearing range. He also promised to give Davis advance notice, although by then the two men had different understandings about what the advance notice referred to. McCrory also complained about how tough this murder business was. Except for the promise to give advance notice, all of McCrory's speech acts were uttered into his body mike while Davis was out of hearing range.

AMBIGUITY PRODUCED BY CONVERSATIONAL STRATEGIES

One commonly used conversational strategy in undercover operations of this type is to block what other persons say by making it impossible for them to finish their statements (Shuy 2005). This blocking strategy was well illustrated in this investigation. A respondent cannot respond to a proposition that he is physically blocked from hearing.

The prosecution treated the simultaneous overlapping dual conversation that took place when Davis left the car as though the two men were interrupting each other. This could give the appearance of a series of interruptions, but as this analysis pointed out at trial, both men were talking independently of each other and oblivious to what the other was saying, which cannot be considered interrupting.

Deceptive ambiguity was also created by McCrory's conversational strategy of using non-proximity to talk about murder while the listener could not hear what he said, a conversational strategy of blocking.

It is not totally clear why the prosecutor didn't try to use the video taken from the van across the parking lot. Perhaps he thought it was useless because the audio portion was so scratchy and hard to hear. Even though McCrory's body mike audiotape was clearer by far, when time-correlated with the few audible words on the videotape it provided unambiguous evidence of the distance between the two men after Davis left the car. McCrory clearly was talking into his body mike hidden under his shirt, for his voice was then slightly louder and clearer than it had been before, while Davis's voice became harder to hear as he moved toward the trunk of his car. But aided by careful listening and electronic amplification, virtually everything Davis said was audibly unambiguous and demonstrated that it had nothing to do with what McCrory was talking about. It is equally clear that McCrory intentionally created this deceptively ambiguous effect.

AMBIGUITY PRODUCED BY LEXICON AND GRAMMAR

Rather than creating ambiguity with lexicon or grammar, this cooperating witness created the deceptive ambiguity by producing simultaneously conflicting speech events; different schemas, agendas, speech acts; and the conversational strategy of blocking Davis's words.

An External Cooperating Witness Uses Deceptive Ambiguity with Yochanan Cohen

In January 2010 twenty-one executives of companies that produce various types of armament for military and law enforcement purposes assembled for a trade show in Las Vegas, Nevada (for more details of this case see Shuy 2015).

The FBI was concerned about illegal armament sales and suspected that in their contracts with foreign countries some of these manufacturers had been violating the Foreign Corrupt Practices Act (FCPA). The subsequent investigation focused on companies that were suspected of making illegal kickbacks to foreign officials in order to obtain lucrative contracts for their armament products. It was not unusual for some governments in Asia, South America, and Africa to require quid pro quo bribes from contractors in order to obtain their business, but the FCPA prohibits American manufacturers from engaging in such activity.

Passing that law was one thing; monitoring it in action was quite another. The FBI determined, quite properly, that the best way to discover violations was to covertly tape-record such transactions as they were taking place. The fact that many of the suspected armament manufacturers were assembled in the same place at the same time provided a golden opportunity for the FBI to troll for suspects and catch those who were willing to commit crimes. The agency decided to use outsider cooperating witnesses in this investigation, men who did not know Cohen personally but were well versed in the armament manufacturing business, had been caught in similar investigations, and were now awaiting their sentencing hearings.

One of the twenty-one targets at the Las Vegas arms manufacturers convention was Yochanan (Yoshi) Cohen, the chief executive of an American company that produces military body armor, most of which was sold internationally. The FBI had no indications that Cohen had any predisposition to commit a crime, although some of the other manufacturers at that meeting may have been suspects. The undercover cooperating witnesses chosen by the FBI to secretly record the executives at this convention apparently were oblivious to which of their targets were suspects. Since it is not uncommon for law enforcement to troll for crime, in the government's way of thinking these arms producers were given the *opportunity* to reveal any illegal predispositions at that time.

The speech event common to such occasions is the business transaction and sales speech event in which the four major phases are: (1) present needs; (2) describe or display the product; (3) negotiate the price and conditions of a sale; and (4) either complete or abort the transaction. The bribery speech event has the same structure but with a huge difference. Usually during phase 3 the agents or cooperating witnesses try to convert the business transaction speech event into a bribery speech event by introducing bribery or kickbacks as part of the conditions for sale. Sometimes it can be easy to convince targets who have violated this law to commit the crime again, while those who are not so predisposed can be more difficult to convince.

Even though Cohen had learned English as a second language he spoke it somewhat awkwardly, and the language evidence revealed by his many telephone conversations with the FBI's cooperating witness made clear that his perception of this as a business sales transaction speech event never varied.

His schema throughout grew out of his understanding that this was a business transaction speech event and his agenda was dominated by his own repeated topics which were: bragging about the quality of his body armor products, describing the legal requirements that had to be followed in such sales, and expressing his business philosophy of fairness.

Examination of all his speech acts demonstrated that he provided no agreement to the cooperating witness's hints and suggestions of illegality, promised to do nothing illegal, and never admitted to having done anything in the past that was contrary to the law. When the cooperating witness finally was clear about his illegal proposition of paying a kickback to get the contract, Cohen's speech act of denial was clear and strong. Nevertheless the prosecutor indicted him for violating the FCPA.

The first strategy of the cooperating witness (CW) began by trying to establish Cohen's past violation of that Act, which would help confirm his predisposition to offer a bribe in this investigation. He did this indirectly, hinting that somebody must have been paid off during Cohen's previous sale of body armor in Peru:

> CW: So there's a lot of happy generals in Peru I think.
> COHEN: I don't care about it.

This obviously was not the response the CW wanted, so he became a bit clearer about kickbacks in Peru:

> CW: In Peru I'm dealing with Carlos too. I mean they're really doing a good job down there. They're taking care of this guy and that guy to make sure everything is okay. How do you deal with money like that?
> COHEN: Everything comes to us.
> CW: And you commission back to them?

The CW introduced the topic that other manufacturers and possibly Cohen as well had filtered their commissions to middlemen and the middlemen then used part of these commissions to pay illegal kickbacks to Peruvian army generals. But Cohen would not admit to doing this himself:

> COHEN: I told them, "listen, I don't care that you make ten times. I just make my money. I don't care about you.

The CW would not take "no" for an answer, and then added:

> CW: And between us girls, I think they told me that the end user payoff was something like $200,000 on that deal.
> COHEN: I believe there was some kind of monkey business because they gave him a letter of credit for much more than he charged.

The CW's "between us girls" was an obvious wink-wink, nudge-nudge expression that he expected Cohen to recognize as confidential enough to encourage him to admit being in on the bribery. This didn't work, for even though Cohen was apparently aware that some "monkey business" was going on in those transactions, he was not involved in it. In a following meeting the CW tried again:

CW: So you're okay, because if we work in the Middle East or if we ever do something in Asia, it's the same thing. You know that they're paying the guys.

COHEN: I don't care. I do not control everything. As long as I don't do that. . . . What the agent does, I don't care. As long as for me it's a straight business, no cash involved with my side . . . I am terrified to do it.

When the CW then told Cohen that certain brokers he knew were paying off the Mexican police, Cohen replied that he did not believe him, saying, "I believe the brokers are enjoying legends about having to pay that amount of money."

Apparently feeling that he was getting nowhere by associating a direct kickback to the buyers, the CW then returned to his strategy of discussing how companies operate illegally when they overpay brokers' commissions so that the brokers can pass along the amounts in excess of their commissions to the buyers as kickbacks. He began by telling Cohen about his own broker in Turkey who did this for him. Cohen apparently missed the CW's point about bribery completely, responding that he always gives his buyers the most attractive price and that if the CW wants to broker his sale to Gabon for him, he'll pay him a normal broker agent's commission:

CW: Do you have a problem building in a 10% commission for me?

COHEN: No, I don't have a problem with that. . . . You can be our agent on this. We need to put you in the contract with Gabon because we need to put the name of everybody that is involved. If there is internal another person involved in Gabon, we need to have his company name and everything like that.

No doubt the CW was disheartened to hear this, for Cohen said he was clearly going to follow the legal procedure. Giving up on this tactic, the CW then switched his strategy to their need for an export license which, as the broker, the CW was supposed to obtain. He kept trying to persuade Cohen that they could sidestep the required process of getting an export license:

CW: Because of the quantity, I don't need pre-approval. I just have to file a report.

COHEN: I don't know that but I know that everything we export requires an export license. First we need the license. Do you know of a law firm in Washington DC that specializes in licenses? We need to show that to someone and therefore would like to have some kind of opinion to help with that.

Over the following three months Cohen continued to ask the CW if he had obtained the export license but the CW kept stalling him until he finally informed Cohen that his contact person in Gabon would be coming to the United States during the Las Vegas convention with the purchase contract. Cohen asked again about the export license adding: "I say for you it is all about the process, as long as the process is correct."

Eight months had passed when a second FBI agent took over in the effort to catch Cohen in illegality. He apparently decided to abandon the first agent's technique of using ambiguity, and instead explicitly discussed the illegality of the proposition:

> CW2: I have to ask for a 20% commission because 10% has to go to Alain, the minister [from Gabon] and then there's 10% for me.
> COHEN: Do you mind if I give Richard [the first agent] a little something?
> CW2: I would rather not.
> COHEN: Because if this is the case, it's really only 10% and you get some of that. Here's my philosophy. I work in the long term. I don't want everybody to grab me and I don't want to grab them. I don't know what's happening—
> CW2: [interrupting] So we have one exception.
> COHEN: [continuing after the interruption]—and I will not say it anymore.

By this time the effort to catch Cohen in illegality had failed twice. So CW 2 tried still another strategy. He ignored both Cohen's refusal to pay a kickback to get the contract and his refusal to sidestep getting the export license and introduced a new topic about how the goods would be transported to Gabon. Cohen, apparently believing he had thwarted the efforts to get him to do something illegal, agreed to send the needed information concerning the sale to the Gabon embassy in Washington, DC. This was a perfectly legal business procedure.

In spite of Cohen's alertness to the efforts to snare him in various types of crime, the government indicted him along with twenty-one other arms manufacturers at the January 2010 Shooting, Hunting, Outdoor Trade Show and Conference in Las Vegas. Cohen was charged with money laundering, conspiracy to violate the Foreign Corrupt Practices Act and aiding and abetting. The following deceptive ambiguities were created by the cooperating witness.

AMBIGUITY PRODUCED BY THE SPEECH EVENT

Throughout the months of conversation during which the first cooperating witness kept offering the *opportunity* for his target to commit a crime, Cohen's language made it clear that he stayed with his perception that this was a legitimate business sales transaction speech event while the cooperating witness created simultaneous deceptive ambiguity. After the second cooperating witness took over and made it clear that this was a bribery speech event, Cohen clearly rejected the idea. In fairness to the FBI, misrepresenting the speech event is considered a standard deceptive procedure in government-run undercover sting operations. However, standard procedure or not, misrepresentation of the speech event can only be considered deceptive.

AMBIGUITY PRODUCED BY SCHEMAS

To both cooperating witnesses, Cohen stayed with his schema that he was in a normal business sales transaction speech event, while the cooperating witness's ambiguously deceptive schema was that Cohen would eventually understand and succumb to their efforts to get him to commit to a crime. The schemas of all the participants were clearly revealed in their agendas.

AMBIGUITY PRODUCED BY AGENDAS

Cohen's agenda, revealed by all of his topic introductions and responses, was to promote his own body armor products and try to get contracts to sell them at the convention. The first cooperating witness's agenda, as revealed by the topics he introduced, was to be deceptively ambiguous in order get Cohen to agree to give Gabon's foreign minister a bribe or kickback in order to get a contract from that country. The second cooperating witness's agenda was more direct and clear about the need for a bribe.

The cooperating witnesses found it necessary change their topic scenario after Cohen clearly rejected the first one, which might be called the "everybody is doing it" strategy. CW1 presented this to Cohen indirectly and ambiguously, probably in the hope that Cohen would admit that he had committed the same illegal acts in his past contracts with overseas governments. CW1's second topic scenario, which might be called the "you can overpay the broker and let him pay the kickback out of his broker's commission" strategy, also was deceptively ambiguous. Here CW1 did not accuse Cohen of doing this but rather ambiguously suggested that it would be profitable for Cohen to take that route. The third topic scenario was CW2's explicit representation that Cohen should offer a kickback, which Cohen clearly rejected. The fourth topic scenario, also by CW2, might be called the "you don't really need to follow the rules" strategy, which he engineered gradually over time by letting Cohen believe that CW2 was slowly obtaining the license until Cohen finally tumbled that he was not. Careful analysis of their taped conversations demonstrated that all four of these topic scenarios went down in flames, leaving one to wonder how many times targets needs to say "no" before the agents realize that they could not be bought.

AMBIGUITY PRODUCED BY SPEECH ACTS

The two cooperating witnesses differed in the ways they used deceptive ambiguity with Cohen. The first cooperating witness used the fishing operation approach of hinting, alluding, and implying in his effort to get Cohen to agree or admit that he had given kickbacks in the past and that he had overpaid his brokers so that they would pass along the extra money to the clients. Since these hinting speech acts didn't work, the second cooperating witness took over and clearly used the speech act of warning Cohen that he would need to pay a kickback to the Gabonian minister of defense if he could hope to get a contract.

In addition to Cohen's many speech acts of reporting that he always conducted his business honestly and his bragging about how good his company and products were, Cohen used the speech act of directly or indirectly denying all of the illegal suggestions made by the cooperating witnesses. It is difficult to understand why the prosecutor's intelligence analysis failed to understand this, but he went ahead and brought charges of bribery against Cohen.

AMBIGUITY PRODUCED BY CONVERSATIONAL STRATEGIES

The two cooperating witnesses' major conversational strategies were their uses of ambiguity and blocking. Their deliberate ambiguity came from hints that Cohen was apparently expected to understand as proof of past bad acts by others and himself. Hinting is deliberately ambiguous because it conveys more than one possible meaning. But Cohen was alert enough to catch the hints and ward them off. The cooperating witnesses also tried to block Cohen from saying something exculpatory by interrupting him and then quickly changing the topic, a form of the hit-and-run strategy (Shuy 2005). When they failed to achieve their goals, the cooperating witnesses used the conversational strategy of ignoring Cohen's responses and going right on as though they had succeeded. Apparently the prosecutor was impressed by the cumulative effect of the cooperating witness's speech acts of offering the *opportunity* and therefore ignored Cohen's speech act responses of rejecting that opportunity. Since this cumulative effect of the offers existed on the taped record, this apparently were enough for the prosecutor to mentally block out Cohen's rejections of those offers from his own awareness of who actually said what.

This form of guilt by association occurs in many undercover operations and it can deceive even the most attentive listeners. For example, during a break in the Senate impeachment hearings of Senator Williams, Senator Hatfield came up to the desk where the senator and I were standing and said, "Senator Williams, why did you have to swear all the time on the tapes in evidence?" I had to point out to Senator Hatfield that Williams was not the person who was doing the swearing. It was FBI agent Amoroso. Although Hatfield was a brilliant and perceptive politician, he watched the tapes but missed that fact entirely. Prosecutors, judges, and juries can be victims of the same guilt by association caused by the way the agents can deceptively color the evidence.

AMBIGUITY PRODUCED BY LEXICON AND GRAMMAR

Perhaps because the cooperating witnesses knew that they and Cohen were in the same business of selling arms and body armor to governments, they used the same specialized vocabulary. Even though the two cooperating witnesses came to understand that their target was not fully competent in English, they used ambiguity in their hints and vague suggestions about the apparent ongoing illegality in their business more than individual ambiguous words or grammatical references. At one point, however, the first cooperating witness began his sentence, "And between us girls," an invitation for Cohen to admit that he was aware of and involved in the illegal kickbacks. This ploy didn't work, however, for Cohen's response was that he doesn't give kickbacks and is terrified to do it.

Although Cohen was indicted, he never had to face trial. The judge had decided to split the twenty-one defendants into three trials in which the government's strongest cases were to be tried first. The first trial ended with a split jury verdict and no convictions. That meant that the prosecutor had to decide whether or not to retry those defendants and then proceed with the other two trials. He decided not to do so. Cohen's defense team was prepared with the foregoing analysis and already had shared some of it with the prosecutor. They were confident that it would prove their client innocent.

An External Cooperating Witness Uses Deceptive Ambiguity with Marwan El-Hindi

The FBI is constantly on the lookout for suspected terrorists, and Arab Americans seem to be high on their list. In 2007 federal prosecutors indicted Marwan El-Hindi, an unsuccessful, middle-age, Toledo Ohio businessman along with two other Arab-Americans, one a local travel agent named Mohammed Amawi and the other a young student named Wassim Masloum, charging them with planning to carry out terrorist activities in the Toledo area. They had no criminal records or any other apparent reasons for the FBI to investigate them.

After the 911 terrorist attacks in the United States, in 2001 Attorney General John Ashcroft advised all senior law enforcement officials about the government's new approach that he called "proactive prevention and disruption." Instead of pursing terrorists after the crime, the new policy tried to use informants to prevent terrorism from happening and arresting the presumed terrorists for conspiracy before any damage could be done. The attorney general referred to this as "strategic overinclusiveness." The government then began to carefully monitor the activities of American Muslims. The Toledo investigation was one of those trolling-for-possible-terrorism operations in which all three suspects were convicted at trial in June 2008.

For this investigation the FBI used Darren Griffin as an outsider cooperating witness. Formerly a member of the US Army's Special Forces, Griffin was reported to have once been a drug user and now had continuing but unspecified financial problems. He had served as a cooperating witness for the FBI in the past and now had a three-year contract to discover terrorist activities in the Toledo area. At El-Hindi's trial, Griffin testified that he was paid some $350,000 for his undercover work in this case, in which he claimed to be running his own private security business.

He began this FBI assignment by hanging around in various Toledo mosques, telling all who would listen that he was a recent convert to Islam and was disenchanted with US foreign policy in the Middle East. He grew a beard, wore Arabic clothing, and began to try to assume a role that could be perceived as an Islamic extremist. He spread the word around that he hated the president and thought that Muslims should bring about violent jihad against the United States. Most people he met at the mosques considered him some type of loony and several of them actually reported him to the FBI. Each time this happened, he had to move his operation to a different mosque.

Eventually Griffin met the three defendants at a Toledo mosque, brought them together, and tape-recorded some 300 hours of fairly innocuous conversations with them. He quickly discovered that the three men didn't exhibit any strong interest in carrying out a jihad. They were devout Muslims, however, and this appeared to support the goal of Griffin's trolling operation. The three men willingly befriended Griffin as a new convert to Islam who claimed to want to learn more about their religion and they often read and discussed passages of the Koran with him.

El-Hindi was a businessman with a very meager income that came from commissions he received by recruiting prospective medical students to attend various European medical schools. He had five children and at that time was going through a difficult and bitter divorce, but he had a deep concern for the education of his own and other poor Muslim children both in the Middle East and in United States. His dream was to create a Muslim school in Toledo, although he was never able to figure out how to do this.

Amawi had recently visited his family in Jordan from whom he learned much about the Iraq war. Griffin tape-recorded his conversations with Amawi separately on several occasions, during which Amawi seems to have provided Griffin with evidence that he might be interested in terrorist activities. When El-Hindi was present, however, Amawi offered no such indications.

Masloum was an overweight young man who was trying to prepare himself physically for immanent military service in the US Army. He seemed to be somewhat of an accidental afterthought who appeared in very few of their recorded conversations.

Griffin began by befriending Amawi, who was an easy target because he was quite vocal about his negative opinions concerning the war in Iraq. When Griffin eventually met El-Hindi, he regarded him as a businessman who might be able to round up the necessary financial resources for his jihad plans. Often El-Hindi invited his friends, including Amawi and Griffin, to talk at his home, where they discussed Islam and listened to the news of the war in Iraq while the others commiserated with El-Hindi about his complicated divorce negotiations. Eventually they added Masloum to the group, at which point Griffin began to hint at his plans to get El-Hindi to recruit additional Muslims to form what Griffin considered a terrorist group, although he never used that term and El-Hindi gave no indication that he understood Griffin's hints. Griffin talked vaguely about using his military experience to "train people" but he carefully didn't mention the nature and purpose of such training.

The word *training* became central to the prosecution's case. Since both El-Hindi and Masloum were seriously overweight, they talked as though *training* referred to physical exercise, for Griffin was a large, trim, and well-built former Special Ops soldier who might be able to provide them such training. Griffin asked El-Hindi to mention the names of several other people he thought might benefit from his training but no matter how many times Griffin reminded him of this, El-Hindi never invited anyone.

Griffin also frequently used the word *security*, presumably hinting that they should avoid being caught planning a jihad. El-Hindi didn't catch the hint, however, for he interpreted *security* quite differently, by responding to it with complaints about the way Muslims were being detained at airports and being attacked on the streets. His understanding of what Griffin meant by *security* was further revealed as he then talked about his own recent mugging by members of the local anti-Arab community, to which Griffin said "there's definitely stuff to teach kids, you know, it's basic stuff as far as weapons training." El-Hindi's language indicated that he understood Griffin's words, *training, security*, and *weapons*, as self-protection strategies that when learned could provide some security to Muslims who were helpless and vulnerable. This led to their discussion of El-Hindi's dream of establishing a private Muslim school that would include physical education instruction in karate for children so that they could defend themselves from muggings like the one he had recently experienced. It was clear that they were on different wavelengths and Griffin's hints were not leading where he needed them to go.

One of El-Hindi's cockamamie business ideas came to him when he found on line a request for proposal from an Egyptian police department asking for bidders on a new training camp for training police officers. In addition to training, bidders were required to supply horses, horse trailers, and trucks. El-Hindi was interested enough in this opportunity to telephone Michigan automotive manufacturers to learn the prices of various vehicles. He also called various horse breeders to learn the price of horses. He mentioned this request for proposal to Griffin at one of their meetings, saying:

> EL-HINDI: They will establish a whole program training for shooting, training for horses, a whole camp. Training for everything, even for swimming. It's going to be a huge camp to train for horses, camels, martial arts and weapons.

The prosecution apparently inferred from this that the words *weapons, camp*, and *training* indicated that even though it was a police training program, El-Hindi was actually planning to create a terrorist cell and operation at that camp. El-Hindi also used the word *training* when he referred to still another of his odd entrepreneurial ideas, training to become a certified translator of English and Arabic. Through the many examples of what El-Hindi indicated *training* meant to him, it is easy to see that none of them came close to Griffin's hints about what he meant by that word.

El-Hindi often talked about finding a suitable location to build a school for Muslim children to study the Koran. He proposed that in addition to schooling it could also provide suitable recreation and also serve as a mosque. Griffin picked up on this and offered to provide the training in physical education. As he made this offer, Griffin dropped another hint that the prosecution considered significant:

> EL-HINDI: The first floor, make it like a prayer area, mosque.
> GRIFFIN: And everything else **training**.
> EL-HINDI: Oh yeah.
> GRIFFIN: 'Cause that's how we could **mask it.**
> EL-HINDI: You will fall in love with that place. Two floors.
> GRIFFIN: We'll do the daycare and use the rest of the money for, you know, the **training** and everything.
> EL-HINDI: I got to get in shape quick.

Here Griffin was a bit more specific with his hint, accompanying the words *mask it* to his previous many uses of the word *training*. He apparently hoped that El-Hindi would finally catch on to his unspoken desire to disguise the mosque as a terrorist cell. El-Hindi was not an attentive listener and his responses gave evidence that he once again missed Griffin's hint. He demonstrated no uptake from the words *mask it* and went on to clearly interpret *training* as physical education for the children and himself. The prosecutor (and later the jury as well) considered this to be a clear and unambiguous smoking gun representation that together they conspired to hide, disguise, conceal, cover up, or camouflage the real purpose of the school as a terrorist training center.

To this point Griffin and El-Hindi had communicated on very different wavelengths about the meaning of both *security* and *training*. Griffin must have sensed this because he stumblingly tried to be a bit clearer about his meaning although his garbled lexicon and syntax didn't help him much:

GRIFFIN: I'm gonna train some other guys, so we'll, and uh, basically we're gonna do it, uh, I found out too is they could be on my VIP protection team.

El-Hindi appeared to be flattered to think of himself as a VIP and wanted to be included with these "other guys," explaining that he had been trying to lose some weight:

EL-HINDI: This is something I want to get into too. I lost about twenty pounds since I came back.
GRIFFIN: It's like you're gonna be in training too.
EL-HINDI: I am. I have to. I have to.

At trial the prosecutor celebrated this exchange as evidence of El-Hindi's desire to join the alleged terrorist group that Griffin had described as "other guys" on his "VIP protection team." Such an inference might be plausible if there had been any clear previous discussion about forming a terrorist group. But there was none. All that Griffin had produced were ambiguous words about *training, security*, and *weapons* and his proposed, but never identified alleged terrorist cell idea.

It is usually the case that undercover operations come to a halt once the government believes the accumulated evidence is enough to bring an indictment. The preceding tape-recordings apparently didn't satisfy the needs of this investigation, so Griffin was sent back to get more. When undercover agents are sent back for more information, it is a clear sign that their previous efforts had not succeeded. Therefore, the four men continued to meet occasionally to talk about Islam until about a year later when the investigator took a new approach.

Griffin's second scenario began when the four men assembled one evening at El-Hindi's home, where he cooked and served dinner while the other three men watched videotapes of the war and discussed religious matters in the house's combined living room and eating area. Griffin covertly (and rather awkwardly) videotaped it all with a device concealed under his shirt. As host and cook, El-Hindi spent a most of the time in the adjoining kitchen, occasionally popping into the eating area as time permitted. Meanwhile, Amawi, the most skilled of the group in electronic matters, searched the Internet for videos about the war in the Middle East. After a while, Griffin asked that certain parts of the programs be downloaded and sent to him by email. Some of these scenes allegedly depicted military tactics used by the US and foreign armies in the Afghan and Iraq war zones. The prosecution later claimed that these videotapes were evidence that the defendants had conspired and participated in what the indictment referred to as *electronic jihad*. El-Hindi was charged with terrorism because, as requested, he subsequently emailed copies of these videos to Griffin, constituting a terrorist act in the mind of the prosecution.

As other cases in this book describe, FBI undercover agents are encouraged to follow a three-step process in their operations (Heymann 1984: 36–39; Shuy 2005: 7–9):

- Let the suspects talk freely and self-generate their own guilt;
- Drop hints that the suspects might be able to understand well enough to then go on to implicate themselves; and
- Represent the illegality of the enterprise clearly and unambiguously.

The evidence tapes indicate here that in his first scenario Griffin had not succeeded in gathering any evidence of the men self-generating their guilt of terrorism. Nor did he ever represent the illegality of the alleged enterprise clearly and unambiguously. As for Griffin's many hints, El-Hindi gave no indication of understanding them in the way Griffin must have intended. During Griffin's second scenario at the dinner table, El-Hindi indeed emailed the videotape to Griffin, but there were serious questions about his presupposition, intention, and voluntariness in doing so. Neither the prosecutor nor the jury recognized the deceptive ambiguity of these hints and as a result the three men were all convicted of terrorism. The prosecution in this case relied heavily on the cooperating witness's following uses of deceptive ambiguity.

AMBIGUITY PRODUCED BY THE SPEECH EVENT

El-Hindi's language throughout their conversations indicated that he believed he was in the benign speech events of instructing Griffin about Islam and trying to determine a way to build a school for Islamic children in Toledo. In contrast, Griffin's language indicated that he was trying to convert their conversations into an illegal speech event showing that El-Hindi was planning to create a terrorist cell. Different aspects of these speech events were going on simultaneously throughout these conversations, with both sides sticking to their own concept of their speech event to the end. Griffin's creating and maintaining simultaneously different speech events creates deceptive ambiguity about what is going on.

AMBIGUITY PRODUCED BY SCHEMAS

El-Hindi's language throughout the topics he raised and his responses to Griffin's topics indicate that he maintained the schema created by his perception of the speech event as legally benign, in contrast with Griffin's schema that El-Hindi was agreeing to create a terrorist cell.

AMBIGUITY PRODUCED BY AGENDAS

In virtually all undercover operations the agent's only serious agenda is to capture targets discussing criminal activities. El-Hindi's benign agendas were revealed by the topics he introduced and by his lack of inculpatory responses to the topics introduced by Griffin. El-Hindi consistently introduced topics of his divorce problem, his dream of building an Islamic school for children, his business plans in response to the Egyptian police department's request for proposals, and his efforts to help Griffin better understand the teachings of Islam. His responses to Griffin's topics revealed his lack of understanding about Griffin's ambiguously deceptive agenda. This was most clearly revealed when Griffin asked El-Hindi to email him the videotapes that the group had been watching in his living room. El-Hindi, who was busy with the cooking and serving, had the opportunity to see very little of what was available on the tapes. He was not a military man and even if he had seen what was on them, he was inept at determining what the government claimed to be tapes purportedly revealing military strategies that could aid and abet terrorism attacks. It is also difficult to understand why videotapes that appeared on publicly accessible television would constitute new information that could be taken as evidence of aiding and abetting the enemy to discover US military tactics.

Like most undercover operations that troll for targets without first establishing their predisposition to commit a crime, the government's single most obvious perception of potential illegality that preceded this investigation was that the targets were Muslims. This lack of known predisposition typically requires agents to proceed cautiously by providing hints of illegality to see what the targets might do with those hints. Griffin's agenda was to fish for illegality by providing hints that were by definition ambiguous. The inexplicit language of hinting requires listeners to infer what those hints might mean. Even more problematic, prosecutors and triers of the fact are also required to infer meaning from ambiguity. Inferences are not always bad, but when there is no explicit evidence to support those inferences, the resulting decision-making can be uneven.

AMBIGUITY PRODUCED BY SPEECH ACTS

El-Hindi never uttered the speech act of agreeing with any of Griffin's ambiguously presented speech acts of offering to create a terrorist cell to train people to do jihad. His language makes it clear that he understood the reason for Griffin's speech act of requesting him to invite more Muslims to their meetings was to do physical exercise that they all needed. At any rate, El-Hindi never invited anyone. Griffin was undaunted and went right ahead as though he actually had received El-Hindi's speech act of agreement to all his ambiguous requests. El-Hindi's only speech acts of promising were to continue to meet with Griffin and to send him a copy of the videotape of which he had only seen parts. He used the speech act of offering Griffin advice about Islam and offered to host a dinner meeting at his home. These speech acts provided nothing to support the prosecution's speech act of accusing El-Hindi of participating in illegal activities.

AMBIGUITY PRODUCED BY CONVERSATIONAL STRATEGIES

Griffin interrupted El-Hindi often, usually at points when El-Hindi was talking about his own various plans to build a school. During these interruptions Griffin suggested that he could do the physical education training, ambiguously hinting that this training could be military in nature rather than the sort of physical education that schools normally might include in their curricula. During their other conversations, the cooperating witness frequently blocked El-Hindi's topics about creating a new school for Muslim children by trying to reinterpret them to match his own hinted topics about developing a terrorist cell. When El-Hindi, his two friends, and Griffin met together at El-Hindi's home, the physical arrangements in the house blocked El-Hindi's ability to know what was going on during the playing of videotapes of the war in the Middle East. As host, he spent most of his time in the kitchen and could gain little if any knowledge about the content of the tapes. None of the comments he made as he went back and forth from the kitchen to the living room supported the accusation that he planned to copy the television programs that were allegedly germane to terrorism.

Griffin also used the conversational strategy of contaminating their conversations by inserting vague hints of terrorism that El-Hindi's responses demonstrated he didn't catch. Griffin's most commonly used conversational strategy, however, was his use of deceptive ambiguity throughout his conversations.

AMBIGUITY BY LEXICON AND GRAMMAR

As noted previously, Griffin failed to identify clearly and unambiguously what he was referring to when he talked about *training, security, weapons*, and *mask it*. Not only did Griffin fail to make clear and unambiguous what he meant by these terms, but he also failed to identify the references to which they related and then ignored El-Hindi's relatively clear representations of what he understood these terms referenced. It is incumbent on the powerful participants in interactions to request clarification when they don't get the responses they are trying to get. Griffin did not do this, perhaps because doing so might have enabled El-Hindi to understand his illegal intentions and then reject them.

It is an indisputable fact that El-Hindi downloaded portions of the videotape they were watching and emailed them to Griffin at his request. The prosecution relabeled this as an intentional act of aiding and abetting terrorism.

Careful analysis of the taped evidence demonstrates that El-Hindi was in the room where the tape was running only part of the time, that he was interested in the war news from his native land, that he gave no verbal indication that he understood military strategy, that he never gave evidence that he understood Griffin's effort to produce a terrorist cell, and that his cooperation with Griffin was to educate him in the Muslim religion. Relabeling this as terrorism can only be considered the result of deceptive ambiguity.

It is possible that the prosecution may have found enough evidence of Amawi's intention to create jihad and could therefore have been justified to indict him. Masloum was such a minor player that his participation caused the prosecutor to include him in the indictment simply because he was present at a few of the meetings. It can be difficult for prosecutors to overlook the possibility that targets who talk with undercover agents are guilty for that reason alone.

7

Complainants Use Deceptive Ambiguity

Sometimes law enforcement doesn't even need to search for crimes because the crimes are reported to them by citizens who complain about alleged offenses committed in the past or about those that are likely to be committed in the future, virtually always by someone they know. In contrast with cooperating witnesses who have much to gain from working with law enforcement, complainants have a more personal stake in the investigations of work associates, family members, or other people they know.

The targets can range from persons who the complainants believe have solicited or offered them bribes to those who have asked them to find someone to commit a murder for them, but one of the most frequent reports from complainants occurs after children tell their parents that someone like an uncle, a cousin, or a family friend has committed a sexual act on them in the past. Commonly such reports relate to current events but occasionally they are recalled at a much later date through a process that psychologists call *recovered memory* (Loftus 1994; Scheflin 1998).

After citizens inform the police about the alleged illegal past act, the police coach them on what to say when they talk with their targets during subsequent electronically recorded confrontation calls or confrontation meetings. If telephone calls are made, the law enforcement officers monitor these calls by sitting near the complainant and whispering or jotting down advice about what to say next. When law enforcement officers videotape confrontation meetings, a police officer is usually unobtrusively monitoring the recording visually and audibly nearby and is poised to assist in case the caller runs into some kind of danger.

Whatever the citizen complaint may be, the police need to collect convincing evidence of it that will stand up in court. The process begins by trying to record confirmation of the claimed past criminal misconduct. Without such evidence the case can result in one of those "he-said, she-said" disputes that courts find difficult to resolve. The police have found that an effective approach is to obtain recorded language of the alleged offenders to obtain proof that they indeed committed that crime. Audio- or videotape recording can provide such evidence if it is done effectively. To accomplish this the police sometimes ask the complainants to personally confront the alleged perpetrators either by telephone or by in-person concealed video or audiotape and try to get them to admit the offense. In this sense the use of complainants as undercover operators is similar to that of cooperating witnesses. One important difference is that the complainants are usually well enough acquainted with the targets that their conversations can start naturally in a friendly and non-threatening manner. In that way complainants also can disguise their conversational power.

Since this approach to recording criminal activity on tape requires clear and convincing language evidence that demonstrates the target's guilt, the recording has to include evidence that both participants were in the same speech event, were on the same topic, and mutually understood what they were talking about. In addition, the purported offenders must provide at least one felicitous speech act of admitting to the offense. If the accusers use ambiguous referencing or manipulate and distort the language evidence in any way, the case against the offenders can be seriously weakened or found to be inadequate. These are areas in which linguistic analysis can be most helpful to the defense, but even prosecutors can benefit from such information if they call on linguistic assistance before making their indictments and especially if they avoid becoming embarrassed by going to trial with questionable language evidence.

In two of the case examples in this chapter, the names of Dora, Sam, and Sheriff Preston as well as other identifying aspects have been changed at the request of the parties involved.

A Complainant Uses Deceptive Ambiguity with Brothel Commissioners John Poli and John McNown

It all began when Janice Chatterton, a San Francisco madam, called two Nevada brothel commissioners to inquire about obtaining a permit to set up her trailers at one of the legal brothels in that state (for a more detailed description of this case see Shuy 1998, 2013). The commissioners, John Poli and John McNown, testified that they were suspicious about Chatterton's call and worried that she might be connected with a known organized crime group in her city. They somehow reasoned that if they requested a bribe for granting her a permit and if she agreed to give them one, they would then know for sure that she was connected to the mafia. The men never denied this ploy, explaining to the investigators that the only reason they requested the bribe during that initial call was to find out whether or not she was connected to the San Francisco mob. There was a reason for this. In the past, the mob had tried unsuccessfully to license a trailer in Nevada and had threatened the commissioners when their bribe offer was rejected. The two commissioners reasoned that if Chatterton was indeed mafia connected, they would try to find reasons to reject her request before any threats might reoccur.

No electronic record was made of Chatterton's first call, but she confirmed that the two men indeed had requested a bribe for granting her the permit, after which she brought the money with her when she came to see them. She quickly reported this first call to the authorities, who wired her up for her meeting with the two men.

Poli and McNown obviously had not thought through their plan very carefully and had failed to consider that a person who was not connected with the mob might report them to the police. Now that the madam was coming to meet with them, they had to figure out a way to tell her that they didn't want a bribe after all. But since they had agreed to meet with her to tell her this, they set up a meeting at a small café in Sparks, Nevada. They later reported that they intended to listen to her plans for setting up brothel trailers but would turn the bribe down if she offered them one. This created ambiguity for later listeners concerning the commissioners' predisposition and motive for initially requesting the bribe. What followed was the commissioners' effort to clarify their actual motive.

Chatterton was already waiting for the men at the café when they drove up in their car. Poli saw her and motioned to her to come to his driver's side window where he suggested that they hold their conversation inside his car. She rejected this proposal, because an FBI agent was sitting at a table in the café waiting to monitor their conversation and protect her if any violence should ensue. She eventually prevailed and they all went inside the café.

McNown selected a table at the edge of the room but Chatterton, realizing that this table was not close enough to the agent, suggested a different more suitable spot. Poli mentioned that some of the people there knew him and he'd rather sit at the edge of the room where he wouldn't be so obvious. His unspoken reason for this, which he later elaborated at trial, was that he didn't want his friends to see him talking with a person who he thought might be a mafia representative. In contrast, the prosecutor interpreted this as a sign that Poli wanted to be bribed inconspicuously, adding to the existing ambiguity of predisposition and motive. Chatterton won the argument and they sat down at the table she picked.

As it turned out the brothel commissioners were very wrong about Chatterton. This madam ran an independent brothel operation that was in no way connected with the San Francisco mob. She simply wanted to expand her business empire into Nevada. The madam began the meeting by asking the men to reduce the $50,000 they apparently had requested in their initial untaped phone call. McNown answered, "What do you got in mind?" She responded that she was afraid that at some later time they would probably come back to her for more money. McNown then inelegantly tried to explain that after they had turned down a previous request to set up trailers, they received a series of threatening phone calls. This vague reference to his previous encounter with a mafia-connected group was the key to understanding why they made their dangerously stupid request for a bribe from her in the first place. He apparently didn't feel that he could tell Chatterton that this is why they asked her for a bribe during their phone call, but he testified at trial that this was indeed the reason. Instead of saying this to her, however, McNown dug a deeper hole by ineptly saying that they had asked her for a bribe because they felt that she could "come up with something that would prove their trust in each other." Almost simultaneously, Poli gave a different answer, saying that they had arrived at this figure ($50,000) on the phone "because that was the offer we had," alluding to that previous caller who then sent them threatening letters. He added, "We figured maybe that's what his fee is." This *pronoun, his,* was Poli's ambiguous way of referring to the mafia without saying it explicitly. His use of *is* rather than *was* supported this ineptly put explanation.

To this point the two men had fumblingly tried to explain why they had originally asked her for a bribe but they had still not retracted their earlier request for it. Since Chatterton had reason enough to believe that she'd have to give them a bribe, she told them that she had $5,000 in cash with her. Poli then backed off, saying that he had told her on the phone that she would get the license "before anything changed hands." Whether or not this was an accurate report of what he told her on the phone, it appeared to support Poli's feeble effort to say that even though they had originally asked her for a bribe, they didn't really mean it. The prosecutor, in contrast, understood it to refer only to the sequence of extorting the bribe money—that Poli had told her that she could pay the bribe money after she got her license.

Undaunted by this ambiguity, Chatterton repeated that she had "the five" with her. At this point the government's transcript differed greatly from the speech on the tape-recording. The transcript showed McNown saying to Poli, "I would take it today, wouldn't you? I'd do it, yes sir." The noise of dishes clattering and people talking made their conversation difficult to hear, but careful listening to the tape demonstrated that he actually said, "I wouldn't take it today, would you? No, I'd wait." The transcript also erred in recording what Poli said next. It read, "We would wait, huh?" when what he actually said was, "We don't want to do anything today."

Immediately following this exchange, Chatterton got up from the table and rushed into the ladies room. Poli rose at the same time and moved in a different direction toward the cashier to pay the bill for the soft drinks they had ordered. McNown was the slowest to get up from the table. As he did so, he saw a roll of money that Chatterton had left on her chair. Before he could pick it and give it back to her, she had already disappeared into the ladies room, where an FBI agent was waiting for her. Confused about what to do with the role of cash, McNown walked outside to the parking lot where Poli had already started the car. As Poli began to drive away he told McNown how fortunate it was that they didn't take that bribe. Then McNown sheepishly showed Poli the roll of cash that he had picked up. Poli immediately turned the car around and drove back to the café, where FBI agents arrested them both for extorting a bribe.

When I testified at the trial, I explained the errors in the government's transcript, pointing out how the tape demonstrated that they had rejected, not accepted, Chatterton's offer of a bribe. The jury verdict was divided, causing the judge to declare a mistrial.

There were many ambiguities in this conversation, several of which were deceptive.

AMBIGUITY PRODUCED BY THE SPEECH EVENT

All of the participants in this conversation shared the knowledge that this would be a bribery speech event. The difference was in the targets' declared intentionality, for the language used by Poli and McNown indicated clearly that they were trying to take back their earlier unrecorded request for a bribe. For them the meeting was a retraction speech event with three phases:

(1) admit that they had made the bribe request earlier (which they did indirectly);
(2) retract their previous bribe request, explaining why; and
(3) refuse to change their minds.

Chatterton agreed with (1), ignored (2) by apparently not recognizing their retraction and change of mind and by going ahead as though it didn't happen, and (3) ignored both their change of mind and their rejection of her bribe as she left the bribe money on her chair and rushed out of the meeting.

This retraction speech event must not have been recognized by the prosecutor, for neither he nor Chatterton gave any evidence of realizing what it was. He apparently was unable or unwilling to understand that they could have retracted a bribe offer after they had made it. He ignored their rather stumblingly indirect explanation for why they requested a bribe in the first place and found it insufficient to protect them from charges of extortion. To him it must have seemed like trying to unring a bell.

AMBIGUITY PRODUCED BY SCHEMAS

The opposing perceptions of this retraction speech event created two simultaneously different schemas about what was happening. After Chatterton agreed to give the men a bribe, the language used by Poli and McNown supported their schema of trying to retract their original schema that Chatterton was from the San Francisco mob. Chatterton's schema created by the original telephone conversation apparently was so strongly embedded that she could not change it based on what the men actually told her during their meeting. These simultaneously contrasting schemas continued throughout their conversation.

AMBIGUITY PRODUCED BY AGENDAS

From the start of their meeting, Chatterton's agenda was obvious—to capture on tape the language of the two men giving her the previously requested bribe. Poli and McNown's language exhibited a different agenda—first to find out whether Chatterton was really from the San Francisco mob and then to retract the bribe offer they had made to her earlier over the phone. During the meeting, their topics revealed that their agenda had shifted as they told her that they would not accept a bribe. Undaunted by this, Chatterton's topics were to insist on giving them the bribe they had requested in their earlier phone call.

There was no ambiguity in the two men's agenda from the beginning of the meeting to the end, but Chatterton created a huge ambiguity as she left the money on her chair for McNown to pick up after she fled the table. The topics introduced by Chatterton indicated that she had bribe money with her and was willing for it to be a quid pro quo for licensing her trailers. Her first topic was to try to negotiate the price down, but after receiving no encouraging response she apparently was so intent on paying the bribe money that she resorted to quickly placing it on her empty chair as they got up to leave the meeting. The topics introduced by Poli and McNown evidenced that they were no longer willing to request a bribe now that they understood she was not connected to the mob.

These conflicting agendas ran through the entire conversation. The prosecution's transcript created the most critical ambiguity concerning the participants' agendas. A reasonable excuse for producing inaccuracies in the crucial parts of the conversation could be that the transcriber was less than competent or that the intelligence analyst, the prosecutor, was careless when he compared the tape with the transcript. The prosecutor denied any error, incompetence, or carelessness, however, and in spite of my teaching the jury how to listen carefully for the linguistic differences between "I would take a bribe, wouldn't you" and "I wouldn't take a bribe, would you?" he remained firm in his claim that his transcript was the only accurate representation of what was said.

His insistence turned what at best might have been considered an ambiguous passage into one that deceived the jury about the words that were actually on the tape. One of the problems with ambiguous expressions is that they can be either ignored or interpreted. When we interpret them, we have a number of tools to call on, one of which is schema and preconception, which may explain why the prosecutor chose to understand the brothel commissioners' words the way he did. A better tool for resolving ambiguity is to make a careful linguistic analysis of the language and context in which it is spoken. The institutional power of the prosecution to interpret evidence by preconception, however, sometimes wins the day. In this case some of the jury interpreted it the same way the prosecutor did while others did not.

AMBIGUITY PRODUCED BY SPEECH ACTS

There was no dispute that in an earlier phone call Poli and McNown had used the speech act of requesting a bribe from the madam. At trial, they admitted that their soliciting a bribe was a stupid way to discover whether Chatterton was associated with the San Francisco crime family. This counted for nothing to the prosecutor, however, for he ignored their later efforts to retract their bribe request and celebrated their initial bribe request as evidence of their unchanged predisposition and motive. When they met, Chatterton clearly used the speech act of offering bribe money to the two men. Once the transcript errors were revealed, it was equally clear that Poli and McNown used the speech act of rejecting the bribe money from Chatterton, who paid no attention to their speech act of rejecting and deposited the roll of money on her chair as they all exited the café. It was also clear that McNown picked it up and looked for Chatterton to return it to her, but by then she had disappeared. The speech act of intentionally accepting as opposed to unintentionally receiving then was disputed at trial, centering on what it means to *take* or *accept* something versus to *receive* it. When McNown picked up the roll of cash, was this an act of intentionally completing the quid pro quo by picking it up, or did it constitute *accepting* a bribe? At trial, I discussed the semantic difference between intentionally accepting the cash and benignly picking up some money that possibly had been inadvertently or intentionally dropped there, and how this related to the fact that both men previously had agreed with each other and in front of Chatterton to reject the madam's offer of bribe money. The madam's action strongly appeared to be an intentionally deceptive effort to trick McNown into reflexively and unintentionally picking up some unguarded money so that his action would give the appearance of taking a bribe. Trickery is one of the definitions of deceit. McNown was nervous, confused, and in a less than rational state of mind when he picked up that roll of money from her otherwise empty chair. This difference between the speech act of intentionally accepting and the speech act of unintentionally receiving was also discussed in the investigation of Senator Williams in chapter 5.

AMBIGUITY PRODUCED BY CONVERSATIONAL STRATEGIES

There was a large amount of overlapping talk in this conversation that made it difficult for the prosecution to produce its transcript. Chatterton's major conversational strategy in this conversation, however, occurred when she non-verbally left the money on her chair as the three of them got up to leave the table. This is a non-verbal version of the common verbal strategy of blocking her conversational partner from responding to her action. It worked in the same way as though she had blocked what the men were trying to say.

AMBIGUITY PRODUCED BY LEXICON AND GRAMMAR

There was no important ambiguous grammatical referencing in the complainant's language with the brothel commissioners. The major lexical ambiguity took place at the trial rather than during their recorded table conversation. As noted previously, the prosecution and the defense were at odds over the meaning of the verb *accept* as in "the defendants accepted the bribe." The conflict was about whether McNown's picking up the roll of money constituted *accepting* a bribe after both men had indicated that they did not intend to give one to Chatterton.

A Complainant Uses Deceptive Ambiguity with Sam

In 2004 Dora, the mother of a nine-year-old girl claimed that her daughter Shawna (names changed) had complained about some nightmares in which she was sexually abused. Shawna's dreams didn't identify the abuser, but her mother suspected that the offender was Sam, the girl's uncle, and reported this to the police. The officer in charge suggested that Dora use the investigative procedure called a *confirmation call*, in which Dora's task would be to telephone Sam and try to get him to admit that he remembered having molested her daughter and to get him to apologize for doing so, despite the fact this alleged act had taken place some four years earlier. A detective coached Dora about how to ease into the topic in a way that wouldn't completely scare Sam away. He also suggested that if Dora failed to get Sam to admit the crime, she should then try to get him to apologize, which could serve the same legal purpose. Dora then called Sam at his office, but she didn't follow the detective's advice. Instead, in her third sentence she launched directly into the accusation:

DORA: She told me that something happened a couple of Halloweens ago with Uncle Sam. I'm going to have to take her to counseling or something if you don't help me out with this. Basically what she told me was that, you know, she was sleeping on the couch and everything and that Uncle Sam woke her by licking her private parts.

SAM: (long pause) I thought I could talk to you right now but I can't talk right now about something like that 'cause I'm not alone in the office.

DORA: Well, you can tell me that's all it was and agree that you'll call me at home tonight and just say to her that you're sorry. She said if she just heard you tell her that you were sorry, it was a mistake or something, she would feel better . . . I'm just asking for your help. . . . Is that what happened? Was there something more?

SAM: Dora, nothing. I mean no.

DORA: Nothing more than that?

SAM: Nothing at all.

DORA: I want to know if that's all that happened and if you'll tell her you're sorry, it was a mistake, and let us move on with our lives.

SAM: Dora, I understand that and I will. Yes on both accounts.

DORA: Yes that it happened and yes you will tell her you're sorry?

SAM: Yes, I'll tell her that.

DORA: Was that all that happened, the licking?

SAM: You can let the entire thing go because nothing happened.

DORA: Well then I need you as a man to tell me as a woman that you didn't have sex with my daughter, that it was just licking her private parts. I just need to hear that from you and then you have to tell her you're sorry, it was a mistake, and we can bury this thing under the rug.

SAM: The answer is yes.

DORA: That's all it was?

SAM: Yes, the answer is yes.

After Dora used the common strategy of minimizing the crime as she shifted her accusation from "if you didn't have sex" to "just licking her private parts," and then minimized this even more by asking only for Sam's apology. Sam's answer of "yes" gave the outward appearance that he had admitted to licking Shawna's private parts. But his *yes* was likely his answer to her second question that asked him if he'd be willing to call Shawna and tell her he was sorry that she was having bad dreams. The strategy of asking two questions at once often yields an answer to the second one rather than the first (the recency effect). The police intelligence analyst apparently wasn't quite sure that this ambiguous admission would stand up in court as Sam's confession to having licked Shawna. When investigations require a return visit, it's a sure sign that the first encounter didn't accomplish its goals. Therefore, the detective told Dora to call Sam again, this time while he was at home that evening. Since Sam had promised to tell Shawna that he was sorry about something still unspecified, Dora put Shawna on the phone and Sam told her:

SAM: So your mom told me that you were having bad dreams. I just wanted to say I'm sorry for that. I'm sorry for making you feel scared and I hope knowing that will stop your dreams. I just want you to know that I really feel bad about your having those dreams. I'm sorry and I hope that helps.

Apparently the detective and Dora were not satisfied with Sam's apology about appearing in Shawna's dreams, so Dora came back on the phone and directly asked for specifics:

DORA: Can you tell her why you licked her private parts?

SAM (to Shawna, who Dora had put on the line): Alright Shawna. I just want to say I'm sorry for the dreams and for you being afraid of me. I just want you to know that that will never happen again.

DORA (back on the line with Sam): But if you'll explain to her that you're not gonna do what you did to her again.

SAM: Yeah, I explained to her that she didn't need to be afraid, that it wouldn't happen and da-da-da.

DORA: Did you tell her specifically why you did what you did? She keeps having nightmares about that. She just wants to know why you did that.

SAM: Okay, put her back on again.

SAM (to Shawna): Just really specifically sweetie, I'm sorry and you don't have anything to be afraid of, you know, that night Uncle Sam was drunk and I didn't mean to scare you or make you afraid, okay?

I'm really sorry.

DORA: Can you just tell her that you're not gonna lick her private parts? That's the dream she's having. Please tell her that.

SAM (to Shawna): Shawna, you don't have to worry about me ever being there at night with you or anything like that, okay? That's never gonna happen, okay? I just want to make sure that you can sleep safe, okay? And I know this is rough and I apologize.

DORA (to Sam): I still don't understand why you did it . . . I just wish you could tell me why. Why?

SAM: I don't want to get into anything that's going to make this type of situation any worse than it is. I just want to make sure that you guys feel that there's nothing to be afraid of from me.

DORA: I'm concerned, you know. Have you licked other children's private parts?

SAM: Dora, I have never done anything like that.

DORA: Then why did you do it to Shawna? I just need to know and then I'll let this go.

SAM: I understand, but I've never ever done that.

DORA: So it's just Shawna that you did it to?

SAM: I've never done it to anybody. Dora, I am not a pedophile. I am not a child molester. I am not any of those things.

DORA: This is the only time that this happened, right?

SAM: (sighing) Yes.

DORA: All right. Well, thank you. Bye.

Finally it apparently seemed to Dora that Sam said what she wanted to hear. He appeared to agree that this is the only time "this" has happened. It is not uncommon for conversations to become ambiguous, but these two were replete with ambiguity created mostly by Dora.

AMBIGUITY PRODUCED BY THE SPEECH EVENT

Confrontation calls have a speech event structure that bears some similarity to the police interview speech event (see chapter 3). The main goal of both is to elicit an admission of guilt and perhaps even an apology. There are also several differences. First, the purpose of a police interview speech event is relatively clear to its participants, while the purpose of a confrontation call speech event is deceptively disguised from the beginning. It usually begins with a deceptively softened tone and appears to be a normal, friendly, and predictable conversation, although this misleads the suspect about the much more serious direction it will eventually take. Its purpose is not to elicit facts as much as to confirm suspected facts. Like many if not most police interview speech events, the suspects are not given an opportunity to tell their own story and the complainant permits them to respond only to requests and accusations. By definition, the act of switching the speech event makes confrontation calls deceptively ambiguous.

Dora followed some of the detective's instructions about how to create the confrontation call speech event as she first deceptively and ambiguously minimized the topic of her daughter's bad dreams about which her uncle might be able to provide enough comfort to make those dreams end. For a minute or so, Sam's language gave evidence that Dora's request for his help did not surprise him, but when he expressed his understanding that Dora was actually accusing him of molesting her daughter in real life, his responses were defensive with strong denials that he had anything to do with molestation.

AMBIGUITY PRODUCED BY SCHEMAS

Dora ambiguously and deceptively put forth her schema that their conversation was about her daughter's dreams, which Sam could understand as being his schema that the conversation was about Shawna's dreams even after it became apparent to him that Dora's schema was that he had actually molested Shawna and that his molestation caused those bad dreams. Consistent with his schema that they were talking about Shawna's bad dreams, he tried to comfort Shawna about those bad dreams but not about Dora's schema that his real life actions allegedly had caused them. Even his fanciful ambiguous addition that he was drunk in her dreams was consistent with his schema of comforting Shawna about her bad dreams. His schema worked against him in the mind of the prosecutor, whose schema caused him to interpret it as evidence that Sam was drunk when he molested the girl. As we've seen in other cases in this book, interpretations can be based either on the listener's predisposition or on the language used in context. Sam's contextual schema here concerned Shawna's bad dreams but not any actual sexual involvement with her.

AMBIGUITY PRODUCED BY AGENDAS

Dora's only agenda was to get Sam to admit that he molested her daughter. We can know this because here could be no other reason for her to make those confrontation calls. When Dora made clear that her agenda was to accuse Sam of the molestation, his consistent response agenda used the speech act of denying the accusations. Disguising the agenda is a deliberate strategy used frequently in confrontation calls and, by definition, disguise is a form of deception. Since targets are unaware that their conversation is being recorded, they are equally unaware of their need to know what the disguised topic is, to try to be constantly on guard to fully understand the caller's intent, and to be careful to clarify any ambiguities that may occur. The government defends this ambiguous deception because it captures criminals. However effective it might be in that effort, it can only be considered as ambiguous deception. Targets are also deceived by being unaware that the conversation is being recorded for the benefit of a future audience of jurors rather than for the persons on the phone with them.

Dora's language indicates that her agenda was to wear down her target's ability to keep resisting. After telling Dora eighteen times that he did not lick Shawna's private parts and that he never did this to anyone else, by the end of the second call he was apparently frustrated at being asked the same question over and over again. Dora had finally worn down his resistance. After taking a meaningfully significant deep sigh, which the government did not include in its transcript, he appeared to agree with Dora that it happened one time when he was drunk. Even though this indefinite pronoun had an ambiguous reference (was it the dream that happened one time or the licking that happened one time?), his response became the prosecution's ambiguous smoking gun evidence. This technique bears a strong similarity to the much-criticized police interrogation approach that wears suspects down to the point that they will admit anything simply to end the interview. The probative value of such ambiguous admissions is highly questionable (Leo 2008). Unless admissions and confessions include exactly what the suspect is admitting and confessing, they cannot be considered admissions and confessions.

AMBIGUITY PRODUCED BY SPEECH ACTS

In her first call, Dora used a mitigated accusation, ambiguously asking Sam if she could call him tonight at home "and just say to her [Shawna] that you're sorry, it was a mistake or something. She would feel better . . . I'm just asking for your help." She later mitigated the accusation again saying, "You as a man tell me as a woman that you didn't have sex with my daughter, that it was just licking her private parts." Here Dora deceivingly suggested that if Sam would confess to a somewhat mitigated charge of licking Shawna one time, it would heal a potential family rift. Innocent targets sometimes admit to a mitigated lesser charge in order to return normalcy to their family life. This deceptive ambiguity failed because Sam did not bite.

When Dora tried to elicit the speech act of an apology, Sam said he was sorry. But what he said he was sorry about was not an apology for what Dora accused him of doing. Dora presented the scenario that her daughter was having bad dreams and strongly suspected that they were caused by an incident four years earlier. It is natural that Sam would then focus on the topic of Shawna's dreams as the topic he was asked to address. He told Shawna that he was sorry that she was having those dreams and that she should be sure that they would not come back. This was far from satisfying the speech act of an apology that he had molested Shawna. In fact, it was not a felicitous apology, because Sam had no right to apologize for what Shawna allegedly dreamed about. The conditions for a felicitous apology are that the speaker identifies the past event, identifies who was offended, takes ownership of the past offensive act, describes actions to be taken to repair the offense, and can promise not to continue such offensive acts in the future.

Sam certainly had a right to apologize for any harm he may have actually caused Shawna in real life, but that's not what he did here. He was sorry about and regretted her bad dreams. Regrets are very different from apologies (Battistella 2014: 61–62). The speech act of regretting refers to the speaker's attitudes toward an action and reports things without assuming agency for them. We can regret that it rained at the outdoor wedding but unless we are some kind of God, we have no right to apologize for it happening. The effect of Sam being sorry about Shawna's dreams provided the prosecutor with an inaccurate interpretation that he took as an accurate apology for the alleged abuse. For the prosecutor to use it in this way deceived the jury, whether intentionally or from ignorance about how the language of a felicitous apology works. Deceptive appearances can cause juries to overlook the factual evidence.

AMBIGUITY PRODUCED BY CONVERSATIONAL STRATEGIES

The major conversational strategy used by Dora was the deceptive ambiguity she created by representing her daughter's dreams as physical reality. Sam eventually caught on to Dora's ambiguity, however, and denied molesting the girl. In addition, Dora used the common conversational strategy of some salespersons who ignore their customers' "no" and go right on as though they never heard it. She also wore Sam down by repeating her accusations eighteen times until Sam finally gave a long sigh and seemingly complied in an effort to end a call that he couldn't know was for the benefit of an audience that was the police and jury rather than for Dora.

AMBIGUITY PRODUCED BY LEXICON AND GRAMMAR

As Sam talked with Shawna, he made it very clear that he was sorry that he appeared in her dreams, but Dora used the deictic references, *this* and *it,* ambiguously without clear noun references. Dora was particularly ambiguous with her follow-up question, "This is the only time this happened, right?" Sam sighed and answered "yes." It apparently was hard for Sam to imagine how he could guarantee that *this* molestation would ever happen again in Shawna's dreams. Nevertheless, the prosecution interpreted Dora's ambiguous deictic references of *this* and *it* as evidence that Sam had admitted to sexually molesting Shawna. Dora's deictic reference, *that,* was also ambiguous. She first asked Sam what had happened. He answered, "Nothing, I mean no." Dora apparently was not satisfied with this response and questioned, "Nothing more than that?" This deceptively created an ambiguity that was not present in Sam's clear answer.

Dora followed with a compound question, first asking if *it* was just licking her daughter's private parts and in that same turn of talk asked Sam to tell Shawna that he's sorry. Sam answered "yes," agreeing to the second and most recent proposition, which Dora misinterpreted as his answer to first proposition of licking her daughter's private parts. His "yes" response was further complicated by the fact that he had already told Dora that he was sorry that he had somehow appeared in her daughter's dream, but at no point did he say that he was sorry for actually committing the molestation that Shawna had dreamed about.

Deceptive ambiguity also can be created by the use of compound questions. Dora asked several of these but Sam managed to handle them appropriately until she asked, "Yes that happened and yes you will tell her you're sorry?" Sam's answer, "yes, I'll tell her that," was equally ambiguous because two questions asked at the same time commonly receive an answer to the most recent one. The *that* used by both Dora and Sam had an ambiguous reference.

Dora was deceptively ambiguous because the context of her topic was about Shawna's bad dream, making it easy for Sam to agree that Shawna had bad dreams. But his "yes" was to Dora's most recent question, that he'd tell Shawna that he's sorry. We can be sure of this because he next continued to tell Dora "nothing happened," "I've never done anything like that," and "I've never done that." Compound questions can be very ambiguous, and sometimes deceptively so.

A Complainant Uses Deceptive Ambiguity with Her Boss

The workplace is a frequent context for sexual offense charges. The power of some bosses enables them to take advantage of their underlings and make various kinds of romantic or sexual advances to the less powerful people who work under them. When this happens, one thing that the powerless employee can do is to accept those advances for various reasons and use them to improve a desired relationship with the boss. Alternatively, the employee can make it very clear from the start that such advances are not wanted. Problems arise, however, when a female employee lets a flirtatious relationship exist for a while, but then changes her mind about it. In the 1990s a 73-year-old, hard-of-hearing sheriff in a small Arkansas town found himself in the latter situation (all names and places are changed).

A secretary in his office made a sexual assault complaint to the local district attorney against her boss. As a result the state police installed video and audio equipment in the sheriff's office area to gather evidence of his behavior toward the woman. Both the video and audio equipment failed, but the secretary managed to record ten minutes of their conversation with a microcassette tape-recorder hidden in her purse. It was a voice-activated machine that cut out when no conversation could be heard and even though it periodically malfunctioned, the police deemed the recording to be adequate for charging the sheriff with sexual misconduct.

This taped conversation revealed that they previously had engaged in some mild hanky-panky in the office that he may have considered as her invitation to move their relationship up to the next level. He had no history of previous sexual misconduct and was not considered lecherous by anyone the police interviewed.

The entire evidence consisted of that tape-recorded conversation in the hallway of the sheriff's office. The secretary purportedly had recently told an office mate about the sheriff's apparent advances, which topic she used to introduce their talk:

> WOMAN: Uh, I want to ask you about something confidential. . . . I kinda decided I want to get this out in the open.
>
> SHERIFF: Huh?
>
> WOMAN: I want to get this out in the open just in case she talks to you.
>
> SHERIFF: Uh-huh.
>
> WOMAN [lowering her voice]: Uh, because, you know, I had told her, you know, what you did that day, you know, you had pulled your penis out and all that stuff, talk about that.
>
> SHERIFF: Huh?
>
> WOMAN: I said I hated talking about that.
>
> SHERIFF: Uh-huh.

After using the excuse that she had told another woman in the office about his behavior, she lowered her volume when she said, "you had pulled out your penis" as part of her ongoing topic of telling her co-worker. This might be considered damaging evidence of the sheriff's sexual misconduct if he admitted that he did this. His response of "huh?" however, is a clue that his hearing difficulty likely didn't allow him to hear these softly uttered words, strongly suggesting that his "huh?" was a request for her to repeat what she just said. If he actually had heard it, his reaction was odd, because what people do not say is often as important as what they do say. Here the sheriff did not say something like, "Oh my God, you shouldn't have told her that." If he had said this, it would have worked against his case, but that's not what he said.

Even though the secretary may have understood the sheriff's "huh?" was an indication that he didn't hear what she said, she chose not to repeat that damaging clause. Instead, she referenced only the part about talking to a fellow officemate, saying that she hated talking about "that." This deictic marker appeared to be clear to the prosecutor, who interpreted it as a reference to the sheriff's pulling out his penis. This understanding not only overlooked the sheriff's request to repeat what the secretary had just said but also the well-known fact of his relative deafness. Apparently the sheriff's poor hearing ability didn't enable him to hear these mumbled words, but instead of responding to his request for repetition, the woman used the unclear deictic reference *that*, and then returned immediately to her ongoing topic of what she told her colleague:

WOMAN: And, uh, and then, you know, I had told her, remember when I had a pain in my side?
SHERIFF: Uh-huh.

Again, what targets don't say is often as important as what they say. In this case, it is significant that the sheriff did not respond to her statement by saying something like, "Why did you tell her about that? His "uh-huh" response showed that he recalled the incident but he gave no indication that he was embarrassed or felt guilty about it. The woman then continued:

WOMAN: And then you wanted to feel it and then you went down **in** my pants and you were feeling (inaudible), uh, you know, I mean—

The above was the prosecution's transcript of this conversation. But upon careful listening to the tape, the word *in,* could not be heard in the transcript's "down in my pants." It is unclear whether the transcriber added the word *in* by mistake or whether the prosecution added it based on a predisposition of the sheriff's guilt. But whatever the reason, the word, *in,* was simply not there. Nor did the sheriff give any evidence of having heard it as he continued talking about the ongoing topic concerning the conversation between the secretary and her co-worker:

SHERIFF: So what did she have to say?
WOMAN: Well, I just told her I wanted somebody to talk to. I didn't want to put her through anything.
SHERIFF: Uh-huh.
WOMAN: And, uh, I mean, hopefully she can keep it hush-hush.
SHERIFF: Uh.

In the secretary's ongoing topic of what she told her fellow employee, her words, "keep it hush-hush" appeared to convey one meaning to the sheriff and a very different meaning to the prosecution. To the sheriff this deictic *it* could have referred to their still unclearly described previous dalliance in the office. To the prosecutor it was the admission that defined the sheriff's sexual offense "going down in" the woman's pants. Complicating matters further, it was never clarified whether the word, *pants,* referred to underpants or to lady's slacks. Despite these ambiguous contrasting meanings, the secretary continued with her ongoing topic about telling her colleague about their past behavior:

WOMAN: So I just wanted you to know.
SHERIFF: Okay. It will not happen anymore.

The sheriff's ambiguous "it" here is significant, because based on the information that he appeared to be able to glean from this conversation, his use of *it* referred to the ongoing and only topic of their conversation—the secretary's report that she had told her colleague something about their past dalliances together in the office. To the prosecutor, this *it* referred to the sheriff's "going down in her pants," even though the tape-recorded evidence strongly suggested that the sheriff couldn't hear the word, *in,* there because it was not audible on the tape. As she continued, the secretary then replaced her ambiguous *it* with an equally ambiguous deictic reference, *that*:

WOMAN: Okay, I, I thank you for that because, I mean, you know, because that scared me.
SHERIFF: There's not gonna be, you know, you know we'd been carrying on and carrying on and I took it the wrong way I think.

Here the secretary's first *that* clearly referred to his promise that *it* will not happen again and her second *that* referred to his alleged sexual misconduct, which both she and the prosecutor interpreted as the sheriff running his hand down in her pants.

The sheriff finally identified what he considered to be their past behavior in the office as "carrying on and carrying on." It is not clear exactly what these words referred to, but at least the sheriff defined the ambiguous *it* in his own terms. The secretary again picked up on her ambiguous pronoun, *it,* and returned once more to the initial topic of their conversation—what she told her officemate and once again used the pronoun, *it*, ambiguously:

WOMAN: Well see, I didn't, that's why I didn't tell the girls over there because I didn't want it to get back to you, you know, I mean, I knew that they would tell you and, but I had to have somebody to talk to and—
SHERIFF: Okay, everything's fine as long as you don't want to testify. That's just fine because it will never happen again, I assure you.

WOMAN: Because I, you know, that's fine. Scared about it.
SHERIFF: Because I think the world of you and I guarantee it will not happen.

Here they both continued to use the pronoun, *it,* with apparently different unspecified noun references. But the sheriff's troublesome words, "as long as you don't want to testify," suggested to the prosecution that his behavior had been more than simply "carrying on and carrying on." There is no way to get into the minds of people to determine what they are thinking, but up to this point the overall context suggests that the sheriff, a law officer who surely knew what sexual misconduct means, did not believe that whatever he and the secretary had done together in the office (by his definition "carrying on and carrying on") had risen to the level of criminal behavior. As a law officer he had possibly used the word *testify* to mean telling the truth on the witness stand. It is at least possible that he now used *testify* in a non-courtroom context to mean going public with the information about their "carrying on" together.

At this point the secretary changed the topic by discussing a letter that the sheriff had just received.

WOMAN: Okay, because I was, you know, scared with, you know, last night, you know, after we talked about it. I didn't even know that letter came to you and, and it scared me so bad last night that I said, oh gosh, I said, you know, I just didn't want this to get back.

This reference to "that letter" was eventually revealed to be an anonymous message that the sheriff had just received. It was hand printed in block letters, claiming that "some people" including one of the sheriff's captains, "were after him" for personal and political reasons. After attempts to identify the author failed, the letter was not used at trial. The secretary vaguely referred to it and apparently tried to use it as part of her fear of the possible discovery about their "carrying on." Since the sheriff shrugged off the letter, the secretary returned to her topic of others who might find out about whatever office dalliance they had together, asking the sheriff who else might know about it:

WOMAN: Okay. Well, I mean does Nancy know or?
SHERIFF: Huh?
WOMAN: Does Janice know?
SHERIFF: No, and I'm not going to tell her anything ... Yeah, I won't tell anything to her. I'm not going to say anything to nobody, to tell you the truth.
WOMAN: I mean, good. You didn't tell Barbara?
SHERIFF: Oh, hell no.
WOMAN: Good. Okay.
SHERIFF: I didn't tell a damn soul.

WOMAN: Oh, good.

SHERIFF: Okay, dear.

WOMAN: I just didn't want anybody just badgering me and—

SHERIFF: Nobody's going to bother you, and me either. And the main thing is I don't want it to get out and you don't either. It would be bad for both of us as far as that goes.

WOMAN: Yeah, I know. That's what I say.

SHERIFF: Look, I appreciate it.

WOMAN: Well, you're welcome.

SHERIFF: Thank you dear.

WOMAN: Thank you. Thank you for promising me not to do it again (laughs) but I should have talked to you about this.

SHERIFF: Okay.

WOMAN: Thanks.

After this last round of ambiguous references to *it* and *anything*, the meeting ended, but the secretary let her microcassette tape keep running as she met with the detective in a nearby room. When undercover operators allow their tape-recorders to keep running, the results sometimes can be useful to the defense, because the discussion often restates what the participants think was said and sometimes they even evaluate what they heard:

WOMAN: (inaudible) I know, I mean, you know, I really didn't have a lot to say, you know, but you've already recorded (laughs). Oh I know, I was sitting there going—

UNIDENTIFIED MALE AGENT: Couldn't figure it out (laughs). Couldn't figure out what you (laughs)

WOMAN: No he couldn't. He couldn't figure out what I wanted to talk to him about but, 'cause I wind up talking to (inaudible; recorder deactivated).

If the secretary and the monitoring detective thought it humorous that the sheriff couldn't figure it out what she wanted to talk to him about, it wouldn't be surprising for the jury to feel the same way. But to make sure, the defense attorney stressed the linguistic features discussed previously and at trial the sheriff was acquitted.

Although the many ambiguities in this conversation were noted earlier, it can be useful to identify them here in the context of the Inverted Pyramid.

AMBIGUITY PRODUCED BY THE SPEECH EVENT

Undercover complainants, whose targets tend to learn quickly that they are being accused of something, often go straight to the accusation and are somewhat less deceptive to their targets about the perceived speech event than are the targets of undercover agents and cooperating witnesses. In the latter investigations the targets sometimes never realize what's actually going on. Confrontation speech events initially come as surprises to the targets when the complainants tend to be clear and unambiguous about their accusations.

The secretary first introduced this speech event as a report of new information in which she admitted that she had shared certain confidential information with a female work colleague. The sheriff indicated that he understood that she had done this but he gave no indication that he considered this new information to be a serious problem. They remained in this speech event until the secretary deceptively tried to convert the reported information speech event into an accusation speech event, reporting that the sheriff pulled out his penis, which she said so softly that the sheriff couldn't hear it, and next that he put his hand down in her pants (which contained no *in*), allowing him to understand this as his benign effort to help diagnose the location of the pain in her leg. Even though both of these reports were accusational speech events, she deceptively let the sheriff continue to understand that they were still in the less serious speech event of her reporting information to her office mate about their past office dalliances that she no longer wished to continue. Unclear speech events an produced unclear, ambiguous, and deceptive results.

AMBIGUITY PRODUCED BY SCHEMAS

The schemas of the sheriff and his secretary grew naturally out of their perceptions of the speech events they each thought they were in and the topics they each thought they were discussing. The secretary first reported ambiguously that she told her officemate about "what happened." This triggered the sheriff's schema to focus on what she told her friend. His schema from that point on was that the event in question was that they had been in his words, "carrying on and carrying on," while her schema was entirely about the alleged predatory sexual events. With these different deceptively ambiguous perceptions of the speech event, the schemas of both the sheriff and the secretary continued to be very different trains passing in the night without seeing each other.

AMBIGUITY PRODUCED BY AGENDAS

Most confrontation meetings and calls do not permit the targets to express their own agendas, for the conversation is dominated by complainants who force their own agendas on their targets. The targets' task is to respond to the complainants' questions that typically require short answers to yes/no or wh- questions. Complainants' agendas do not produce useful evidence, however, unless their questions and observations are represented clearly and unambiguously.

In this case the employee introduced all the topics as she confronted the sheriff about his alleged sexual offense. The sheriff, who had hearing problems, provided responses only to what he was apparently able to hear and understand. During the complainant's taped conversation with the monitoring law enforcement officer after the sheriff had exited the conversation, she admitted that she had not made her agenda clear to the sheriff. As in most confrontation meetings and calls, the targets' agendas are seldom clearly articulated. If the sheriff had an agenda at all, his responses indicated that he was unaware that he had committed any offense other than their previous "carrying on and carrying on," an expression he didn't define, possibly because it would not be necessary to specify the details of it to the person with whom it had happened. Ambiguity such as this is common between conversational partners who share the same knowledge and therefore don't need to present it fully. In confrontation calls and meetings, however, such assumed shared knowledge can benefit the prosecution because it allows them to infer something bad, even if it was actually benign.

AMBIGUITY PRODUCED BY SPEECH ACTS

The secretary who worked in the same office with the sheriff must have known that he was hard of hearing when she lowered her voice and softly reported, "You pulled your penis out." The sheriff's "huh?" response to this was his speech act of requesting repetition of what she said. But she did not repeat. Instead, she referred to what she had just said as "that," which does not qualify as either a repetition or a clarification. Her response violated the standard and expected speech act that had requested her to repeat or clarify her previous statement. Her subsequent reference, *that,* gave the deceptive impression that the sheriff accepted and agreed with her unrepeated "you pulled your penis out" as though he had heard what she had said. The complainant's only goal in this conversation was to get the sheriff to admit that he had pulled out his penis and ran his hand in her pants. Since his "huh?" response conveyed his inability to hear what she said, he obviously couldn't use the speech act of denying or even apologizing for something he didn't hear. Evidence of this is that he then said nothing about the accusation created by her reference to his penis and returned immediately to the initial (and for him continuing) topic of her conversation with a fellow worker and then asked her, "So what did she have to say?" The sheriff then promised, "It will not happen again," in which his *it* was ambiguous. Since the sheriff clearly used the speech act of promising something, the legal issue became what he promised. The key to what the sheriff's *it* promised is found in his follow-up response, "There's not gonna be, you know, we'd been carrying on and carrying on and I took it the wrong way I think." His promise is determined contextually as a promise to discontinue their past office flirtations or dalliances and not, as the prosecution argued, to never again pull out his penis or put his hand in her pants. Later in the conversation the secretary used the speech act of thanking him for "promising not to do it again," once again not specifying the reference to her ambiguous *it.*

The prosecutor also misinterpreted the sheriff's speech act of apologizing for "carrying on and carrying on" with his employee in the past as the speech act of apologizing for putting his hand *in* her pants, even though the government's own taped evidence demonstrated that he ran his hand "down" her pants leg in an effort to be diagnostically helpful to her after she had complained about a sharp pain in her leg.

Even stronger evidence that the secretary had been deceptively ambiguous is her speech act of admitting being ambiguous found in the brief conversation between the secretary and her monitoring agent after the sheriff had left the area. Prosecutors usually don't disclose transcripts of portions of the conversation that continue after the target leaves. They are required, however, to turn over to the defense all of the tape-recordings used as evidence. Occasionally the defense finds a few gems in what was said in those recordings. On this tape the secretary and her monitoring detective both admitted that she had been deceptively ambiguous as they laughed about the fact that the sheriff couldn't figure out what the secretary was talking about.

AMBIGUITY PRODUCED BY CONVERSATIONAL STRATEGIES

In addition to the many other deceptive ambiguities noted previously, the complainant used several deceptively ambiguous conversational strategies to support her claim of sexual misconduct. One obvious strategy was to block the sheriff from answering her accusations. She did this by not answering his request for clarification, by using the deceptively ambiguous pronoun *it* and the ambiguous deictic reference *that,* and by distorting information ("ran your hand down in my pants") that the sheriff would need to understand in order to provide an exculpatory response. Since she knew the sheriff, she likely knew he might not be able to hear what she said to him when she lowered her voice at the crucial moments. This blocked his ability to respond. She used the conversational strategy of going right on, however, as though the sheriff had heard and understood what she said, leaving on the record what appeared to the prosecutor to be evidence of the sheriff's sexual misconduct.

AMBIGUITY PRODUCED BY LEXICON AND GRAMMAR

The complainant's confrontation with Sheriff Preston produced no lexical ambiguity but plenty of ambiguity stemming from the complainant's grammatical references to *it* and *this*, as well as the transcript's inaccurate representation of going "down *in* her pants" as opposed to the taped evidence that he said "down her pants." The sheriff's hearing problems were not the cause of this transcription error. In this case he didn't hear the word, *in,* here simply because the tape demonstrated that it wasn't there. He didn't deny that he touched her leg when she complained about the pain, but his response gave no evidence that he recognized this event was a predatory sexual act.

In an attempt at fairness, this complainant was less sophisticated about how to use language unambiguously than a powerful policeman, prosecutor, or experienced undercover agent might be. Therefore, she might have been less likely to be aware of the ambiguities she created by her uses of *it* and *that* in her conversation. There is no excuse, however, for the government's intelligence analyst to overlook the possibility that these references were ambiguous. Unless this prosecutor was linguistically unsophisticated, his schema of guilt apparently overwhelmed his sense of fairness and accuracy as he performed his intelligence analysis of this conversation. As a result, he interpreted these ambiguities to suit his own prosecutorial schema and purpose.

There is no ambiguity when the language is clear and accurate, but when the actual spoken words are interpreted inaccurately, the result creates ambiguity that can only be considered deceptive. One question is whether the deceptive ambiguity in this case was intentional. Even though in our legal system it is necessary for the lawyers to advocate for one position or the other, both sides can create the possibility that they are using ambiguity to their own advantage in order to oppose a competing interpretation. The advocate's schemas may lead them to take their respective positions, but accurate transcripts and linguistic analyses trump the lawyer's advocacy, no matter which side they represent.

8

Deceptive Ambiguity in Language Elements of the Inverted Pyramid

Chapters 3 to 7 described fifteen investigations in which police, prosecutors, undercover agents, cooperating witnesses, and complainants used deceptive ambiguity in their interactions with suspects, defendants, and targets. In contrast, this chapter focuses on the linguistic elements of the Inverted Pyramid in which uses of deceptive ambiguity were found rather than on the fifteen investigations themselves. These elements, the speech events, schemas, agendas, speech acts, conversational strategies, and lexicon and grammar, together provide individual snapshots of the interactive communications in which the deceptive ambiguity took place. It should be mentioned that deceptive ambiguity is also created by the socio-cultural differences that are discussed separately in Appendix A.

Assembling the snapshots together can reveal important aspects of the investigations that might otherwise go unnoticed, particularly on matters of predisposition and intentionality of the participants as well as on the voluntariness of the target's language when the interactions were located in a police station, a courtroom, or at undercover sites. This brief summary demonstrates how during these different types of interactions with targets the government representatives produced varying amounts of deceptive ambiguity, some more than others.

Deceptive Ambiguity in Speech Events

The following reprises the importance of identifying the speech events found in investigations carried out by both transparent and camouflaged representatives of the legal institution. As noted throughout this book, the speech event is central to understanding what is said during the ensuing interactions. For this reason, it is the logical first element of language to examine. Representatives of the legal institution are deceptively ambiguous when they encourage their suspects, witnesses, and targets to believe that the speech event they are in is different from the announced or expected speech event. It can be equally deceptive when the government agents switch the speech event during the interaction. As the cases described in this book demonstrate, more deceptive ambiguity is found when the power of the institution is hidden than when that power is transparent.

DECEPTIVE AMBIGUITY CREATED BY SWITCHING SPEECH EVENTS DURING TRANSPARENT POLICE INTERVIEWS

The physical setting of the police station makes the institutional power of police interviewers appear to be more transparent and unambiguous than in undercover operations. On the surface at least, it should be clear to those being questioned that they are in a police interview speech event and respond accordingly. In such interviews the recognized task of the police is to gather information up to the point that they believe their suspects appear to be guilty, at which point the interview event changes from one of information gathering to that of an interrogation speech event that can contain accusations that attempt to elicit confessions. Police interviewers (and prosecutors as well) create deceptive ambiguity when they begin by identifying their interactions as information-gathering speech events in which they lead their suspects and witnesses to believe they are not the subjects of this speech event, but then switch the speech event into an interrogation speech event in which the subjects are the real targets. When this happens, the interviewees find themselves in the awkward and uncomfortable position of needing to quickly adjust their schemas as well as their language. Because the communication playing field is no longer level, such adjustments require a considerable amount of linguistic and social skills that many subjects simply do not possess and others find difficult to call upon. Police and prosecutors may consider switching the speech event a standard and acceptable procedure, but it also creates ambiguity about the nature of the event about which the police can only benefit.

Because the police provided no tape-recording of their interview with Kevin Rogers, there is no way to know exactly how this speech event was defined or how it took place. Rogers's written confession, however, suggests that from the start it was an accusatorial interrogation speech event (we are here to accuse you) rather than an information-gathering speech event (we are here to find out what happened). In contrast with the interview of Rogers, the police tape-recorded the first part of their interaction with Michael Carter, demonstrating that this also was an entirely interrogation speech event rather than an information-gathering speech event.

Although the record is far from clear, Rogers and Carter apparently were not deceived about the speech event they were in, because the evidence shows that however deceptive the police may have been, they were unambiguously accusatorial throughout. In contrast, in his initial interview Jokic was deceptively led to believe that he was a friendly witness helping law enforcement discover facts about criminals in the Srebrenica massacre, an information-gathering speech event. Early during their second interview, however, the information interview abruptly changed to an accusatorial interrogation. If the officers had discovered Jokic's culpability during their information-gathering interview, it may have been appropriate for them to have then switched to an interrogation. As the language evidence demonstrated, however, even after the speech event was switched Jokic did not provide evidence of his guilt although the interviewers apparently thought he did.

DECEPTIVE AMBIGUITY CREATED BY SWITCHING SPEECH EVENTS DURING TRANSPARENT COURTROOM QUESTIONING

Like law enforcement officers, prosecutors also convey their transparent institutional power of complete control when they question witnesses and defendants. The physical courtroom itself strongly conveys this power and the prosecutors' total control of the interactions in that courtroom underscore it. But prosecutors can be equally capable of ambiguously and deceptively misrepresenting the announced speech event as they examine their witnesses, as was illustrated in their courtroom questioning of Steven Suyat, Larry Gentry, and Father Joseph Sica.

Suyat was called as the government's own friendly witness in an information-gathering speech event relating to charges being brought against his fellow union representatives. Similarly, the police told Gentry that they were not after him and that this was only an information-gathering speech event concerning a murder committed by someone else. Father Sica was told he was in an information-gathering speech event concerning what he could tell them about a known criminal that he had met twenty years earlier at his ordination ceremony.

During these information-gathering courtroom speech events the prosecutors encouraged the interviewees to understand that they were not the subjects of their investigations and that they were not participating in the speech event of an accusation. Nevertheless, these three witnesses were accused and indicted, indicating that the prosecutors were doing considerably more than gathering facts relating to the cases of other different suspects. Like changing rules halfway through a game, changing the speech event in progress can be deceptively ambiguous.

DECEPTIVE AMBIGUITY CREATED BY MISREPRESENTING THE SPEECH EVENT DURING CAMOUFLAGED INTERACTIONS WITH UNDERCOVER AGENTS

In all undercover operations, government agents deceptively disguise their institutional power. By the government's own admission, this camouflage is intended to create speech events that are ambiguous and deceptive. From the start, undercover agents intentionally try to convert benign speech events, such as business transaction speech events, into discussions of bribery, narcotics sales, or tax fraud.

The government's ambiguously deceptive misrepresentation of the speech event was clearly intentional in the undercover investigation of Senator Harrison Williams, who was told that he was going to participate in a business progress speech event while John DeLorean and Vernon Sligh were led to believe that they were participating in business assistance speech events. The FBI agent posing as a banker deceptively led DeLorean to understand that the product of his many meetings would be loans or investors in his financially troubled company. The IRS agent initially gave Sligh no reason to think that he was in any speech event other than a business consultation speech event of requesting and obtaining help to file his taxes.

DECEPTIVE AMBIGUITY CREATED BY MISREPRESENTING THE SPEECH EVENT DURING CAMOUFLAGED INTERACTIONS WITH COOPERATING WITNESSES

During investigations in which cooperating witnesses are used as stand-ins for undercover agents they also camouflage their derived institutional power as they introduce their speech events with the same intentionally ambiguous deception used by government agents. Cullen Davis's language indicated that he believed that he was in a report-of-progress speech event in which his employee would tell him where things stood in his investigation of his wife's romantic liaison with a judge. The cooperating witness tried to create the ambiguous deception that their speech event was a discussion about killing people, which he accomplished by deceptively uttering the critical part of their conversation outside Davis's hearing range.

Yochanan Cohen's language consistently indicated that he thought he was in a business sales speech event and he maintained this perception even after the cooperating witness made it clear that his own version of the speech event was bribery.

Marwan El-Hindi's language made it clear that he understood that he was in the business speech event of trying to find resources in Toledo to build a school for Islamic children, while the cooperating witness consistently used deceptive ambiguity to try to make that speech event appear to be one of planning to set up a terrorist cell.

DECEPTIVE AMBIGUITY CREATED BY MISREPRESENTING THE SPEECH EVENT DURING CAMOUFLAGED INTERACTIONS WITH COMPLAINANTS

Perhaps because they are not skilled in the crimes they are trying to catch, complainants tend to represent their speech events less ambiguously than do government agents and cooperating witnesses. Their uses of deception, however, are similar in other ways. The complainant in the investigation of John Poli and John McNown was exceptionally skilled in at least one aspect of deceptive ambiguity. The two men had planned and tried to produce a retraction speech event concerning their earlier bribery request to the madam, but she ignored their retraction speech event and tried to convert it into a bribery speech event by providing what the government considered a bribe even after the two men had verbally rejected it. The ultimate act of deception, however, occurred when the madam left a roll of cash on her chair for the men to pick up, which physically (rather than verbally) converted this into what the government believed to be a bribery speech event. At trial the deceptive ambiguity of the madam's switched speech event became one of the defense lawyer's central issues.

There was somewhat less deceptive ambiguity of the accusation speech event in which Dora claimed that Sam had sexually abused her daughter. The major ambiguity came when the government deceptively misrepresented Sam's apology for appearing in the daughter's dream as his apology for committing the sexual act itself.

Sheriff Preston's secretary produced a very deceptively ambiguous accusation speech event during which the sheriff admitted that in the past he had been "carrying on and carrying on" with her, although he didn't admit to her more specific accusation of sexual misconduct, largely because the secretary never made this unambiguously clear to him. Evidence of the complainant's deceptive ambiguity in taking advantage of the sheriff's hearing difficulty was verified by her conversation with the agent after her meeting with the sheriff had ended.

Deceptive Ambiguity in Schemas

As noted throughout this book, participants reveal their schemas through the language that reflects their attitudes, beliefs, and assumptions. Schemas grow naturally out of the speech events that the participants are led to believe they were in. Schemas relate directly to the cornerstones of criminal investigations: motive, means, and method. Analysis of the schemas of the participants also can play an important role in determining their predisposition and willingness to commit a crime. But when representatives of the law use ambiguity in their exchanges, the evidence of suspects' predisposition easily can be misperceived. The following reprises the importance of pointing out the schemas found in investigations carried out by both transparent and camouflaged representatives of the legal institution.

DECEPTIVE AMBIGUITY OF SCHEMAS CREATED BY POLICE DURING TRANSPARENT INTERVIEWS

Conventionally the police hold the schema that their suspects are predisposed to commit the crime, for otherwise there would be no purpose for their interviews with them. With little else to go on, the police ambiguously and deceptively represented Kevin Rogers's schema in killing his neighbor lady as his predisposition to retrieve his pellet gun that she had confiscated at some earlier time. Even based on the meager language evidence found in that confession statement, however, there was no evidence that he was so predisposed because the police found Rogers's pellet gun exactly where the victim and left it in a place clearly visible for the killer to have seen.

The police also held the schema of Michael Carter's guilt when they interviewed him as the last of the four suspects they questioned. By that time the other boys had pinned the blame on him and the police apparently accepted their account that Carter had shot the policemen out of his fear of being shot himself. During the recorded part of the police interview, Carter admitted his predisposition to join with the other boys to rob some houses, but he strongly denied that he shot the policeman or held any schema or predisposition to do so.

In contrast with the police interviewers' consistent schemas of guilt during their interviews with Rogers and Carter, Dragan Jokic's interviewers changed their purported schema from information gathering to that of accusation, which introduced ambiguity for Jokic as he suddenly found himself in a surprisingly different and uncomfortable situation. During their first interview with him, the questioners encouraged him to embrace their purported schema that he was being questioned only so that the authorities could learn further information about details of the massacre at Srebrenica. He began the second interview with that same schema but had to change it quickly when he realized that it had morphed into an accusation in which the questioners claimed that Jokic was predisposed to cover up his own involvement in the massacre and that he was one of the guilty participants. Despite his surprise at the need to suddenly abandon his schema about the interview event, Jokic's language indicated that he consistently managed to maintain his schema as an outsider to the massacre.

DECEPTIVE AMBIGUITY OF SCHEMAS CREATED BY PROSECUTORS DURING TRANSPARENT COURTROOM INTERVIEWS

The prosecutors held schemas of Steven Suyat's, Larry Gentry's, and Father Joseph Sica's guilt, apparently believing that these defendants were predisposed to protect other people from being indicted and charged with crimes. The defendants' language indicated that their schemas were that their role in these speech events was to help the police gather information about the real suspects rather than the role of protecting their own interests.

When prosecutors base their charges on the evidence gathered by police interviewers, they commonly agree with and adopt the police interviewers' schema of the guilt of their subjects. But prosecutors also serve as information analysts whose task is to evaluate the information gathered by the police. As such, their responsibility is to discover any ambiguity in that evidence and to determine whether it was deceptive. The prosecutors of Suyat, Gentry, and Sica did not take into account the defendants' language indicating their consistent schemas that lacked evidence of any predisposition to commit crimes for which they were accused.

Even though Suyat failed to catch on to the direction the prosecutor was leading him, he remained constant in his schema of helping law enforcement. Since he didn't seem to understand that he was being accused, he didn't exhibit an accused person's tendency to try to defend himself against the detective's charges. This lack of defense, however, only assisted the prosecutor's claim that Suyat was predisposed to commit the crime of perjuring himself to protect his colleagues.

After a murder took place, Gentry first made his schema of innocence clear by voluntarily meeting with the police to report that he suspected some things about the murder but didn't know for sure how it was carried out or who did it. When he appeared at the search warrant hearing, he continued in his schema that he would be helping the police capture the killer, now even more so because of his recent visit from an undercover cooperating witness who had caused him to fear for his own life. During the critical hearing before the judge, Gentry gave no evidence of understanding that he was being accused of his involvement in the killing. Gentry maintained his schema of assisting in the investigation even during his trial. It is difficult to determine the schema of the detective who provided the inaccurate information to the judge, but he appeared to believe that Gentry was predisposed to play a knowingly significant role in the killing and it was that detective's inaccurate report to the judge that led to Gentry's conviction. A possible alternative could be that the detective was linguistically inept when he ambiguously reported to the judge that Gentry would describe "his role in the murder." Whatever the reason, the judge then found it easy to hold the schema that Gentry had played a significant role in the murder and was predisposed to hide it. The prosecutor's schema of Gentry's guilt derived naturally from the detective's inaccurate report to the judge.

Father Sica's language during his first grand jury hearing indicated that his schema was to be helpful to the prosecution by his willingness to describe what little he knew about a known criminal named Bufalino. His schema was the same during his own grand jury hearing, except that he now realized that he was being accused of perjury based on his testimony during the previous grand jury hearing. The prosecutor's schema was virtually the same in both courtroom events—that Father Sica was so predisposed to protect his "close personal relationship" with Bufalino that he would commit perjury to hide it. The prosecutor's schema about Sica's perjury likely prevented him from understanding the priest's attempts to clarify his relationship not only with the now deceased Bufalino but also with DeNaples, the primary target of that investigation. The prosecutor created this ambiguity about Sica's schema and in the end was adversely affected by it when the district attorney, who was skeptical about the prosecutor's evidence, asked linguists to analyze the language evidence. Based on that analysis, the district attorney withdrew the charge of perjury.

DECEPTIVE AMBIGUITY OF SCHEMAS CREATED BY AGENTS DURING CAMOUFLAGED INTERACTIONS

Unlike the transparent context of police and courtroom questioning, undercover operators camouflage their schemas to make them appear to be something they are not and misinterpret their target's schemas as well. The agent in Senator Williams's investigation used deceptive ambiguity to misinterpret the senator's schema as his predisposition to make a huge amount of money from the cockamamie mine project planned by the senator's associates. Similarly, the agent ambiguously misinterpreted John DeLorean's schema to find investors or get a loan in his desperate effort to save his failing company as his predisposition to solve his problem by engaging in a drug transaction. The IRS agent used deceptive ambiguity to misrepresent Vernon Sligh's schema that she could help him with his tax form as his predisposition to bribe her.

These three targets' schemas were clearly revealed in the language they used, none of which demonstrated any predisposition to commit a crime. The language of all three indicated their very different schemas growing out of their perception of the speech event they were led to believe they were in.

DECEPTIVE AMBIGUITY OF SCHEMAS CREATED BY COOPERATING WITNESSES DURING CAMOUFLAGED INTERACTIONS

The cooperating witnesses also began with schemas that their targets held predispositions to commit a crime even though they had considerable difficulty finding the evidence to support this. Cullen Davis had no love for his estranged wife or the judge with whom she allegedly was having a romantic relationship, but his language revealed the schema that he and his employee were in the speech event of reporting that employee's progress in spying on Davis's wife, which was very different from the prosecution's schema that he was predisposed to have them killed.

Yochi Cohen's language made it very clear that his only schema was to sell his company's body armor as opposed to the agents' schema that he was predisposed to offer a kickback to anyone who could help him get the contract.

Marwan El-Hindi's language demonstrated that his schema and predisposition throughout his conversations with the cooperating witness was to build a school for Islamic children in Toledo, while the cooperating witness held the schema that El-Hindi was predisposed to create a terrorist cell in that city.

DECEPTIVE AMBIGUITY OF SCHEMAS CREATED BY COMPLAINANTS DURING CAMOUFLAGED INTERACTIONS

Although the complainants were not as skilled in undercover operations as agents or cooperating witnesses, their schemas were much the same, because such investigations wouldn't be carried out if the complainants didn't hold schemas of their targets' predisposition of guilt. The complainants' language supported their schemas.

The initial, clearly admitted schema of John Poli and John McNown was to find out whether the complainant was connected with the mob in San Francisco. They carried out their plan ineptly, but their language evidence demonstrates that after they met with the madam their schema and predisposition was to withdraw their earlier request for a bribe. In the investigations of Dora and Sam as well as that of Sheriff Preston, the targets transparently revealed schemas and predispositions that were contrary to those of the complainants.

Deceptive Ambiguity in Agendas

When suspects and targets are confronted, one of the important analytical tasks is to determine any available clues to their intentions revealed by the topics they bring up and their responses to the topics introduced by the other participants. There is little reason to need to infer their agendas when actual language evidence is available, because the participants' own language provides the strongest available clues to their intentions. This is a compelling reason to determine the participants' agendas during police interviews, courtroom questioning, and undercover conversations. In all of the investigations described in this book, the topics and responses of the suspects and targets provided strong clues that their intentions were to not carry out illegal acts. As the targets tried to do this, the institutional representatives often misrepresented their agendas and deceptively tried to replace them with their own.

The conventional transparent structure of police interviews and courtroom interactions allows representatives of the law to control the agendas of suspects and defendants. This is not surprising in adversarial legal processes where institutional representatives hold the power to do so. Problems arise, however, when they block, ignore, or misrepresent what the suspects and defendants try to say.

Although police interviewers purportedly give suspects the opportunity to tell their own stories before they begin to probe and accuse, it seldom happens that way during most such interviews. More commonly, the police present their own agendas to suspects who have little or no opportunity to offer their own, even when they try to do so. Prosecutors also hold a distinct advantage over the defendants they question, for they have that same institutional power to control the interactions.

Whether undercover investigations are carried out by agents, cooperating witnesses, or complainants, their camouflaged agendas have a powerful potential to mislead targets with deceptive ambiguity. The major task of all three types of undercover investigations is to get targets to say something inculpatory on tape. Guilty targets often do so. But in some investigations the targets are far from clear about their guilt. To them, the government representatives usually introduce most of the topics while some targets, who don't perceive the agent's hidden agendas, often try to respond to these topics by assuming that they are talking about something legally benign. Although such targets' eventually may catch on to the agents' agendas and deny any implications of guilt, not all of them are that perceptive and alert. When they are not, their agendas are allowed to remain unclear. Oddly enough, if their defense lawyers call attention to the conversational asymmetry in which the illegality is introduced only by the undercover operatives with no positive responses from their targets, the result can actually benefit the defense cases, because the targets' own topic introductions can indicate that they were not about the same things as the agents' allegedly illegal topics. Pointing out this contrast can help demonstrate that the targets lacked motivation and predisposition to commit the crimes for which they are accused.

The following reprises the importance of pointing out the agendas found in investigations carried out by both transparent and camouflaged representatives of the legal institution.

DECEPTIVE AMBIGUITY OF AGENDAS CREATED DURING TRANSPARENT POLICE INTERVIEWS

Because the police made no recording or transcript during their interview with Kevin Rogers, later listeners were prevented from learning what Rogers's agenda may have been. The police stopped taping Michael Carter's interview while it was still in progress, also hampering later listeners from learning his agenda. Because of the government's decision to omit important evidence, all we can know about Carter's agenda was that he had planned to rob houses but that he denied shooting the patrolman. In contrast, interviewers allowed Dragan Jokic to explain that his agenda was to simply describe his day-duty job to them, but they then overpowered him with their own agenda that accused him of actively participating in the criminal massacre.

DECEPTIVE AMBIGUITY OF AGENDAS CREATED DURING TRANSPARENT COURTROOM QUESTIONING

During direct examinations, defendants' defense attorneys may try to get their clients to reveal their agendas, but when the prosecution takes over, their responses to prosecutors' questions allows little or no chance for defendants to state what they may be trying to say. Prosecutors' control of the questioning is even greater during grand jury hearings where defendants are not represented by lawyers.

Steven Suyat did not get a chance to reveal his own agenda because he was not allowed to introduce any topics. His agenda could be made only partially apparent by his responses to the prosecutor's deceptively ambiguous questions, to which Suyat tried to indicate that the proper job of union representatives is to organize workers rather than contractors and that Nishibayshi's logbook had stated this incorrectly. The prosecutor's questions, which Suyat had difficulty understanding, did not permit him to adequately express his own agenda.

Larry Gentry ineptly attempted to explain his own agenda but because the police deceptively misrepresented what he had said earlier to them, the prosecutor converted this misstatement into his own agenda that Gentry was guilty of aiding and abetting the murder. Gentry's mental and social slowness apparently didn't enable him to understand how the prosecutor was doing this.

Father Sica was perceptive enough to tacitly indicate what a "close personal relationship" meant to him by providing an example of his close personal relationship with person other than the target that the prosecutor was pursuing. The prosecutor's schema of Sica's guilt probably prevented him from comprehending the priest's clarification as he subsequently misrepresented the Sica's involvement with the target as a close and personal one, leading to charges of perjury.

DECEPTIVE AMBIGUITY OF AGENDAS CREATED DURING CAMOUFLAGED INTERACTIONS WITH UNDERCOVER AGENTS

The schemas and agendas of undercover agents apparently lead them to ignore, misunderstand, or misrepresent their targets' agendas. Because the underlying purpose of their investigations is to capture language evidence of guilt, agents typically begin with a schema of their targets' guilt and then ignore, divert, or try to convert the targets' agendas into their own.

Senator Williams was told in advance that his agenda was to meet with a foreign dignitary to report on progress in his associates' mining venture. This agenda lasted only a minute or so, at which point it became clear that the agent's competing agenda was to ask Williams for his help in obtaining political sanctuary in the United States. Williams adjusted his agenda quickly by explaining how the relevant legal process works and what the sheik would need to do for this to happen. At that point the agent's real agenda emerged—to give the senator a bribe for sponsoring the legislation required to accomplish this. After Williams forcefully rejected the bribe, the agent switched his agenda back again to an effort to get the senator's agreement to sponsor the needed legislation for him. The senator agreed to do what he could to help him meet the requirements, but only after he could learn more facts about the sheik and his situation. He told the sheik that until he had this information to work with, neither he nor any other congressman could do anything for him, which effectively rejected the agent's apparent quid pro quo agenda. Although the sheik camouflaged his ambiguous deceptive agenda, the senator was able to see through and thwart it. The language of Williams's agenda revealed both his lack of predisposition to commit a crime and his clear rejection of the opportunity when it was offered.

From the beginning of the investigation of John DeLorean, the FBI agent's ambiguously deceptive agenda was to entice DeLorean into participating in a drug transaction that would provide enough profits to save his company from bankruptcy. DeLorean's language demonstrated that his very different agenda was to obtain a loan or investors for his company. When the agent's associate, DeLorean's former neighbor finally became clear about the illegal drug transaction, DeLorean rejected it, and in the process demonstrated neither a criminal predisposition nor the willingness to commit a crime.

Vernon Sligh's clearly articulated and repeated agenda was to get the help he needed from the IRS agent so that he could use it to satisfy his tax burden. The agent, who had just taken a course about how taxpayers try to bribe IRS investigators, translated what she learned from this course into her ambiguously deceptive agenda in which she scripted Sligh with the only possible solution to his problem—to bribe her. In spite any evidence that he was predisposed to do so, Sligh then saw no other way out and finally bribed the agent. This investigation better demonstrated the dogged predisposition of the IRS agent to create a crime than Sligh's predisposition to commit one.

DECEPTIVE AMBIGUITY OF AGENDAS CREATED DURING CAMOUFLAGED INTERACTIONS WITH COOPERATING WITNESSES

When Cullen Davis met with his employee, his agenda, as revealed by the topics he introduced, indicated that he was predisposed only to learn about the progress his employee had made while spying on the amorous activities of his wife and the judge handling his divorce proceedings. The employee's sole agenda was to capture on tape Davis's agreement to have those two people and two others killed. The one and only time the employee mentioned the killing was when Davis was out of hearing range. This produced a classic example of deceptive ambiguity for the jury to try to unpack.

Yochi Cohen's agenda, revealed by all of his topic introductions and responses, was that he was predisposed only to promote his company's body armor products and try to obtain sales contracts at the convention. The agenda of the cooperating witnesses was to get Cohen to agree to give Gabon's foreign minister a bribe in order to obtain a business contract from that country. By staying with his own agenda even after the bribery offer was suggested, Cohen provided no evidence that he was willing to commit a crime.

Marwan El-Hindi articulated his own agenda consistently as his desire to create a school for Islamic children in Toledo. The cooperating witness held the very different deceptively ambiguous agenda of trying to get El-Hindi to establish a terrorist cell, although he never said this directly or explicitly enough for El-Hindi to catch his meaning. The jury then had to distinguish the agent's deceptively ambiguous agenda from El-Hindi's.

DECEPTIVE AMBIGUITY OF AGENDAS CREATED DURING CAMOUFLAGED INTERACTIONS WITH COMPLAINANTS

The complainant's covertly recorded conversation with John Poli and John McNown was unusual because these targets admitted that they had actually requested a bribe from her in a previously unrecorded telephone call. The complainant's task was to confirm this bribery request on tape and complete the bribery event by bringing cash with her and give it to the men as a bribe. All of the topics she introduced were about her bribery offer. Even though many of the topics introduced by Poli and McNown were denials that they would ask her for a bribe, the IRS agent was undaunted and left a roll of cash on her chair as they got up to their leave the restaurant, physically supporting her agenda while creating deceptive ambiguity in the process.

Dora introduced all of the topics in her confrontation call to Sam, while Sam had no agenda other than to play defense as he tried to respond to her accusations. At Dora's insistent request, Sam told her daughter that he was sorry about appearing in her dream. That was the only topic Sam introduced and it failed badly as a felicitous apology for committing a crime.

The complainant who tried to get Sheriff Preston to admit that he had committed sexual misconduct with her also introduced all her topics using such deceptive ambiguity that he could not even recognize what she was trying to accomplish. Curiously, even the complainant admitted her deceptive ambiguity during her brief discussion with the agent after the conversation with the sheriff had ended.

Deceptive Ambiguity in Speech Acts

The speech acts of participants flow naturally out of their agendas, where speech acts illuminate the meaning of their topics and responses to the topics introduced by the other speakers. The following reprises the importance of pointing out the speech acts found in investigations carried out by both transparent and camouflaged representatives of the legal institution.

DECEPTIVE AMBIGUITY CREATED BY SPEECH ACTS DURING TRANSPARENT POLICE INTERVIEWS

Although there was no tape-recorded evidence in Kevin Rogers's murder investigation, his signed confession indicated he was "sorry for what I did" and that he was "sorry for what happened." The police celebrated these statements as the speech acts of apologies that represented his admission of guilt even though they both failed the felicity conditions of the speech act of apologizing. The written confession statement that he signed created ambiguity by not saying what he apologized for, leaving the police to infer that it was for the murder. Since the police did not electronically record this interview, it was not possible to assess the felicity of the detectives' speech acts of questioning, the time sequences in which they asked their questions, and the verbal context surrounding what Rogers allegedly admitted. Rogers was convicted at trial in spite of the deceptive processes used by the police during this interview.

Michael Carter's frequently repeated speech act was to deny that he was the one who shot and killed a police officer. The police interviewers' primary and frequently repeated speech acts were to accuse him of doing it. Carter's written speech act of confessing eventually was demonstrated to have been deceptively ambiguous because it was created and worded by the officer and not by Carter himself.

Dragan Jokic's investigators tried hard to convert his speech act of reporting that his superior had used the speech act of requesting information from him into the speech act that he was ordered to do this. They also deceptively misinterpreted Jokic's several speech acts of giving opinions ("I think," "I assume") as speech acts of reporting facts that he allegedly knew.

DECEPTIVE AMBIGUITY OF SPEECH ACTS CREATED DURING TRANSPARENT COURTROOM QUESTIONING

Steven Suyat's courtroom testimony speech event revealed the prosecutor's deceptive unwillingness to respond to Suyat's speech act of requesting clarification concerning which part of the prosecutor's true or false question relating to his colleague's logbook Suyat was asked to answer. The logbook contained two statements, one of which, in Suyat's opinion, was false and one of which was true. After the prosecutor did not clarify what Suyat indirectly requested, Suyat reluctantly answered, "false," which the prosecutor deceptively went on to interpret as perjury.

Larry Gentry's language indicated that he tried to convey the speech act of denying having any knowledge of the murder before it happened. The prosecutor created ambiguous deception by misinterpreting Gentry's efforts as a speech acts of admitting such knowledge.

Father Sica's prosecutor failed to use the speech act of requesting clarification when he apparently didn't understand what the priest was saying. He then proceeded to assume that his misperception of the priest's statement supported the charge of perjury. This prosecutor also deceptively misinterpreted the priest's "I don't recall" as an evasive response that supported his charge of perjury.

DECEPTIVE AMBIGUITY OF SPEECH ACTS CREATED DURING CAMOUFLAGED INTERACTIONS WITH AGENTS

Both the undercover agent and the prosecutor created deceptive ambiguity by misrepresenting Senator Williams's very unambiguous speech act of rejecting the sheik's bribe offer and then proceeded as though the senator had used the speech act of agreeing to accept it. The agent and the prosecutor also deceptively misrepresented the process in which the valueless stock certificates thrust upon the senator by surprise as Williams's nonverbal speech act of agreeing to accept something of value, the basic requirement of a quid pro quo bribe. The prosecutor also deceptively claimed that Williams had used the speech act of promising to sponsor legislation for the sheik in spite of the language evidence showing that the senator clearly indicated that he promised only to help the sheik compile the information needed in order to become ready for consideration before any such legislation for citizenship could be introduced in congress. Finally, the prosecutor created deceptive ambiguity to the jury when he criticized the senator for not strongly rebuking the phony sheik after he offered Williams the bribe. The cumulative effect of these deceptions created ambiguity in the minds of the prosecutor, judge, jury, and even his colleagues in the US Senate.

Similarly, John DeLorean was indicted and tried for using the speech act of agreeing to participate in the drug transaction even though the taped evidence shows that he actually used the indirect speech act of rejecting the opportunity given him ("I'm getting the money from an Irish group"). The government also created deceptive ambiguity by claiming that after the agent showed DeLorean a suitcase full of drugs, his response, "It'll be dangerous," was his speech act of agreeing to continue their discussion rather than his evaluative comment about how dangerous such drug programs really are.

The IRS agent who spoke with Vernon Sligh deceptively reinterpreted his speech act of requesting help with his taxes as his speech act of offering to give her a bribe for falsifying his tax record. She also used deceptive ambiguity by consistently refusing to answer Sligh's speech act of requesting clarification.

DECEPTIVE AMBIGUITY OF SPEECH ACTS CREATED DURING CAMOUFLAGED INTERACTIONS WITH COOPERATING WITNESSES

Cullen Davis's only speech acts were those of advising and requesting information. He first advised McCrory that he told his boss that he should be treated like any other employee. Davis's speech act of requesting information about McCrory's progress in spying on Priscilla and the judge went unanswered, as did his speech act of requesting McCrory to give him advance notice about when he planned to miss work so that Davis could explain this to McCrory's boss. McCrory's speech acts, spoken out of Davis's hearing, were those of reporting that he got Priscilla and the judge dead, and promising to get other people dead. After Davis came back into hearing distance, McCrory also promised to give him advance notice about when he would next miss work. Even though their conversation was simultaneous and overlapping, analysis of it made clear that the two men held very different understandings about what that ambiguous advance notice referenced. Out of Davis's hearing, McCrory also used the speech act of complaining about how hard the murder business was. Except for McCrory's promise to give advance notice, all of his crucial speech acts were uttered into his body mike while Davis was out of hearing range, which can be considered the ultimate act of deceptive ambiguity.

The two cooperating witnesses investigating Yochi Cohen provided various uses of deceptive ambiguity. The first cooperating witness deceptively reinterpreted Cohen's speech act of agreeing to give him a commission as his agreement to give an illegal kickback to the Gabon defense minister. This cooperating witness also tried to get Cohen to use the speech act of admitting that he had given kickbacks in the past by ambiguously hinting, alluding, and implying that Cohen had overpaid his brokers so that they would illegally pass along the extra money along to the foreign ministers as a kickback. Later he used the speech act of advising Cohen that he really didn't need to get a legally required export license. Since these efforts were not successful, the second cooperating witness took over and clearly and unambiguously advised Cohen that if he wanted to get the contract, he needed to pay a kickback to Gabon's minister of defense, which yielded Cohen's speech act of denial. In addition to Cohen's many speech acts of reporting that he always conducted his business honestly and his bragging about the superiority of his company and products, Cohen's speech acts were denials of all the illegal suggestions made by both cooperating witnesses. It might seem that the intelligence analyst, the prosecutor, should have noticed Cohen's speech acts of rejecting the opportunities to act illegally, for such analysis might have clarified any possible ambiguity, but he ignored them and brought charges of bribery against Cohen.

El-Hindi never uttered the speech act of agreeing to any of Griffin's deceptively ambiguous hints for him to create a terrorist cell to train people for a violent jihad. El-Hindi's language indicates that he understood that Griffin's speech acts of requesting were for him to invite more Muslim Americans to their meetings in order to get the physical exercise that they all needed. Even so, Griffin's ambiguous requests failed because El-Hindi invited nobody. Griffin was undaunted and proceeded as though he had received positive speech act responses to all of his deceptively ambiguous requests. El-Hindi's only speech acts of promising were to continue to meet with Griffin and send him a copy of the allegedly important videotape he had only partially viewed. Throughout their relationship, El-Hindi used the legally benign speech act of advising Griffin about Islam and finally used the speech act of offering to host a dinner meeting at his home.

DECEPTIVE AMBIGUITY CREATED DURING CAMOUFLAGED INTERACTIONS WITH COMPLAINANTS

The complainant/madam in the bribery investigation of John Poli and John McNown created deceptive ambiguity by misrepresenting their speech act of denying to bribe her as their speech act of agreeing to do so. Her non-verbal speech act of offering consisted of leaving a roll of money on her chair as she left the meeting, which created deceptive ambiguity for the prosecutor and jury to try to resolve.

The complainant and the prosecutor in Sam's sexual misconduct investigation deceptively misinterpreted Sam's speech act of apologizing for appearing in the little girl's dream as his speech act of apologizing for committing that act in real life.

Similarly, the complainant and prosecutor in the sexual misconduct case of Sheriff Preston deceptively reinterpreted the sheriff's speech act of apologizing for "carrying on and carrying on" with her in the past as his speech act of apologizing for putting his hand *in* her pants, even though the government's own taped evidence demonstrated that he ran his hand *down* her pants leg at a previous meeting in an effort to be diagnostically helpful to her after she had complained about a sharp pain in her leg. The complainant was equally ambiguously deceptive by lowering her voice while she uttered words that the hearing-impaired sheriff gave evidence of being unable to hear. To this she then ignored his speech act of requesting repetition or clarification.

Deceptive Ambiguity in Conversational Strategies

Conversational strategies are used either consciously or unconsciously to persuade. In the legal setting the targets of such persuasion are not only the audience being addressed but also later listeners such as prosecutors, judges, and juries. This type of persuasion is most evident in undercover operations, when the effort is actually to obtain language evidence that will persuade later listeners about the guilt of the targets. But conversational strategies are also used by police and prosecutors during their questioning in an effort to create the impression of their subjects'guilt. There is nothing wrong with persuasion, but certain types of persuasion can convey degrees of questionable fairness. Being intentionally ambiguous during persuasive efforts can give speakers an advantage over listeners when that ambiguity invites later listeners to misperceive the meaning.

Certain conversational strategies are used to convey deceptive ambiguity. As the investigations in this book illustrate, the most common deceptive conversational strategies are the creation of ambiguity by blocking what the other person is in the process of trying to say, employing the hit-and-run technique, contaminating the conversation, withholding important information, deliberately lying, and others (Shuy 2005). Such conversational strategies can produce deceptive ambiguity not only for participants in the conversations but also for later listeners, especially for juries. The following reprises the importance of pointing out the conversational strategies used by investigators in both transparent and camouflaged exchanges.

DECEPTIVE AMBIGUITY OF CONVERSATIONAL STRATEGIES CREATED DURING TRANSPARENT POLICE INTERVIEWS

Based on the sparse evidence provided by the police interviewers in Kevin Rogers's case, it was not possible to determine what possible conversational strategies the police may have employed. It is clear, however, that the first deception was conveyed when they did not record their interview, which successfully blocked Rogers's defense attorney and any other later listeners from knowing what the officers' questions were as well as precisely what Rogers's answers were to those questions. Blocked evidence creates deceptive ambiguity by leading listeners to infer what that language evidence might have conveyed.

Michael Carter's partially taped interview also contained deceptive ambiguity created by blocking later listeners, including his defense attorneys, from knowing what the police asked Carter and what he answered after the tape-recorder was deactivated. This form of blocking bears some similarity to the conversational strategy of interrupting suspects' efforts to continue sentences that they have started. The police also constantly interrupted Carter's efforts to talk during the recorded part of their interview with him. These deceptive blocking strategies enabled the prosecutor to infer Carter's guilt based on ambiguous interview evidence that could not be authenticated or verified. Perhaps the most deceptive blocking strategy, however, occurred when the police interviewer claimed that he produced a verbatim confession using

Carter's own words, which a comparison of a sample of the detective's language with Carter's language demonstrated to be a clear example of creating deceptive ambiguity.

There appeared to be no instances showing that Dragan Jokic's interviewers used the conversational strategy of blocking his efforts to talk, although it is difficult to be certain about this because the only evidence was a transcript containing an English translation that could have omitted or cleaned up any interruptions, hit-and-run questions, and other conversational strategies that may have occurred in the original language. By not presenting the taped evidence in the original language used in the interviews for verification and comparison with the English transcript, the legal system created still another possible form of deceptive ambiguity created by the conversational strategy of blocking.

DECEPTIVE AMBIGUITY OF CONVERSATIONAL STRATEGIES CREATED DURING TRANSPARENT COURTROOM QUESTIONING

The prosecutor used the conversational strategy of blocking Steven Suyat's speech act of requesting clarification about the prosecutor's unclear question by insisting that Suyat answer only *true* or *false* to a question that contained two deceptively different propositions. Suyat found it impossible to answer with the *true* or *false* answer that the prosecutor demanded. Suyat's attempt to clarify his own response to the question about what the word, *scab,* means was also interrupted and blocked by the prosecutor's widely used and deceptively ambiguous courtroom strategy: "No further questions."

The prosecutor similarly blocked Larry Gentry's inept, tacit definition of what he meant by the verb, *know,* by deceptively converting it into a totally different meaning of this verb. The prosecutor also used the common conversational strategy of asking two questions at the same time, to which Gentry, like most respondents, answered the most recent question (the recency effect), giving the false impression that his answer was to the first question. The most egregious blocking strategy, however, occurred when the information Gentry gave during his initial police interview was reported to the prosecutor in an ambiguously deceptive and inaccurate manner. The prosecutor then passed this same inaccurate, deceptively ambiguous information along to the judge.

The prosecutor blocked Father Sica's tacit definition of *a close personal friendship* by redefining it in a way that served his prosecutorial purposes, thus creating a deceptive ambiguity that was central to his prosecution of perjury. Although prosecutors have the right to sequence their questions however they want, this prosecutor produced deceptive ambiguity by using the conversational strategy of withholding certain detailed questions until Sica had given earlier less detailed answers. This strategy produced a deceptive impression that Sica had lied about what he had said up to that point, even though he previously had not been asked to provide detailed information. This deceptively ambiguous courtroom conversational strategy of withholding the exact information wanted in the question can lead to an effective prosecution, but it also must be recognized as a deceptively ambiguous prosecutorial tactic. Fortunately for Sica, he eventually was able to repair this misperception about what the prosecutor was trying to elicit. Not all defendants have Sica's language skills.

DECEPTIVE AMBIGUITY OF CONVERSATIONAL STRATEGIES CREATED DURING CAMOUFLAGED INTERACTIONS WITH UNDERCOVER AGENTS

In Senator Williams's investigation the conversational strategy of deceptively ambiguous blocking was done by an outsider to the conversation. While the senator was trying to explain why he could not take a bribe from the sheik, another agent in an adjoining room telephoned the sheik, interrupting and thereby blocking what Williams was trying to explain to the sheik about why bribery was not acceptable in the United States. After his clear rejection of the sheik's bribe offer, this conversational strategy of interrupting and blocking what the senator was trying to say created deceptive ambiguity for later listeners who therefore would not be able to hear his explanation about why bribery is illegal. Hearing such missing information could have supported their understanding about why Williams had actually rejected the bribe offer.

The first FBI agent in DeLorean's investigation used deceptive ambiguity with his target for several months, making it appear that he was trying to help DeLorean get a loan or investors for his company. But apparently his conversational strategy was to wait until the point at which DeLorean's company would be so desperate for money that the second agent then could introduce the drug scheme that DeLorean would be forced to agree to. Since the first deceptively ambiguous conversational strategy yielded no evidence against DeLorean, the government brought in a second operative who eventually made it clear that the only solution to DeLorean's financial problems would be for him to buy into the proposed drug scheme, which offer DeLorean clearly rejected. The agent's conversational strategy then was to ignore this rejection and, like some salespersons, he continued the conversation as though had actually received DeLorean's agreement. This conversational strategy apparently created for the prosecutor the deceptively ambiguous impression that DeLorean had actually agreed with the cooperating witness's offer.

The IRS agent used the conversational strategy of blocking Sligh's requests to discover the *reasons* articulated in the IRS guidelines that might help him resolve his tax burden. She then deceptively and ambiguously tried to misinterpret Sligh's own word, "reasons," to mean reasons why she should agree to accept a bribe from him. The agent also used the conversational strategy of scripting Sligh about what he needed to tell her in order to successfully extract himself from his tax problems. This scripting is similar to the technique used by some police interviewers who script their suspects to use the certain words and sentences in their confession statements. Police are now expected to heed more closely to Wigmore's ancient admonition about this (1904: 308): "an acknowledgement in express words by the accused in a criminal case" (Shuy 2014: 207, 2015: 28–29). Contrasting with this admonition, the IRS agent used deceptive ambiguity by scripting Sligh with the exact words to use in his eventual offer of a bribe to her.

DECEPTIVE AMBIGUITY OF CONVERSATIONAL STRATEGIES CREATED DURING CAMOUFLAGED INTERACTIONS WITH COOPERATING WITNESSES

One of the most outrageous forms of the conversational blocking strategy is illustrated in the investigation of Cullen Davis. Here cooperating witness McCrory waited until Davis was outside the car and therefore out of hearing range to mutter the incriminating words into the recording device hidden under his shirt. This deceptive conversational strategy created ambiguity that convinced the prosecutor to charge Davis with soliciting murder.

During Yochi Cohen's investigation, the cooperating witness used the conversational strategy of ignoring Cohen's clear statement that he would not offer a kickback in order to get a Gabon contract for body armor. The cooperating witness used the conversational strategy of ignoring Cohen's rejection and proceeded as though his target had not rejected it. The cumulative effect of the cooperating witness's many efforts to solicit bribery apparently was enough to block from the awareness of the prosecutor what Cohen actually responded. In undercover cases it sometimes happens that later listeners become confused about who uttered the inculpatory words. The cooperating witness also used the conversational strategy of ambiguously hinting about kickbacks done by other arms manufacturers and even hinted that Cohen had done this himself. Hinting, a common practice of fishing for guilt in undercover operations, is by definition ambiguous and in criminal investigations it can be a deceptively ambiguous practice.

Similarly, the cooperating witness who tried to inculpate Marwan El-Hindi used the conversational strategy of ignoring El-Hindi's consistent failures to catch on to his deceptively ambiguous fishing hints about illegality. When El-Hindi, his associates, and the cooperating witness met together at El-Hindi's home, the room arrangements blocked El-Hindi's ability to know what was going on during much of the playing of videotapes about the war in the Middle East. As host, El-Hindi spent most of his time in the kitchen and could have little if any knowledge about the specific content on those tapes. As he went back and forth from the kitchen to the living room, none of his comments supported the accusation that he planned to copy television programs that were allegedly germane to the charge of terrorism or that he even understood that the tapes had any significance about the agent's concept of jihad. In fact, it's hard to imagine that recordings of the publicly presented television programs about the war in the Middle East could be considered *electronic jihad* containing secret information that would aid and abet the enemy. During their other conversations, the cooperating witness used the conversational strategy of frequently reinterpreting and therefore blocking El-Hindi's own topics about creating a new school for Muslim children by trying to recast them into his own hinted but never clearly articulated topics about the need to develop a terrorist cell.

DECEPTIVE AMBIGUITY OF CONVERSATIONAL STRATEGIES CREATED DURING CAMOUFLAGED INTERACTIONS WITH COMPLAINANTS

During her investigation of John Poli and John McNown, the complainant used the conversational strategy of blocking the suspects' efforts to revoke their earlier offer to elicit a bribe from her by ignoring what they told her. She also used the strategy of blocking by covertly placing a roll of cash on her chair as she left the meeting, thereby both ignoring and blocking the brothel commissioners' efforts to act legally. She used the conversational strategy of blocking any possible effort of McNown to return money to her by deftly disappearing before he had any opportunity to do so.

Dora's conversational strategy of conflating her daughter's dreams with an actual sexual event was deceptively ambiguous. Cooperating witnesses also often use the conversational strategy of wearing their targets down by repeating their accusations over and over again after they receive only denials as responses. After denying Dora's accusation eighteen times, Sam appeared to be emotionally worn down and finally gave up and tried to get Dora off the phone weakly by admitting to her that he did *it* one time when he was drunk. His meaning of the word, *it,* was ambiguous about whether he admitted being drunk in the little girl's dream or that he admitted being drunk when he committed the sexual act. The prosecutor interpreted this ambiguity in his own way, using it as evidence that Sam finally admitted to molesting the girl.

In the investigation of Sheriff Preston the complainant used the conversational strategy of blocking in a way similar to that used by the cooperating witness in Cullen Davis's case. Whereas Davis was too far away to hear the critical words, the sheriff's responses made it clear that he was too hearing impaired to know what the complainant had said to him. She blocked his request for repetition or clarification and went right on, however, acting as though he actually had heard and understood what she said, leaving on the record a deceptively ambiguous exchange that the prosecutor took as evidence of sexual misconduct. The government's deceptively inaccurate transcript saying "you went down **in** my pants," also contributed to blocking what later listeners could understood in that conversation, as did the complainant's continuously interrupting the sheriff from answering her deceptively ambiguous accusations.

Deceptive Ambiguity in Lexicon and Grammar

Finally, we address the smaller elements of the Inverted Pyramid by examining the language that has been most commonly used by prosecutors as smoking gun evidence. The language of words, phrases, and sentences is the area of ambiguity most studied by linguists. Although standard and predictable uses of syntax, pronoun referencing, conditionals, deixis, hypotheticals, lexicon, and others are important in effective communication, these linguistic features normally are embedded within the larger units of speech events, schemas, agendas, speech acts, and conversational strategies. This is not to say that lexicon and grammar are unimportant, for in some law cases, especially in civil torts such as contract and trademark disputes, lexicon and grammar can play a very significant role. But there are also occasions such as interviews and conversations in which the meanings conveyed by lexical and grammatical ambiguity can be more clearly understood when they are contextualized within the overall discourse. The following reprises the importance of pointing out the lexical and grammatical features found in investigations carried out by both transparent and camouflaged representatives of the legal institution.

DECEPTIVE AMBIGUITY OF LEXICON AND GRAMMAR CREATED DURING TRANSPARENT POLICE INTERVIEWS

In criminal cases the words and expressions of the *Miranda* warning are among the most commonly celebrated sources of confusion and complaint. Many of the words are inherently ambiguous even without considering them in the larger context in which those words occur. Part of the legal lexicon is simply difficult for some people to understand at all, especially when their referents are unclear or missing.

In Kevin Rogers's murder case, the police reported that they read Kevin his rights using the critical words and expressions *consult with, voluntarily, right, freely,* and *knowingly*, also claiming that Kevin understood them. The legal meanings of these expressions are not easy for most suspects to unpack, but for this mentally slow juvenile they could be even less clear, as a tape-recorded interview of Rogers might have been able to indicate.

The police did not record their reading of the *Miranda* rights to Michael Carter, but based on the tape-recording of the police interview with him it is difficult to know what lexicon and grammar Carter may have found ambiguous because he gave only minimal responses of denial to the police while crying and vomiting throughout. During the evidentiary hearing, however, it became clear that some of the lexicon and grammar items found in Carter's signed confession statement were those of the detective, not Carter. The officer who wrote the statement created the deceptive ambiguity that Carter had knowingly signed a confession statement that he was not physically, cognitively, or emotionally able to understand.

The interviewers of Dragan Jokic reinterpreted his expressions, *hearing about*, and *assuming*, to create deceptive ambiguity that he was certain about crucial facts. They preserved their misinterpretation of Jokic's meaning of *know* in the official record of the interviews with him. They also reinterpreted Jokic's expression, *passing an order along*, which he used while describing how he carried out his required job as duty officer, as his intentional, active participation based on a presumably important and partially coded directive rather than as his routine secretarial activity that didn't involve his decision-making capacity. The law officers also created critical deceptive ambiguity in their ambiguous representations of the referencing and time sequences they talked about with Jokic. They deceptively misrepresented Jokic's conditional statements as factual by misinterpreting his own words, *could, might*, and *possibly*, as terms of actuality, and reinterpreted as causals his description of events that did not reference causes. Jokic's interviewers also used deceptive ambiguity in their own uses of lexicon and grammar. For example, they used present tense verbs to ask him about what happened in the past, produced ambiguous deictic referencing, and treated what Jokic told them about what he learned about the massacre after it happened as what he knew while it was happening. They also interpreted his 'I don't know' responses to their questions as evidence of his evasiveness, distorted his expression, *passed on the information,* as though he admitted responsibility for its content, reinterpreted his hypotheticals as factuals, and twisted Jokic's description of his actions as causations for the crimes.

DECEPTIVE AMBIGUITY OF LEXICON AND GRAMMAR CREATED DURING TRANSPARENT COURTROOM QUESTIONING

During Steven Suyat's testimony, the prosecutor indirectly asked him to define the word, *scab*, in a manner that caused Suyat to fail to supply an answer to what he apparently thought required a more learned dictionary definition than he was able to provide. The prosecutor also ambiguously misinterpreted the meaning of *to organize contractors* to refer to organizing workers rather than Suyat's understanding that contractors were business owners or officers who were not the proper targets of the union's efforts to organize workers.

Similar to Jokic's investigation, Gentry's prosecutor created lexical ambiguity by redefining Gentry's use of the contextually ambiguous verb, *know,* to mean that he knew with certainty that the murder would take place even though Gentry said that he suspected but wasn't sure that it might even happen. The prosecutor then inferred Gentry's "by the time it was gonna happen, yeah . . . I'd done figured it out" as evidence that he actually knew the details of the intended killings before they took place. The prosecutor also distorted

Gentry's pronoun, *it,* to refer to something that Gentry's own language contextually did not reference.

Father Sica's prosecutor created lexical ambiguity by claiming that the priest had *a close personal relationship* with a known criminal who had attended the priest's ordination service some twenty years earlier. The priest, however, was alert enough about this misinterpretation to try to repair the prosecutor's undefined and therefore deceptively ambiguous expression.

DECEPTIVE AMBIGUITY OF LEXICON AND GRAMMAR CREATED DURING CAMOUFLAGED INTERACTIONS WITH AGENTS

The undercover agent posing as an Arab sheik offered Senator Williams a bribe to which the senator said "no" four times. It is difficult to fathom how the relatively unambiguous word, *no*, could be misunderstood as agreement, but nevertheless the prosecutor indicted Williams for bribery. He also claimed that Williams accepted the worthless stock certificates for the nonexistent mining venture even though his friends unexpectedly had forced these worthless papers on him while his full attention was on hurrying to board a train. The difference between *accepting* stock certificates and unwittingly *receiving* them made no difference to either the agent or the prosecutor in this case.

The undercover agent in John DeLorean's investigation created deceptive ambiguity by reinterpreting the car manufacturer's agreement that it would be good to get investors in his failing company to mean that he agreed to the agent's offer to invest in the drug scheme. The agent also used the expression, *interim financing,* in a deceptively ambiguous way. Throughout the sixty-four recorded conversations, DeLorean consistently used this expression to refer to investors who could provide interim financing to save his company from bankruptcy. In contrast, in the final conversation the agent used *interim financing* to convey the meaning that DeLorean would provide an interim financing investment in the drug operation that would then to be followed by his subsequent reinvestments after he received the profits from his first interim investment in the scheme. The agent also used deceptive ambiguity to misinterpret DeLorean's need to *confirm* his arrangement with the Irish group that had already promised to fund him to mean that DeLorean intended to confirm his participation in the drug transaction. Additional deceptive ambiguity was created with the agent's ambiguous referencing of *other funds*, which could refer to either the agent's funds or DeLorean's. The agent also misinterpreted DeLorean's pronoun, *it* when he said, "I want to do it," as an indication that he wanted to do the drug transaction instead of DeLorean's clear contextual reference to his plan to get his funds from the Irish group.

In the investigation of Vernon Sligh the IRS agent ambiguously redefined Sligh's reference to her institutional *power* as her power to create a false tax record for him. She also introduced the word, *favor,* and reinterpreted the benign meaning of this word into an illegal one, suggesting that she could do him a big favor by giving him an illegal tax break that deviated from IRS rules and procedures. Even after she used the word *deviated*, Sligh's response gave no indication that he understood what she meant by it. The agent's request for *reasons* to help him was also deceptively ambiguous, for Sligh's response made it clear that he meant reasons to help him with his tax problem, not reasons to do anything illegal.

DECEPTIVE AMBIGUITY OF LEXICON AND GRAMMAR CREATED DURING CAMOUFLAGED INTERACTIONS WITH COOPERATING WITNESSES

When cooperating witness McCrory talked with Cullen Davis, the prosecution concluded that the alleged smoking guns were Davis's words, *good, alibi,* and *all right,* which the prosecutor cited in the indictment as evidence of his guilt. The words, *good* and *all right*, are indeed words of agreement, but analysis of the discourse context made it clear that these words were not agreements to what McCrory was saying. Contrary to the prosecutor's claim, Davis spoke these words as part of his ongoing topic of dealing with McCrory's boss, Art, who had complained about McCrory's absence from his job. As for *alibi,* Davis's discourse context made it clear that he was trying to provide McCrory with an acceptable reason to give his boss for missing work to spy on Davis's wife and not, as the prosecution claimed, as an alibi for the proposed killer to use.

In Cohen's investigation, the cooperating witness used deceptive ambiguity in his many hints and vague suggestions about ongoing illegality in their business rather than using specifically unambiguous words. At one point, however, the cooperating witness uttered the wink-wink, nod-nod code expression, *between us girls*, apparently as an indirect invitation for Cohen to admit that he was involved in the illegal kickbacks. This ploy didn't work, however, for Cohen responded that he doesn't give kickbacks and the very idea of doing so terrifies him.

In Marwan El-Hindi's investigation the cooperating witness used the ambiguous nouns *training, security,* and *weapons* and the verb phrase *mask it* in deceptively ambiguous grammatical contexts. El-Hindi's responses made it clear that he understood these words to be benign and in no way related to setting up a terrorist cell.

DECEPTIVE AMBIGUITY OF LEXICON AND GRAMMAR CREATED DURING CAMOUFLAGED INTERACTIONS WITH COMPLAINANTS

At the trial of Poli and McNown there was much disagreement over whether the two brothel commissioners said "I would take a bribe, wouldn't you" or "I wouldn't take a bribe, would you?" This crucial difference didn't involve lexicon but went deeper into the phonetic supersegmentals of intonation, stress, and meter as well as the transposition of the negative morpheme. Another lexical ambiguity conflict also took place at trial rather than during their recorded conversation in the café. The prosecutor and the defense attorneys were at odds over the prosecutor's use of the verb *accept* when he claimed the defendant McNown "accepted" the bribe when he picked it up after the madam left it on her empty chair. The defense lawyers agreed that the men had the money in their possession (received it) but strongly disagreed with the prosecutor's claim that the men knowingly *accepted* the bribe, which was made especially clear by the discourse context in which they had just rejected it.

In Dora's confrontation call she told Sam about her daughter's dream and asked Sam if it represented an actual event. He answered, "Nothing, I mean no." Dora apparently was not satisfied with this response and asked, "Nothing more than that?" creating a grammatical ambiguity that was not present in his answer. She then continued with a deceptively ambiguous compound question, first asking if the "nothing more" meant that all he did was lick her daughter's private parts. She immediately asked him to tell her he's sorry for *that.* Sam answered "yes," agreeing to Dora's second and most recent proposition (he'll tell her he's sorry), which Dora (and the prosecutor) took to be his answer to first proposition that he licked her daughter's private parts. His *yes* was further complicated by the fact that he had already told her that he was sorry that he appeared in her daughter's dream, not that he was sorry for committing the act she dreamed about. Dora then used the ambiguous deictic referent, *this,* twice when she asked Sam whether this was the only time this happened. Sam paused, sighed, and said "yes," creating ambiguity about whether he was responding to Dora's *this* as a reference to his sexual misconduct or to her daughter's dream about it.

The complainant's confrontation with Sheriff Preston produced no obvious lexical ambiguity but a great deal of ambiguity relating to the complainant's grammatical references of *it* and *this*, along with the prosecution's inaccurate and creative interpretation of his "going down in her pants" versus the taped evidence that demonstrated that the word, *in,* was not present in that sentence. The secretary actually said "going down her pants." The sheriff couldn't hear the word, *in,* here because it wasn't even there. He didn't deny that he had touched her leg when she had complained about the pain, but this brief incident apparently didn't register to him as sexual misconduct. All of this was confused by the sheriff's difficulty in hearing what the complainant was saying.

Following this reprisal of the police interviewers', prosecutors', and undercover operators' major uses of deceptive ambiguity in the context of speech events, schemas, agendas, speech acts, conversational strategies, and lexical/grammatical evidence, the final chapter first summarizes the role of deceptive ambiguity in relationship to the legal institution's need to discover predisposition, intentionality, and voluntariness. It then compares the relative frequency of the government representatives' uses of deceptive ambiguity found in the six elements of the Inverted Pyramid. Finally, it summarizes and compares the government's uses of deceptive ambiguity when the legal institution's power is transparent in police interviews and courtroom examinations with instances when this institutional power is hidden in undercover interactions with targets.

9

The Effects, Frequency, and Power of the Government's Uses of Deceptive Ambiguity in Criminal Investigations

This book points out that although most past studies of deception in the legal context place their focus on the deception created by suspects and defendants, representatives of the legal institution are equally proficient at being deceptive and do so by using ambiguity to help accomplish their goals. These fifteen investigations demonstrate how police officers, prosecutors, and three types of undercover operatives used various types of deceptive ambiguity during their interactions. The extent to which this ambiguity is intentionally deceptive can be argued, for it is impossible to get into anyone's minds, but it is clear that representatives of the government use ambiguity that often deceives their subjects.

The preceding chapters have illustrated how these officers of the law produced deceptive ambiguity in the elements of their speech events, schemas, agendas, speech acts, conversational strategies, lexicon, and grammar. This chapter first reprises how this deceptive ambiguity relates to the important legal criminal categories of predisposition, intentionality, and voluntariness of the subjects with whom these representatives of the government interacted. This reprise is followed by the admittedly limited evidence suggesting the frequency of the use of deceptive ambiguity in the six elements of the Inverted Pyramid, noting whether more or less ambiguity is used when the government transparently expresses its power than when that power is opaque, hidden, or camouflaged. Finally, the chapter reprises the topic of the legal institution's power, noting how that power is manifested as it creates and manages deceptive ambiguity to achieve the government's purposes.

The Effects of Deceptive Ambiguity on Predisposition, Intentionality, and Voluntariness

Because words and phrases can be contextualized within the larger discourse elements of the Inverted Pyramid, smoking gun evidence normally found in the lexicon and grammar can be a risky place for government investigators to place their confidence. Here we discuss the smoking gun evidence first, since prosecutors commonly consider smoking gun evidence as the most likely indicator of suspects', defendants', and targets' predispositions, motives, intentionality, and voluntariness. After first briefly examining the ways predisposition, intentionality, and voluntariness are purported to exist in the smoking gun evidence of lexicon and grammar, we turn to the contextualizing ways these important legal concepts occur in the larger language elements of the Inverted Pyramid, beginning with the speech event and followed by the elements that systematically grow out of it—schemas, agendas, speech acts, and conversational strategies where deceptive ambiguity can affect our understandings of how predisposition, intentionality, and voluntariness can be adduced.

As the police interview their suspects, they sometimes bring up previous bad acts as evidence of their predisposition, but prosecutors are usually prohibited from reporting defendants' previous bad acts in the context of a trial. Things are a bit different, however, in undercover investigations in which the very reason for targeting a possible perpetrator relies on demonstrating that the targets were predisposed to accept the opportunity given them to commit a crime. Without such a predisposition, there would seem to be little or no justification for pursuing them, for without it the investigators then can be criticized for merely trolling for crimes among citizens who had evidenced no particular predisposition to commit one. In spite of such criticism, the government has indeed trolled for possible crimes at least since the early 1980s during the FBI's massive and expensive undercover operations named Frontload, Speakeasy, Whitewash, Recoup, Colcor, Resfix, Greylord, and the most famous of all, Abscam (Shuy 2013, 28–38). The FBI may have slowed down such trolling for a while after the severe criticism given that agency by the US House of Representatives' Subcommittee on Civil Rights of the Committee on the Judiciary in 1984, but it has intensified since the 9-11 terrorist attacks on the United States, and government agents are now allowed to infiltrate groups whose participant's viewpoints are only inferred or suspected without any preceding proof, including domestic advocacy organizations, churches, mosques, groups that oppose the death penalty, organizations favoring gun control, and others. The government defends this practice of trolling by claiming that its agents do nothing more than provide targets what it calls the *opportunity* to commit crimes.

The legal interpretation of predisposition was first revealed in *Sorells v. United States*, 287 U.S. 435 (1932), as the court discussed the inevitable problems that result when the legal analysis is inappropriately focused upon the predisposition of defendants. In 2002 the Ninth Circuit Court of Appeals also weighed in on this in *United States v. Poehlman*, 217 F.3d 692, saying: "Government agents may not originate a criminal design, implant in an innocent person's mind the disposition to commit a criminal act, and then induce commission of the crime so that the Government may prosecute." Doing this can open the door for the defendant to claim entrapment.

Predisposition bears a direct relationship to intentionality. If it can be shown that a suspect is predisposed to commit a crime, the task of establishing intentionality becomes easier. If there is no evidence of the suspect's past predisposition to commit the crime, undercover agents often try to elicit it during conversations with them. In doing this, however, the agents sometimes stretch the limits of their targets' voluntariness.

LEXICON AND GRAMMAR: THE COMMON SMOKING GUN EVIDENCE REVEALING INTENTIONALITY, PREDISPOSITION, AND VOLUNTARINESS

As indicated throughout this book, I have recommended that the smoking gun evidence usually existing in lexicon and grammar is not optimally the first language element to analyze. I deal with it here first, however, because that is where many prosecutors and even defense lawyers usually begin their examinations of the spoken language evidence. This is not to say that smoking gun expressions are never a problem for the defense. Of course they can be a problem, and once they are noticed they can discourage and even thwart any other analysis even though there may be other language evidence that can refute the prosecution's interpretation. But in many cases such as those illustrated in this book, such smoking gun evidence is not always the straightest path to a conviction because analysis of the entire context sometimes can paint a very different picture. During these fifteen investigations, representatives of the legal institution deceptively used ambiguity themselves and misrepresented and otherwise created lexical and grammatical ambiguity by misrepresenting or misunderstanding the language used by their suspects, defendants, and targets that offered the surface smoking gun appearance that they were predisposed to commit crimes. The following briefly reviews how they accomplished this, leading to the indictments of their subjects.

As noted in chapter 3, police interviewers created ambiguity by misinterpreting and misrepresenting both Jokic's and Gentry's expressions, *hearing about* and *assuming*, as evidence that these suspects actually knew critical facts that would indicate that they were predisposed and intentionally involved with murders.

In much the same way, prosecutors deceptively misrepresented Suyat's definitions of *scab* and *organize* and ignored Sica's tacit definition of the meaning of a *close personal relationship* in ways that created the appearance of smoking gun evidence purportedly showing that these defendants were predisposed to intentionally commit perjury.

Both the undercover agent and prosecutor deceptively reinterpreted Williams's repeated use of *no* to mean his agreement to accept a bribe and they deceptively treated his receipt of stock certificates as though he was predisposed to accept them in spite of the fact that they were unexpectedly and unwillingly thrust upon him without his knowledge that this would happen. The IRS agent produced purported smoking gun evidence by deceptively decontextualizing and reinterpreting Sligh's words, *power, favor*, and *reasons,* as evidence of his predisposition and intention to bribe her.

Undercover agents created deceptive smoking gun evidence by redefining DeLorean's meaning of *investment* and by misinterpreting other references and expressions as his predisposition, intention, and willingness to get involved in a drug transaction.

Cooperating witnesses deceptively wrenched Davis's words, *good, alibi*, and *all right,* from both their physical and discourse contexts to create the appearance of smoking gun evidence that he was predisposed to solicit murder. The cooperating witnesses in Cohen's investigation produced deceptively ambiguous hints to which Cohen gave no language evidence that he understood their illegal association, much less that he had any predisposition to commit a crime. To El-Hindi the cooperating witness used the ambiguous expressions, *training, security, weapons*, and *mask it*, as smoking gun evidence of his predisposition even though El-Hindi's responses clearly demonstrated that he had no idea that these ambiguous expressions referred anything illegal.

A complainant converted the awkward efforts of Poli and McNown to revoke their previous bribery request into smoking gun evidence of their predisposition and willingness to preserve and continue that bribe request. She then deceptively placed the bribe money on her empty chair as they all left the café table, undoubtedly realizing that they would not be able to leave abandoned money lying there unguarded but instead would pick it up and therefore be accused of intentionally accepting her bribe.

Dora's major deceptive ambiguity was to get Sam to apologize for appearing in her daughter's bad dream, after which she used deceptive ambiguity to reinterpret this as his smoking gun apology for being predisposed to commit the sex act that her daughter had purportedly dreamed about.

To Sheriff Preston the complainant created smoking gun evidence of his purported predisposition by deceptively using the ambiguous references *it* and *this* and by inaccurately claiming that when she complained of a pain in her leg, the sheriff put his hand down "in her pants," even though the tape-recorded evidence contained no *in* in that utterance. She also deceptively spoke these purported smoking gun words in a lowered tone of voice to which the sheriff's responses gave no evidence that he could hear what she had said or that he was predisposed to commit sexual abuse when he admitted that he had tried previously to diagnose the problem of the pain in her leg.

The government used these deceptively ambiguous purported smoking gun expressions as proxies for the subjects' predisposition, intentionality, and voluntariness. Isolating smoking guns from the overall language context is a version of proof texting, a technique that uses isolated out-of-context quotations from a conversation or text to try to prove a certain point. However, when these isolated words and expressions identified as smoking guns are properly placed in the overall language context in which they appeared, the alleged predisposition and intention of the speakers can evaporate.

In each of the foregoing investigations, these alleged smoking gun expressions were wrenched from overall contexts that showed that they were not smoking guns at all. The subjects' language gave evidence that their perceptions of the speech events in which they found themselves encouraged them to talk, listen, understand, and react in ways that the government representative's uses of deceptive ambiguity had not made clear. Throughout their interactions, their language revealed their schemas and illustrated their benign predispositions and intentions that grew naturally out of those speech events. Their agendas provided the best available evidence that their motives and intentions were not illegal. Their speech acts supporting the motives that they expressed in their agendas also provided evidence of their lack of predisposition and intention to commit crimes. When the representatives of the legal institution resort to using the conversational strategies of blocking, interrupting, or hit-and-run questioning, it seriously called into question the voluntariness of what the subjects tried to say. It is also of considerable importance that there would have been no need for the government representatives to have used these conversational strategies if the participants had already demonstrated their predisposition and intention to be involved in a crime. The fact that the government representatives resorted to using these strategies suggests that at least up to that point in the conversations the targets had not revealed any criminal predispositions and intentions.

When this purported smoking gun evidence was contextualized within the entire discourse, it was shown to be inadequate evidence of the subjects' predisposition, intentionality, and voluntariness. We next describe how the government representatives could have noticed how the important elements of the speech events and their resulting schemas influenced their own understanding of the issues of predisposition, intentionality, and voluntariness.

SPEECH EVENTS AND SCHEMAS REVEAL PERCEPTIONS OF INTENTIONALITY, PREDISPOSITION, AND VOLUNTARINESS

In this book I have repeatedly stressed that identifying the speech event is the first important task in analyzing spoken language evidence because the speech event determines and influences the language used by the participants and enlightens the understanding of later listeners about that evidence. The speech event also sets the stage for determining the vitally important aspects of predisposition, intentionality, and voluntariness.

The clearest evidence of the representatives of the legal institution's intentional use of deceptive ambiguity occurs during undercover operations carried out by the agents, cooperating witnesses, and complainants who intentionally camouflage their speech events. All nine of the investigations reported in chapters 5, 6, and 7 provide examples of their uses of deceptive ambiguity. When targets are deceived about the speech events that they are led to believe they are in, they become easy prey, because their schemas about what is happening and their subsequent agendas derive from those perceived speech events and these can be very different from the schemas and subsequent agendas of the government's representatives. And when the targets' efforts to express their own agendas are restricted, ignored, or blocked, later listeners can misperceive or misattribute their predispositions and intentions, resulting in the outward appearance of something that the targets' voluntary expression of their own agendas may not have otherwise revealed. The occurrence of undercover operators' intentional uses of deceptive ambiguity is not surprising, however, because law enforcement authorizes its undercover agents, cooperating witnesses, and complainants to be deceptively ambiguous in order to provide their targets the alleged opportunity to engage in criminal behavior.

When the legal institution's power is clear and opaque, as in police interviews and prosecutorial questioning, these speech events provide somewhat less deceptive ambiguity than is found in undercover operations, although there is still considerable evidence of its presence. For example, during courtroom hearing speech events in which prosecutors initially identify their speech events as efforts to discover the culpability of suspects other than the individuals they are questioning, they sometimes then convert that speech event into one of accusing those witnesses who previously had been led to believe that they were being questioned in order to assist the prosecution about a different suspect.

Steven Suyat, Larry Gentry, Father Sica, and Major Jokic suddenly realized that the prosecutors had switched their speech events away from the one that was announced. Although they were led to believe that they were in information-gathering speech events, they suddenly found themselves in accusation speech events. This surprising, abrupt change disadvantaged them emotionally and linguistically as they suddenly needed to adjust their response strategies from being helpful to the government to now needing to defend themselves against the accusations that were thrust upon them. The previously cooperative speech event playing field then became very different, requiring different language skills and strategies, to say nothing of sudden psychological adjustments created by what could seem like an ambush to them. When the speech event is initially disguised as something different, the sudden and surprising shift from the announced cooperative speech event to a very different oppositional one not only hampers subjects from making their predispositions and intentions clear but also creates a cumulative effect on later listeners, including juries, that they must have been guilty from the start. Although the practice of switching the speech event may be justified as a conventional courtroom tactic used by prosecutors, it also must be recognized as one that involves deceptive ambiguity.

Evidence of the schemas of suspects, defendants, and targets grow out of their perceptions of the announced speech event and are primarily revealed in the language they use to represent their agendas and speech acts. The common and predictable schemas of police interviewers, prosecutors, and undercover agents are that their suspects, defendants, and targets are very likely guilty, for otherwise there would be no need to talk with them. One of their tasks is for these representatives of the government to find evidence of predisposition in their subjects and to attribute this as their motive for committing the alleged crimes. The fifteen cases described in this book demonstrate that when the language evidence of suspects, defendants, and targets offered no indication of schemas that would support their predisposition or motive to commit the crimes, the police, prosecutors, and agents often ignored this and resorted to various types of ambiguous deception to try to produce evidence of such predisposition.

AGENDAS REVEAL INTENTIONALITY, PREDISPOSITION, AND VOLUNTARINESS

When suspects, defendants, or undercover targets do not explicitly admit their guilt, it can be useful to both the prosecution and the defense to try to discover clues that can discover what their intentions may have been. Since it is relatively rare that criminal intentions are stated performatively, as in "I intended to rob the bank," one of the best if not the only available way to discover clues to such intentions is to carefully examine the topics that the speakers introduce and their responses to the topics introduced by others (Shuy 2013, 2014). In the cases described in this book, police, prosecutors, and undercover agents sometimes deceptively ignored or blocked the efforts of their suspects, defendants, and targets to express their own agendas. When this important element of interactive exchanges is omitted, the result can be an incomplete and ultimately negative impression of a speaker'intentions and predisposition that creates an equally negative effect in the official record that jurors eventually have to assess. When the subjects' responses are blocked, evidence of their voluntariness can be questioned. Without contextual evidence provided by the participants' agendas, later listeners are required to infer their intentions, and it is well recognized that inferences can be very wrong.

Because they had total control of the questioning process, the powerful police interviewers had the discourse advantage of putting forth their own agendas and at the same time downplaying, blocking, or ignoring the efforts of suspects like Jokic to describe his own agenda and predisposition that might be able to have provided evidence of his intentionality. Based on the only records that the interviewers made available, the police appeared to have used their institutional power to block Rogers and Carter from even trying to introduce their own agendas. Subjects such as Suyat, Gentry and Jokic are particularly vulnerable to deceptive ambiguity when they are used as friendly witnesses for the prosecution, or when, like Gentry, they are required to participate in a search warrant hearing. One problem is that in such instances the purportedly friendly witnesses are not represented by an attorney and therefore are not protected by that attorney's presence and advice. Even at their own subsequent trials Suyat, Gentry, and Jokic were disadvantaged by having their agendas either blocked or misrepresented by their prosecutors, leaving absent the crucial avenues for revealing their intentions as well as calling into question their voluntariness.

In the cases described in this book, all of the undercover agents, prosecutors, police, cooperating witnesses, and complainants at some points deceptively and ambiguously blocked or misinterpreted the agendas of their targets, preventing later listeners from discovering their lack of intentions to commit the crimes for which they were accused and thereby leaving whatever intentions they may have had unavailable for the jury to consider. Determining intentionality is important in all types of criminal cases. When there is a lack of clear and unambiguous evidence that demonstrates predisposition, intentionality, and voluntariness, it necessary to try to discover these important matters through police interviews, questioning at trial, or undercover operations. But when the legal institution uses deceptive ambiguity, such efforts can be seriously challenged by calling on linguistic analysis. By far the least satisfactory way to adduce individual intentions, predisposition, and voluntariness, however, is to infer them, as happened in the cases of Williams, DeLorean, Sligh, Davis, Cohen, El-Hindi, Poli and McNown, Sam, and the sheriff.

SPEECH ACTS REVEAL PREDISPOSITION, INTENTIONALITY, AND VOLUNTARINESS

As the cases described in this book point out, linguistic analysis of speech acts can help reveal clues about whether individuals are predisposed to take an action and what their motives and intentions were to take such action. Like agendas, individual speech acts can be blocked and when their conversational partners do this we have no way to be sure what those intentions and predispositions may have been. Such blocking also raises the obviously important issue of voluntariness. In addition to blocking speech acts, the police interviewers, prosecutors, and undercover operators sometimes deceptively misrepresent or ignore the speech acts of suspects, defendants, and targets. Such deception creates ambiguity for later listeners and eliminates what could have provided further indications of the subjects' predisposition, intentionality, and voluntariness.

The police omitted any possible understanding of Kevin Rogers's speech acts by leaving no evidence of the questions that generated his unrecorded and therefore not verifiable speech acts. It is important to know how they may have asked those questions that elicited Rogers's alleged responses, and the time sequences and topic contexts in which those exchanges took place. Ironically, this blocking also blocked the government's own effort to establish evidence of his predisposition, voluntariness, and intentions, leaving these only to be inferred.

During the brief recorded portion of Michael Carter's interview during which he was crying and vomiting, Carter produced the speech act of denying his guilt many times. Although his written confession purportedly was derived from the unrecorded part of the interview that allegedly contained his speech act of admitting, it failed to report the speech acts of the officer's questions that Carter allegedly answered. This omission produced deceptive ambiguity for later listeners such as jurors, who were thereby prevented from knowing the actual questions and answers that related to his intentionality and predisposition. And, of course, this also created serious doubts about Carter's voluntariness.

Dragan Jokic's questioners created deceptive ambiguity by misrepresenting his speech acts of requesting information and his speech acts of giving opinions by mistakenly treating the latter as his speech acts of reporting factual knowledge. This strategy actually hindered the discovery of his actual intentionality, his predisposition to become involved in the Srebrenica massacre, and invited the question of the voluntariness of Jokic's responses.

Prosecutors created deceptive ambiguity by ignoring Steven Suyat's and Father Sica's speech acts of requesting clarification and by misrepresenting Larry Gentry's speech acts of denying his guilt as his purported speech act of admitting it. They misinterpreted and inferred Sica's speech act of not recalling a specific event that took place some twenty years earlier as evidence of his perjury. When law officers ignore and misrepresent what the subjects say, it casts serious doubt on their predisposition, intentionality, and voluntariness.

The undercover agents ignored Senator Williams's speech acts of rejecting the bribe offer as well as John DeLorean's speech act of rejecting the agent's speech act of offering him the opportunity to purchase illegal drugs. They misrepresented DeLorean's speech act of opining about the value of the drugs by interpreting it as his willingness to purchase them. The IRS agent misrepresented Vernon Sligh's repeated speech acts of requesting help about how to report his taxes as his efforts to bribe her. When brought to light, the misrepresentations of these speech acts cast doubt on the prosecution's claim that Sligh had the intention and predisposition to commit bribery and that he acted voluntarily when he actually offered the IRS agent a bribe.

Cullen Davis's investigation illustrated how the cooperating witness's speech acts suggesting that Davis agreed to hire a hit man were made meaningless because these speech acts were deceptively spoken outside the hearing range of the target. Yochi Cohen's investigation illustrated how his speech act of agreeing did not connect with what the agents perceived that agreement to be for. And Marwan El-Hindi's case demonstrated how his speech acts of agreement could not be grammatically connected with the discourse topics being discussed. Predispositions and intentions to commit crimes were not evident in these instances and voluntariness could be called into question.

The trial of John Poli and John McNown revealed how the undercover complainant failed to interpret accurately the suspects' speech act of revoking their earlier bribe request. Instead, the madam used deceptive ambiguity to make their revocation appear to be the speech act of their agreement. She also was deceptively ambiguous in her non-verbal speech act of trying to complete the bribery event by leaving that bribe money on her chair as they all left the table where they had been sitting and talking. We can even ask whether picking up this money was a voluntary act.

Ambiguous deception was also evidenced by the complainants' misattributing the objects of the speech acts of apologizing made by Sam and by Sheriff Preston.

When such deception is evident, predisposition, intentionality, and voluntariness are questionable. All of these instances of the government's deceptively ambiguous treatment of speech acts pose serious questions about the subjects' predisposition and intentionality to commit the crimes as well as the alleged voluntariness of statements that the prosecution judged crucial to the investigations.

CONVERSATIONAL STRATEGIES CALL VOLUNTARINESS INTO QUESTION

As these investigations demonstrate, conversational strategies used by representatives of the government can strongly influence the voluntariness of the persons upon whom such strategies are used. Conversational strategies fall under the discourse category of efforts to persuade others to accept the speakers' own positions. There are perfectly appropriate ways to persuade, but there also are strategies that are highly questionable, especially in the legal context (Shuy 2005: 11–29). Here I refer to the government's questionable conversational strategies that influenced the voluntariness of those who were subjected to them.

The most common questionable conversational strategy is the use of ambiguity, the central focus of this book. However, there were other questionable conversational strategies used as well, including various types of blocking what the subjects were trying to say, interrupting them during their turns of talk, failing to provide contextual information that was important for them to know, using the hit-and-run strategy, offering ambiguous hints (hinting is ambiguous by definition), asking two or more questions at the same time, and scripting their targets with what they should say.

These conversational strategies can often give later listeners the false impression that the targets were voluntarily implicated in criminality when the contextualized language evidence indicates otherwise. Ambiguity, blocking, interrupting, hit-and-run questioning, and hinting contaminate important parts of the language evidence that the government representatives could have avoided because these conversational strategies directly hampered the voluntariness of their subjects.

To Michael Carter the police used the conversational strategy of blocking his opportunities to respond their questions during his interview and then blocked any knowledge of what happened after that by turning the taperecorder off. In addition, the detective blocked Michael's own words found in his confession statement by writing it himself. These acts call to question Michael's voluntariness. Whether or not they blocked Kevin Rogers's words during his interview is not clear, because the police preserved no verifiable records of it. As a result, later listeners could not learn how voluntarily this suspect would have responded because the conversational strategy of blocking prevented any way to discover it. The interviewers blocked Major Jokic's responses by continuously interrupting his efforts to talk and by asking him hit-and-run questions (changing the subject before he could answer), thus providing the false impression that he had been evasive.

In the same way, the prosecutor distorted Suyat's voluntariness by using the conversational strategy of blocking Steven's efforts to request clarification about the prosecutor's ambiguous questions as well as his efforts to clarify his own incomplete answers. Larry Gentry's prosecutor used the conversational strategy of asking two questions at the same time, to which Gentry followed the conventional recency principle of answering only the second question, leaving the first and more potentially damaging question unanswered. This provided the false impression to later listeners that he had been voluntarily evasive. Father Sica's prosecutor used the conversational strategy of ignoring the priest's tacit definition of a critical phrase by redefining it in his own way, thereby producing the false effect that Sica was voluntarily agreeing with him.

In Senator Williams's investigation, the pre-arranged telephone interruption made by a second agent monitoring their exchange from an adjacent room enabled the sheik to employ the conversational strategy of blocking Williams's attempt to explain the reason why he could not accept the sheik's offer of a bribe. This interruption created deceptive ambiguity for later listeners, including the jury, about Williams's voluntariness. The agent tried to block John DeLorean's rejection of the drug scheme and then went on talking as though his target hadn't rejected it, causing the resulting deceptive ambiguity that DeLorean voluntarily had agreed to participate in the scheme. Similarly, the

IRS agent ignored Vernon Sligh's many efforts to act legally and then used the deceptively ambiguous strategy of scripting him about how to offer her a bribe.

The cooperating witness used the conversational strategy of deceptively blocking Cullen Davis from hearing the smoking gun words that he uttered outside of Davis's hearing range, creating deceptive ambiguity for the jury to untangle about Davis's voluntariness to commit the crime of soliciting murder. The cooperating witness used the conversational strategy of ignoring Yochi Cohen's rejections of the bribe offer and threw in a number of deceptively ambiguous hints to which Cohen gave no language evidence that he understood, thereby creating the deceptively ambiguous impression that Cohen would voluntarily commit a crime. Marwan El-Hindi's cooperating witness also used the conversational strategy of producing many deceptively ambiguous hints that the target's language gave no indication that he understood. This cooperating witness's critical deceptive conversational strategy, however, was to manipulate a physical setting in which El-Hindi was blocked from knowing what was actually going on during a group conversation that took place in an adjacent room during the playing of the allegedly crucial videotapes. This gave the impression that El-Hindi was voluntarily committing the terrorist act that the prosecution called "electronic jihad."

The complainant used the conversational strategy of blocking the efforts of John Poli and John McNown to reject her bribe offer when she deceptively and ambiguously left the rejected bribe money on her chair, after which the prosecutor charged the two targets with voluntarily accepting her bribe. After Dora was ambiguously deceptive to Sam by conflating her daughter's dream about sex abuse with the actual event, she employed the conversational strategy of repeating her accusations over and over again, a familiar conversational strategy borrowed from the tactics of clever salespersons. This conversational strategy eventually wore down Sam's resistance to the point that he appeared to voluntarily agree with her, even though this apparent agreement gave every reason to be considered his effort to get rid of her annoying and often irrational phone call. The complainant who talked with Sheriff Preston used the deceptively ambiguous conversational strategy of uttering the smoking gun words so softly that the hearing-impaired sheriff gave no evidence of hearing what she said (similar to the conversational strategy used in the investigation of Davis). Nevertheless, it gave the appearance of the sheriff's voluntary admission of guilt. She then refused to respond to his speech act of requesting repetition of what she said, leaving her accusation on the tape as deceptively ambiguous evidence that he had admitted his guilt.

These conversational strategies went far beyond the benign definition of persuasion and are better classified as deceptively coercive because they created ambiguity while encouraging later listeners to get a false impression that the suspects, defendants, and targets were voluntarily acknowledging their own guilt.

The powerful prosecution gains a distinct advantage when it uses deceptive ambiguity to block suspects, defendants, and targets from expressing what they may have intended to say, thereby creating the impression that they were predisposed to commit the crime intentionally and that they voluntarily admitted it. Since jurors come to the trial knowing that an indictment has been made, they too have predictable predispositions about the subject's predispositions and intentions. When there is tape-recorded evidence, they naturally assume that the police, prosecutors, and undercover operatives have elicited the critical language fairly and have captured admissions of guilt voluntarily. When jurors perceive that there is evidence from these suspects, defendants, and targets indicating that they had a predisposition or intention to commit the crime, they may not realize that the government representatives' used deceptive ambiguity to create it and that these subjects did not understand what was happening to them. Even when undercover targets like Cohen, Williams, and DeLorean came to understand the criminal opportunity and then rejected the offer to become involved in it, the fact that the event took place gave the appearance of criminality that remained so fixed in the jurors' minds that it became difficult for them to separate this fact from what actually occurred.

Frequency of the Government's Uses of Deceptive Ambiguity in Each of the Six Language Elements of the Inverted Pyramid

Perhaps it is not surprising that the government's use of deceptive ambiguity in these fifteen criminal investigations can go relatively unnoticed. First, since representatives of the law have the advantage of carrying out the necessary and acceptable regulatory task of unmasking and prosecuting criminal behavior, society is predisposed to believe they have reason to do this in an aboveboard manner. It is natural and easy to expect the legal institution to do its work fairly and properly.

A second reason that the public has not focused on deceptive ambiguity used by the legal institution is that the tasks and methods of institutionally powerful police officers, prosecutors, and undercover agents have been passively and conventionally understood and accepted. The public is aware that its legal officials are accustomed to interviewing their subjects but are less familiar with the idea that these subjects are relatively unfamiliar with task of interacting in the legal context. This important ballgame is played on the home team's field, by the home team's rules, and with the home team's umpires.

A third reason is that the tactic of successfully using deceptive ambiguity to accomplish conversational goals has not been fully recognized by the public in the legal arena. The public may understand that police and prosecutors are legally restrained from using certain of the more obvious forms of deception and coercion and that if they risk doing this, they are likely to suffer reprimands or be challenged by defense lawyers or judges. Much less is known, however, about how police and prosecutors subtly produce ambiguity in the hope that suspects, defendants, and targets will fail to notice it and respond in ways that either inculpate or appear to inculpate themselves.

Having illustrated how the government representatives use deceptive ambiguity, it may be helpful to learn whether it is found more in police interviews, prosecutorial questioning, or undercover operations. The fifteen representative interactions described in chapters 3 through 7 indicate that the quantity of deceptive ambiguity used by police, prosecutors, and all three types of undercover agents varies somewhat. The only goal here is to provide a broad-brush comparison of the relative frequency of deceptive ambiguity in these types of investigations. It does not take this comparison to the next possible quantitative step, a study that could better describe ratios of such usage in relationship to each other and to other aspects of the interactions.

Although this book does not claim to present a comprehensive quantitative analysis of the frequency of the government's use of deceptive ambiguity, this rough comparison uses the subjective indicators of the broad categories of *consistently, frequently*, and *sometimes* to represent the frequency of occurrence of the deceptive ambiguity revealed in these fifteen example cases.

Table 9.1 roughly demonstrates that the three types of camouflaged undercover operators used relatively more deceptive ambiguity than was found in the more transparent interviews by police officers and prosecutors. One explanation for the fact that prosecutors use comparatively less deceptive ambiguity is that a judge is present during their interactions to monitor this courtroom speech event. When police interviews are recorded, the intelligence analyst (the prosecutor) performs similar monitoring of these interview speech events although this happens after they have already taken place. The presence of contempory or later evaluation apparently serves as an umpiring function to limit the use of using deceptive ambiguity in some of the elements of the Inverted Pyramid.

In contrast, undercover agents, cooperating witnesses, and complainants are given carte blanch to be deceptively ambiguous about the speech events that they introduce to their targets. As Table 9.1 shows, they also use deceptive ambiguity more frequently in the manipulation of their targets' schemas and agendas primarily because their deceptively camouflaged speech event nicely sets the table for these elements of the Inverted Pyramid. But undercover agents are not alone in frequently using deceptive ambiguity. The speech events conducted by police and prosecutors with suspects and defendants also contain instances of deceptive ambiguity when they give their subjects false conceptions about the speech events they were led to believe they were in.

The frequency of deceptive ambiguity relating to speech acts and conversational strategies distributes rather equally across all five types of interactions, while police and prosecutors appear to rely more heavily on deceptive ambiguity located in their uses of ambiguously deceptive lexicon and grammar.

TABLE 9.1

Frequency of deceptive ambiguity used by representatives of the legal institution with these suspects, defendants, and targets

Inverted Pyramid	Government Representatives				
	Police	Prosecutors	Undercover Agents	Cooperating Witnesses	Complainants
Speech events	Frequently	Consistently	Consistently	Consistently	Consistently
Schemas	Sometimes	Consistently	Consistently	Consistently	Consistently
Agendas	Sometimes	Sometimes	Consistently	Consistently	Consistently
Speech acts	Sometimes	Sometimes	Sometimes	Sometimes	Frequently
Conv. strat.	Frequently	Frequently	Frequently	Sometimes	Sometimes
Lex., & Gr	Frequently	Frequently	Sometimes	Sometimes	Sometimes

However quantitatively oversimplified Table 9.1 may be, it shows that undercover operators use deceptive ambiguity more frequently than do the police in their interviews with suspects and the prosecutors in their courtroom questioning. It is noteworthy, however, that not one of these categories is empty. We can take from this that all representatives of the legal institution use varying amounts of deceptive ambiguity during their interactions with their suspects, defendants, and targets.

The Role of Power in the Context of Police Interviews, Courtroom Examinations, and Undercover Operations

Since chapter 2 identified the characteristics of power as control, authority, domination, reinterpretation, inequality, and persuasion, it can be useful to briefly review how these definitions of power are reflected in the way police, prosecutors, and undercover agents use these elements of institutional power.

CONTROL AND INEQUALITY

Language power is most easily recognized when it is distributed unequally. The first benefit of power is that speakers who have it can control and direct the interaction however they choose, while less powerful speakers cannot. The communicative control of police interviewers and prosecutorial examiners is obvious not only because of the power provided by the physical settings in which they apply their status as officers of the law, but also by the way they use language to control the speech event, set the agenda, and ask most or all of the questions. Because this control is transparently obvious to all, police and prosecutors must try to give the appearance of not misusing it in obvious ways. As chapters 3 and 4 illustrate, police and prosecutors can supplement their already present advantages of control by using deceptive ambiguity to help them achieve their goals. Considerably less transparent and obvious, however, is the way undercover operatives establish their control. Since they do not share the advantage of the transparent control afforded to police and prosecutors, camouflaged agents find it necessary to use even more deceptive ambiguity to achieve their goals, beginning with the deceptively ambiguous speech event and the other conversational advantages that grow out of it.

AUTHORITY AND DOMINATION

Those who have power to control interactions with others have the unquestioned authority to dominate those with whom they interact, which is especially evident when the communicative events involve conflicts of interest. This authority and domination is obvious during police interviews and prosecutorial courtroom examinations, permitting those representatives of the legal institution to introduce all of the topics, to control the flow of the interactions, and to block any resistance or objections. Even with this great advantage, however, chapters 3 and 4 provide illustrations in which police and prosecutors used deceptive ambiguity to supplement the power given by their authority and domination. As chapters 5, 6, and 7 illustrate, undercover operators had to disguise their authority in order to preserve their appearance as conversational and social equals. This apparently led them to use even more deceptive ambiguity in order to accomplish their goals.

REINTERPRETATION AND PERSUASION

Powerful speakers who have the control and authority to dominate others also have the power to get their subjects to reinterpret their own points of view. In many interactive situations this is called the power to persuade people to change their opinions, values, or beliefs about such things as purchasing products or changing their religious orientations. In situations that involve serious conflicts of interest, however, such persuasion can take on different attributes that are evident when police and prosecutors try to persuade suspects and defendants to admit or otherwise reveal their guilt. As chapters 3 and 4 indicate, when police and prosecutors tried to reinterpret what their subjects said in ways that suited the purposes of their questioning, they found deceptive ambiguity a useful way to accomplish this. As chapters 5, 6, and 7 point out, when undercover agents tried to get targets to reinterpret their predispositions and intentions to indicate illegality, these agents also used several types of deceptive ambiguity to accomplish this. Among other methods, it was particularly effective for them to employ the conversational strategies of blocking, interrupting, hit-and-run, and compound questions that encouraged their respondents to follow the recency principle of responding to the last (most recent) question while overlooking the other more critical (least recent) part of these compound questions.

Previously Underrecognized Power of the Legal Institution

Fairclough (2015: 73–89) points out that there is a difference between transparent power *in* discourse and power *behind* discourse. His meaning of power *in* discourse refers to unequal encounters, such as those found in the classroom or job interviews, where one participant shapes the discourse event by controlling the contributions of others. He defines the power *behind* discourse as power that is hidden and therefore not apparent at the surface level of the interactions (27).

In his discussion of power *behind* discourse, however, Fairclough does not treat institutional power in the context of exchanges between representatives of the legal institution and the individuals with whom they interact. This book therefore provides an additional dimension to his differentiation between power that occurs *in* discourse and the often unseen or unrecognized power *behind* it. Police, prosecutors, and undercover agents certainly hold indisputable institutional power over the individuals with whom they talk which, according to Fairclough, makes such encounters unequal. As the cases in this book illustrate, the representatives of the legal institution also hold hidden power *behind* their discourse as well as *in* it. Their power to be deceptively ambiguous is an important form of power that seems not to have been fully recognized in past research about institutional power.

Another previously underdeveloped issue is whether institutional power is manifested more frequently when the identity of the institution is transparent than when it is opaque. One might expect that the physical settings of the police station and courtroom, along with the clear presence and obviously recognized authority held by law enforcement officers and prosecutors, would exhibit more institutional power over individuals who come before them than would undercover operations in which that institutional power is not at all evident. But this seems not to be the case. Table 9.1 provides evidence that when we account for the use of the conversational use of deceptive ambiguity, we find that the presence of institutional power thrives even during undercover interactions in which the physical symbols of the courthouse and authority of government representatives are not present.

Apparently in undercover operations the intentionally camouflaged use of deceptive ambiguity enables institutional power to exist just as well as it does during transparent police interviews and prosecutorial questioning. The interactions during all three types of undercover operations demonstrate that agents, cooperating witnesses, and complainants relied on deceptive ambiguity to assert their power even when it was not accompanied by the cover of powerful institutional support. One way they did this was by creating misperceptions of the speech events that led to inaccurate schemas about what was going on. These inaccurate schemas about what was happening then limited subjects' ability to demonstrate their own relevant agendas and speech acts that could have supported their legally benign intentions. In addition, the undercover agents used questionable conversational strategies to produce perceptions of agreement, which was a very effective way to create a false impression that the targets had voluntarily expressed their guilt. Therefore, even though the undercover agents surrendered their institutional transparency, virtually all of them compensated by using deceptive ambiguity in all the elements of the Inverted Pyramid.

Chapter 2 cited van Dijk's observation (2008: 41) that sociologists and political scientists commonly study power at the macro level of institutions while linguists examine it from the micro level of individual use. He observed that a huge gap remains between the more linguistically oriented micro-level studies of text and talk and the institutional studies of macro-level power. The interactions examined in this book provide at least one instance to help fill the missing connection between the macro level of institutional power and the micro-level power of individuals who are outsiders to the legal institution. Although macro institutional power is made transparently visible in the physical context of a police station and a courtroom and in the widely recognized and understood power invested by the power, authority, and control of law, the examples in this book indicate that police and prosecutors exerted their macro institutional power not only through these transparent ways but also through the use of more micro, subtly created language featuring deceptive ambiguity that was not obvious to their individual subjects.

Deception used by police and prosecutors is not usually accomplished through outright lies, because doing so could create serious legal repercussions about the way the evidence was gathered and the way it was presented in the courtroom. Instead, the examples in this book demonstrate that deception operated in the ways the police and prosecutors used ambiguity to misinterpret how their suspects and defendants interacted to their speech events, schemas, agendas, and speech acts. This deception is even more obvious when representatives of the law used deceptive conversational strategies to persuade their subjects and to influence or alter their responses.

The government's use of non-transparent undercover operations has opened the door to even more deceptive ambiguity through the intentional deception it authorized, beginning with the creation of false speech events that, as the cases demonstrate, invited targets to have equally false schemas about what was going on. Undercover agents deceptively took the opportunity to block their targets from revealing their own agendas and then reinterpreted and restated whatever aspects of their targets' agendas managed to emerge in ways that appeared to support the idea that they had guilty intentions. These undercover agents also deceptively misinterpreted their targets' speech acts and revealed their own deception in the ways they used ambiguous conversational strategies to give the impression of voluntariness.

These fifteen investigations also offer the opportunity to reprise the observation made by Bogoch (1994) that the concept of strong institutional power, distance, and solidarity that is reportedly dominant in many parts of the world may be diminishing in Western democratic countries. This book provided examples of cases that do not support Bogoch's observation. Based on this admittedly small sample in the American context of police interviews, courtroom interactions, and undercover operations, the legal institution is apparently managing to firmly hold onto its power rather well. The findings here demonstrate that institutional power appears to remain strong both when its representatives use it transparently and especially when they hide it from the awareness of those with whom they interact. It shows how law's institutional power survives and is maintained in all of these interactive settings by manifesting itself through deceptive uses of ambiguity.

In addition to the power of the commonly emphasized linguistic features of words and grammar, the power of deceptive ambiguity is clearly revealed through the discourse elements that include the speech events, schemas, agendas, speech acts, and conversational strategies found in interactions in which the macro-level institution exists side by side with the micro-level individuals. Comparing the uses of deceptive ambiguity in its transparent versus opaque institutional settings demonstrates that it is generated by a much larger language context than words, phrases, and grammatical constructions. Although those language elements also can produce deceptive ambiguity, analysis of the larger context of these fifteen interactions demonstrates that deceptive ambiguity often originates in the elements of the contextualized larger units of language—speech events, schemas, speech acts, and agendas—and that when the entire language evidence is analyzed, the smoking gun accusations found in the lexicon and grammar sometimes can be more fully and satisfactorily explained.

APPENDIX A

Deceptive Ambiguity Created by Socio-cultural Differences

Socio-cultural differences between the language used by representatives of the legal institution and the people with whom they interact can also provide evidence of deceptive ambiguity. Differing schemas based on prior knowledge, values, attitudes, and beliefs play a large role in this.

Although socio-cultural issues do not fit heatly into the Inverted Pyramid approach discussed in this book, they provide additional evidence of ambiguity that can be deceptive. Sociolinguists have been identifying socio-cultural forms of lexicon and grammar of for many years (Labov 1972; Wolfram and Fasold 1974; Baugh 1983; Fasold 1990, and many others). Kecsckes includes such socio-cultural differences in what he calls "pragma-discourse" (Kecskes 2014: 8). The following summarizes the ways socio-cultural language differences revealed deceptive ambiguity in the fifteen cases described in this book.

Deceptive Ambiguity Created by Police Interviewers

Perhaps the most obvious socio-cultural differences occur when white majority interviewers talk with minority suspects, when adult interviewers speak with juvenile suspects, when native English speakers talk with non-native English speakers, and when mentally competent speakers interact with the less mentally competent. All of these come together when law enforcement representatives interact with individuals of any race, age, or intellectual capacity and these socio-cultural differences become apparent during their interactions.

Kevin Rogers's confession statement provided no indication of whether or not the police took into consideration that he was an African American minor, that he was mentally slow, or that his non-standard use of English varied widely from that of his questioners. It can be easy for police interviewers to ignore important socio-cultural communication differences, especially when the suspects are juveniles, are emotionally distraught, are impaired by alcohol or drugs, or, as in Kevin Rogers's case, are mentally slow (Shuy 2014). Even if Rogers's mental handicap had been considered by the prosecutor at trial (which it was not), it was deceptive for the detectives and prosecutors to omit such consideration during their interview with him and during his trial. Nor did the white, middle class detectives who interviewed the emotionally distraught juvenile, Michael Carter, demonstrate any evidence that they took into account their subject's African American vernacular and culture. In both of these cases the white police officers used a dialect and style of English very different from that of these young boys. Their sociolinguistic differences demonstrated that the resulting alleged confession statements were actually constructed in the words of the powerful police officers rather than in the language of their suspects. This produced deceptive ambiguity not only for the suspects but also for the subsequent prosecutors, judges, and triers of the fact. In contrast, Dragan Jokic and his interviewers appeared to be relative social equals and this produced no ambiguity of this type during their interactions.

Deceptive Ambiguity Created by Prosecutors

Steven Suyat was a relatively uneducated man who grew up on a Hawaiian backwater island speaking Hawaiian Pidgin, making him sociolinguistically vulnerable to the expert language skills of his well-educated, powerful prosecutor. Even so, Suyat knew enough to realize that he should try to answer the questions asked him compliantly and to the best of his ability. His problem was that his powerlessness to engage with the prosecutor on equal sociocultural terms caused him to not try to challenge the prosecutor with requests for clarification but rather to try to infer what the prosecutor meant by his questions that were not made clear to him. This resulted in Suyat's inability to recognize the ambiguity created by the prosecutor's use of the crucial expression, *organize contractors*. Suyat apparently assumed that the prosecutor obviously would know that unions organize rank-and-file workers rather than their contractors. He also was not up to the task of getting the prosecutor to clarify his ambiguous two-part question that demanded a yes or no answer, even though either answer by itself would not represent what he needed to say. Such questions are not limited to less educated defendants, of course, but they are especially deceptively ambiguous to less educated defendants who find it difficult to request clarification. Nor did Suyat give evidence of understanding the prosecutor's English effectively enough to grasp the subtle nuances conveyed in his question about what Suyat meant by the word *scab*. Suyat apparently understood that the question demanded a fancy dictionary definition that he felt incompetent to provide.

Larry Gentry had a different socio-cultural problem when the prosecutor questioned him. Since Gentry had borderline intelligence and very poor language and social skills, his responses showed that he was unable to see the implications of his rather inept answers to the prosecutor's questions and was unable to explain that he had been misquoted in an earlier interview with the police that contained crucial deceptive ambiguity concerning his involvement in the crime. Conversational repair is not easy for even intelligent speakers of the same socio-cultural status with the prosecutor, but for Gentry it proved to be impossible to manage with his powerful and articulate adversary.

During Father Joseph Sica's testimony before the prosecutor, the socio-cultural differences were reversed. Here it was the prosecutor who apparently did not know the culture of the priesthood well enough to understand that priests can be obliged to write thank you notes for ordination gifts, give the last rites to those who are on their death beds in hospitals, and write character witness letters for those who have befriended them even in minor ways. The prosecutor mischaracterized these priestly socio-cultural activities as evidence that Father Sica had a "close personal friendship" with a known criminal.

Deceptive Ambiguity Created by Undercover Agents

Ambiguity occurs frequently between speakers of the same language, but when second-language speakers are involved, the opportunities for misunderstanding can increase dramatically. In the legal setting there is probably no more prominent example of this than when the police read second-language speakers their *Miranda* rights in English. Statements like "you have the right to remain silent" and "you have the right to have an attorney present" have been shown to be ambiguous even to native English speakers, but much more so to non-native English speakers. When the police then ask suspects if they understand these rights, they usually compliantly agree, whether or not they understand the significance of their agreement. In such cases not only are the suspects deceived by what they didn't understand, but the police, prosecutors and juries also are deceived into thinking they have heard the suspect's felicitous agreement to waive their constitutional rights.

This type of ambiguity is equally deceptive when native English-speaking agents fake foreign cultural and language interference as they talk with targets during undercover sting operations. Even when targets are able to predict the potential problems of non-native speakers' English pronunciation, vocabulary, and syntax, agents who fake their non-nativeness often fail to produce it in the way that genuine non-native speakers do. And when a listener is not familiar with a non-native speaker's language, such as Spanish or Arabic, the agent's faked, less than accurate, and therefore unpredictable representation of foreignness can further reduce the listener's chances of accurately decoding what that speaker is saying. This creates deceptive ambiguity and incomprehensibility.

Senator Harrison Williams found himself in exactly that situation when he talked with the native English-speaking FBI agent who was disguised in typically Arab clothing and tried to fake a non-standard rendition of English. The senator revealed that he was unfamiliar with the Arab culture by the way he pronounced Emirates with four syllables as "em-er-*ate*-ies," with stress on the third syllable. He was apparently equally unfamiliar with the problems that native speakers of other languages have when they try to speak English. Nor did he know that the sheik was actually a native speaker of English who was faking his foreign accent. A listener familiar with Arabic likely would have recognized this accent as fake, but the senator was no linguist and he missed all the available clues. It is natural for a native speaker to try to be polite and understanding to accommodate the stumbling efforts of non-native speakers (Giles and Coupland 1991). It is even more predictable that a US senator would try to socially and politically accommodate a purported foreign dignitary such as a visiting Arab sheik.

Senator Williams managed to understand one thing, however. He believed he was talking with an educated foreign dignitary whose culture may not have allowed him to understand that bribery was a crime in America. This degree of cross-cultural sensitivity caused Williams to treat the sheik with dignity rather than to excoriate him for offering a bribe. The prosecution failed to recognize this socio-cultural conflict and claimed that if Williams really were an honest man, he would have strongly criticized the sheik. Such an accusation might be justified in a mono-cultural context, but the senator was well aware that this was one of those cross-cultural events in which the alleged Arab sheik's understanding of bribery laws in America could be very different.

John DeLorean and the first FBI agent posing as a banker were at least roughly equivalent in social status and language, for they both appeared to know the fields of banking and investment well. Even when the second agent, Hoffman, appeared on the scene in the final tape, the two men had at least the same background knowledge relating to the time they had lived near each other in San Diego a few years earlier. But when Hoffman launched into his drug discussion, DeLorean appeared to be puzzled, perhaps because of the shock of coming face to face with the real drug culture and language for the first time. His lack of predisposition to commit a drug-related crime also could be understood by the fact that earlier in his career DeLorean, who hated the drug problem in America, had sold his interest in a professional football team after some of the players got involved in drug transactions.

The middle-class, female, Caucasian IRS agent who interviewed the working-class, African American taxpayer, Vernon Sligh, began this interaction with socio-cultural advantages. She was in the racial majority and was also an expert in tax matters about which Sligh was admittedly ignorant. This power imbalance was clear from the start and was even recognized by Sligh when he described to her how difficult it was for "black men like me to find the answers we need." During his initial rejection of the agent's request for a bribe, he lamented that a black man "stood a poor chance of survival in prison." Rather than taking advantage of her socio-cultural difference, the agent might have been expected to accommodate Sligh's difference in knowledge and background by adjusting to it. Instead, she operated in the murky area of socio-cultural ambiguity.

Deceptive Ambiguity Created by Cooperating Witnesses

Although Cullen Davis was owner of a company in which McCrory was only a mid-level employee, the two men possessed little or no important language and cultural differences. Unlike his father from whom he inherited the company, Davis was not the usual CEO. He mingled with the lower-level employees and chose his friends from among the working classes. For these reasons the tape-recordings of their conversations revealed no serious socio-cultural miscommunications.

In contrast, the investigation of Yochi Cohen displayed important socio-cultural contrasts. Cohen, born in Israel, was a second-language speaker of English. He managed syntax fairly well but was relatively weak at understanding the ambiguous inferences, nuances, and presuppositions made by the two native English-speaking cooperating witnesses. Despite this, he muddled his way through their hints about illegality well enough to distance himself from their inferences about any past illegal involvements or him about some of the other arms contractors they both knew. When the second cooperating witness tried to get him to bribe the Gabon minister of defense and to skip the process of obtaining the required export license, Cohen clearly rejected those offers to be personally involved in illegality. The prosecutor may not have understood Cohen's different sociolinguistic manner of rejecting the opportunity to bribe the Gabonian official, for he interpreted Cohen's odd and less than fully competent use of English as his ambiguous willingness to offer the kickback. But throughout this investigation the cooperating witnesses and eventually the prosecutor were the ones who created the deceptive ambiguity, for they were the ones who misunderstood the cross-cultural exchanges.

Because the first cooperating witness's major undercover strategy was to hint about illegality, his conversation with Yochi Cohen contained many referential ambiguities such as "happy generals in Peru," "taking care of this guy and that guy," and "between us girls," all without specific noun references. When the second cooperating witness took over, this ambiguity stopped, at which point Cohen strongly rejected that man's much clearer suggestion of offering a kickback to the Gabonian minister of defense. But even Cohen's rejection was misinterpreted as his agreement by the government representatives who may have been reflecting their own cross-cultural problems.

Although Marwan El-Hindi was fairly proficient in English, it was his second language. His use of English evidenced that he was not good at recognizing nuances provided by presuppositions, hints, and implicatures. Griffin, the cooperating witness, took full advantage of this and produced deceptively ambiguous language that the prosecution used to indict El-Hindi. Griffin and El-Hindi were from two very different cultures. Griffin was a native speaker of African American English who let El-Hindi believe that he wanted to learn more about Islam. He proposed two things that were attractive to El-Hindi. He said he wanted to learn more about Islam and that he could use his military background to aid El-Hindi's dream of building a school for Islamic children by providing physical education training for it.

El-Hindi's lack of American socio-cultural understanding contributed to his consistently missing Griffin's use of nuances, hints, presuppositions, and implicatures. Nevertheless, this somehow gave the prosecution the impression that he had agreed to help set up a terrorist cell to train people for violent jihad. Griffin's deceptive ambiguity also took advantage of El-Hindi's various emotional stresses growing out of his recent divorce, his inability to see his five children, his financial difficulties, and his non-native English skills that might allow him to achieve a clearer uptake about Griffin's indirectness and hints.

In both the Cohen and El-Hindi investigations, the prosecutor also apparently had great difficulty understanding the socio-cultural differences between the targets and the cooperating witnesses.

Deceptive Ambiguity Created by Complainants

There were no apparent socio-cultural differences between complainant Janice Chatterton and her targets, John Poli and John McNown. They were all familiar with the brothel business and their uses of English did not appear to provide any comprehension problems. Chatterton's refusal to understand Poli when he told her that they would not accept her bribe appeared to be deceptive ambiguity on her part that was not based on any confusion caused by sociolinguistic interference.

Dora and Sam were relatives, who no doubt shared the same socio-cultural context. The main socio-cultural problem stemmed from the inappropriateness of the setting of their first conversation. Dora initiated her confrontation call to Sam to the public space of his office, where he was socially handicapped in trying to respond to her highly sensitive, private topic of sexual abuse. This strategy of situating a private, intimate topic in a socially inappropriate public setting created deceptive ambiguity for Sam. He was immediately placed in a difficult social position in which it would have been easy for him to dismiss the significance of her call by agreeing with her accusation to get rid of her call and then to try to clarify the matter later in a private context. In past confrontation calls that I've analyzed, the strategy of initiating the call in a public setting is socially advantageous to the prosecution because the targets, who have no perception of the significance of the call and don't know that it is being recorded, tend to provide quick and less thoughtful responses in the effort to get rid of the caller as quickly and safely as possible. This socio-cultural strategy is commonly used in confrontation calls and it is likely that the investigators knew this and planned it that way, for in a public office space it would have been easy for Sam to have simply agreed to get rid of Dora's call without bothering to provide any exculpatory information. Trying to obtain a confession in a public context is clearly a deceptively ambiguous law enforcement violation of socio-cultural norms.

The complainant and Sheriff Preston worked in the same law enforcement office and no doubt shared most elements of their socio-cultural backgrounds. The major socio-cultural difference was that the sheriff was hard of hearing of which the complainant took full advantage. This is similar to the way the cooperating witness in the investigation of Cullen Davis took advantage of his target by lowering his voice when he was outside the car and therefore out of hearing range when he uttered on tape the words that led to Davis's prosecution.

REFERENCES

Adams, Susan and John P. Jarvis. 2006. "Indications of veracity and deception: an analysis of written statements made to police." *The International Journal of Speech, Language and Law* 13(1), 1–22.

Ainsworth, Janet. 2008. "You have the right to remain silent . . . but only if you ask it just so." *International Journal of Speech, Language and Law* 15(1), 1–15.

Ainsworth, Janet. 2010. "Curtailing coercion in police interrogation: the failed promise of Miranda v. Arizona." In *Handbook of Forensic Linguistics*, Malcolm Coulthard and Alison Johnson (eds.), 111–126. London: Routledge.

American Heritage Dictionary of the English Language. 2011 Fifth Edition. Houghton Mifflin Harcourt: New York.

Ariel, Mira. 1990. *Assessing NP Antecedents.* London: Routledge.

Atkinson, J. M. and Paul Drew. 1979. *Order in the Court: The Organization of Verbal Interaction in Judicial Settings*. London: Macmillan.

Austin, J. L. 1962. *How To Do Things with Words.* Cambridge, MA: Harvard University Press.

Bailin, Alan and Ann Grafstein. 2001. "The linguistic assumptions underlying readability formulae: a critique." *Language & Communication* 21, 285–301.

Bakhtin, M. 1981. *The Dialogic Imagination.* Austin: University of Texas Press.

Bartlett, Frederick. 1932. *Remembering: A Study in Experimental and Social Psychology.* Cambridge: Cambridge University Press.

Battistella, Edwin. 2014. *Sorry About That*. New York: Oxford University Press.

Baugh, John. 1983. *Black Street Speech.* Austin: University of Texas Press.

Berk-Seligson, Susan. 1990. *The Bilingual Courtroom: Court Interpreters in the Judicial Process.* Chicago: University of Chicago Press.

Berk-Seligson, Susan. 2009. *Coerced Confessions: The Discourse of Bilingual Police Interrogations.* Berlin: Mouton de Gruyter.

Black's Law Dictionary (8th ed.). 2004. St. Paul, MN: Thomson West.

Bogoch, Bryna. 1994. "Power, distance and solidarity: models of professional-client interaction in an Israeli legal aid setting." *Discourse and Society* 51(1), 65–88.

Bok, Sissela. 1982. *Lying*. New York: Vintage Books.

Briere, Eugene. 1978. "Limited English speakers and the Miranda rights." *TESOL Quarterly* 12, 235–245.

Brown, R. and A. Gillman. 1960. "The pronouns of power and solidarity." In *Style in Language*, T. Sebeok (ed.). Cambridge: MIT Press.

Brown, Gillian and George Yule. 1983. *Discourse Analysis.* Cambridge: Cambridge University Press.

Buller, D. B. and J. K. Burgoon. 1996. "Interpersonal deception theory." *Communication Theory* 6, 203–242.

Burbules, Nicholas.1984. "Toward a theory of power in education." In *Philosophy of Education*, Emily Robertson (ed.), 79–89. Normal, IL: Philosophy of Education Society.

Burgoon, J., J. Blair, T. Qin, and J. Nunamker. 2003. "Detecting deception through linguistic analysis." In *Proceedings of the Symposium on Intelligence and Security Informatics*, 91–101. New York: Springer-Verlag.

Carter, E. 2014. "When is a lie not a lie? When it's divergent." *Language and Law/Linguiagem e Direito* 1(1), 122–140.

Chafe, Wallace. 1972. "Discourse structure and human knowledge." In *Language Comprehension and the Acquisition of Knowledge*, Roy Freedle and John B. Carroll (eds.), 67–81. Washington, DC: V.H. Winston.

Chafe, Wallace. 1996. "Inferring identifiability and assessibility." In *Reference and Referent Accessibility*, Thorstein Fretheim and Jeanette Gundel (eds.). Amsterdam: John Benjamins.

Charow, Veda and Robert Charow. 1979. "Making legal language understandable: a psycholinguistic study of jury instructions." *Columbia Law Review* 79, 1306–1346.

Chomsky, Noam. 1965. *Aspects of a Theory of Syntax.* Cambridge, MA: MIT Press.

Cloud, Morgan. 1994. "The dirty little secret." *Emory Law School Journal,* 1311–1349.

Cole, Peter (ed.). 1978. *Syntax and Semantics, vol 9 Pragmatics*. New York: Academic Press.

Coleman, Linda and Paul Kay. 1981. "Prototype semantics: the English word lie." *Language* 57(1), 26–44.

Conley, John and William O'Barr. 1998. *Just Words: Language and Power.* Chicago: University of Chicago Press.

Cotterill, Janet. 2003. *Language and Power in Court.* Houndmills: Palgrave Macmillan.

Cruse, D. A. 1986. *Lexical Semantics*. Cambridge: Cambridge University Press.

Danet, Brenda and Byrna Bogoch. 1980. "Fixed fight or free-for-all? An empirical study of combativeness in the adversary system of justice." *British Journal of Law and Society* 7, 36–60.

DePaulo, B. M., J. J. Lindsey, B. E. Malone, L. Muhlenbruck, K. Charton, and H. Cooper. 2003. "Cues to deception." *Psychological Bulletin* 129(1), 74–118.

Dickson, Paul. 2003. *The Hidden Language of Baseball.* New York: Walker and Company.

Drew, P. and J. Heritage (eds.). 1992. *Talk and Work: Interaction in Institutional Settings*. Cambridge: Cambridge University Press.

Dumas, Bethany. 1992. "The adequacy of cigarette package warnings: An analysis of t he adequacy of federally mandated cigarette package warnings." *Tennesse Law Review* 59, 261–265.

Dumas, Bethany. 2000. "Jury trials: lay jurors, pattern jury instructions and comprehension issues." *Tennessee Law Review* 67(3), 701–742.

Eades, Diana. 2010. *Sociolinguistics and the Legal Process*. Bristol: Multilingual Matters.

Ehrlich, Susan. 2001. *Representing Rape: Language and Sexual Consent.* London: Routledge.

Ekman, Paul and W.V. Friesen. 1969. "Nonverbal leakage and clues to deception." *Psychiatr*, 32, 88–105.

Ekman, Paul, M. O'Sullivan, and M. Frank. 1999. "A few can catch a liar." *Psychological Science* 10, 263–266.

Ekman, Paul, M. O'Sullivan, W. V. Friesen, and K. Scherer. 1991. "Face, voice and body in detecting deception." *Journal of Non-verbal Behaviour* 15(2), 125–135.

Fairclough, Norman. 1989. "Language and power." In *Language and Social Life Series*, Christopher Candlin (ed.). New York: Longmans.
Fairclough, Norman. 2015. *Language and Power.* London: Routledge.
Farnsworth, Ward, Dustin Guzior, and Anup Malani. 2010. "Ambiguity about ambiguity." *Journal of Legal Analysis* 2(1), 1–43.
Fasold, Ralph. 1990. *Sociolinguistics of Language.* Cambridge: Basil Blackwell.
Felsenfeld, Carl and Alan Siegal. 1981. *Writing Contracts in Plain English.* St. Paul, MN: West.
Fillmore, Charles. 1968. "The case for case." In *Universals in Linguistic Theory,* Emmon Bach and Robert Harms (eds.), 1–88. New York: Holt, Rinehart and Winston.
Fowler, Roger. 1985. "Power." In *Handbook of Discourse Analysis*, Teun van Dijk (ed.), Vol. 4, 61–82.
Galasinski, Dariusz. 2000. *The Language of Deception.* Thousand Oaks, CA: Sage.
Galbraith, J. K. 1985. *The Anatomy of Power*. London: Corgi.
Garner, Bryan. 1995. *Dictionary of Modern Legal Usage.* New York: Oxford University Press.
Garner, Bryan. 2009. *Garner's Modern American Usage.* New York: Oxford University Press.
Gazdar, Gerald. 1979. *Pragmatics: Implicatures, Presupposition, and Logical Form.* New York: Academic Press.
Gibbons, John. 2003. *Forensic Linguistics: An Introduction to Language in the Justice System.* Oxford: Blackwell.
Giles, Howard and Nikolas Copeland. 1991. "Accommodation theory: communication, context, and consequence." In *Contexts of Accommodation*. Howard Giles, Justine Coupland, and Nikolas Copeland (eds.). New York: Cambridge University Press.
Goffman, Erving. 1974. *Frame Analysis.* New York: Harper and Row.
Green, Georgia. 1989. *Pragmatics and Natural Language Understanding.* Hillsdale NJ: Lawrence Earlbaum Associates.
Greene, Robert W. (1981). *Sting Man.* New York: Ballentine Books.
Grice, H. Paul. 1975. "Logic and conversation." In *Syntax and Semantics: Grammatical Relations*, Peter Cole and Jerry Morgan (eds.), Vol. 8, 41–58. New York: Academic Press.
Grice, H. Paul. 1989. *Studies in the Way of Words.* Cambridge, MA: Harvard University Press.
Gudjonsson, Gisli. 1993. *The Psychology of Interrogations, Confessions and Testimony.* New York: Wiley.
Gumperz, John. 1982. *Discourse Strategies.* Cambridge: Cambridge University Press.
Gumperz, John. 1990. *Language and Social Identity.* New York: Cambridge University Press.
Gumperz, John and Dell Hymes. 1964. *The Ethnography of Communication.* Washington, DC: American Anthropological Association.
Gumperz, John and Dell Hymes. 1972. *Directions in Sociolinguistics: The Ethnography of Communication.* New York: Holt, Rinehart and Winston.
Gundel, Jeanette, Nancy Hedberg, and Ron Zacharski. 1993. "Cognitive status and the form of referring expressions in discourse." *Language* 69, 274–307.
Hall, Harold V. and David A. Pritchard. 1996. *Detecting Malingering and Deception.* Boca Raton, FL: St. Lucie Press.
Handel, M. 1982. "Intelligence and deception." *Journal of Strategic Studies* 5/1, 122–154.
Hansel, Mark and Cheryl Ajirotutu. 1982. "Negotiating interpretations in inter-ethnic settings." In *Language and Social Identity*, John Gumperz (ed.), 85–94. Cambridge: Cambridge University Press.

Haworth, K. 2006. "The dynamics of power and resistance in police interview discourse." *Discourse and Society* 17(6), 739–759.

Heffer, Chris. 2005. *The Language of Jury Trial.* Houndmills: Palgrave Macmillan.

Heffer, Chris. 2015. "Authority and accommodation: Judicial responses to juror's questions." In *Speaking of Language and Law*, Lawrence Solan, Janet Ainsworth, and Roger Shuy (eds.), 289–292. New York: Oxford University Press.

Heffer, Chris, Frances Rock and John Conley (eds.). 2013. *Legal-Lay Communication.* New York: Oxford University Press.

Hess, John E. 1997. *Interviewing and Interrogation for Law Enforcement.* Cincinnati: Anderson Publishing.

Heydon, Georgina. 2005. *The Language of Police Interviewing: A Critical Analysis.* Basingstoke: Palgrave Macmillan.

Heydon, Georgina. 2011. "Silence: Civil right or social privilege? A discourse analytic response to a legal problem." *Journal of Pragmatics* 43(9), 2308–2316.

Heymann, Philip. 1984. "FBI Safeguards." In *FBI Undercover Operations: Report of the Subcommittee on Civil and Constitutional Rights of the Committee on the Judiciary, House of Representatives*, 36–39. Washington, DC: U.S. Government Printing Office.

Hockett, Charles. 1958. *A Course in Modern Linguistics.* New York: Macmillan.

Hopper, R. and R. A. Bell. 1984. "Broadening the deception concept." *Quarterly Journal of Speech* 70, 288–302.

Huddleson, Rodney and Geoffrey K. Pullum. 2002. *The Cambridge Grammar of the English Language*. Cambridge: Cambridge University Press.

Hymes, Dell. 1972. "Models of Interaction of language and social life." In *Directions in Sociolinguistics,* John Gumperz, Vera John, and Dell Hymes (eds.), 35–71. New York: Holt, Rinehart and Winston.

Inbau, Fred, John Reid, and Joseph Buckley. 1986. *Criminal Interrogations and Confessions.* Baltimore: Williams & Wilkins.

Kassin, Saul and Katherine Kiechel. 1991. "The social psychology of false confessions: Compliance, internalization, and confabulation." *Psychological Science* 7, 125–128.

Kates, Carol. 1980. *Pragmatics and Semantics: An Empiricist Theory.* Ithaca, NY: Cornell University Press.

Kecskes, Istvan. 2014. *Intercultural Pragmatics.* Oxford: Oxford University Press.

Keenan-Ochs, Elinor and Bambi Schieffelin. 1976. "Topic as discourse notion: a study of topic in the conversations of children and adults." In *Subject and Topic,* Charles Li (ed.). New York: Academic Press.

Klass, Gregory. 2012. "Meaning, purpose, and cause in the law of deception." *Georgetown Law Journal* 100, 449–496.

Kreedens, Krzysztof. 2015. "Scarlet letter or badge of honor? Semantic interpretation in changing contexts of culture." In *Speaking of Language and Law*, Lawrence Solan, Janet Ainsworth and Roger Shuy (eds.). New York: Oxford University Press.

Labov, William. 1972. *Sociolinguistic Patterns.* Philadelphia: University of Pennsylvania Press.

Leal, S. and A. Vrij. 2008. "Blinking during and after lying." *Journal of Non-verbal Behavior* 21, 87–102.

Leo, Richard. 2008. *Police Interrogation and American Justice*. Cambridge MA: Harvard University Press.

Leo, Richard and Richard Ofshe. 2001. "The truth about false confessions and advocacy scholarship." *The Criminal Law Bulletin*. 37, 293–370.

Levi, Judith and Anne G. Walker (eds.). 1990. *Language in the Judicial Process*. New York: Plenum.

Levinson, Stephen. 1983. *Pragmatics*. Cambridge: Cambridge University Press.

Lofus, Elizabeth. 1994. *The Myth of Repressed Memory: False Theories ad Allegations in Sexual Abuse*. New York: St. Martin's Press.

MacDonald, J. M. and D. L. Michaud. 1992. *The Confession: Interrogation and Criminal Profiles for Police Officers*. Denver: Apache Press.

Marder, Nancy. 2006. "Bringing jury instructions into the twenty-first century." *Notre Dame Law Review* 81, 449–511.

Marder, Nancy. 2009. "Jury reform: the impossible dream?" *Tennessee Journal of Law and Policy* 5, 149–183.

Matoesian, Gregory. 1993. *Reproducing Rape*. Chicago: University of Chicago Press.

Matoesian, Gregory. 2001. *Law and the Language of Identity: Discourse in the William Kennedy Smith Rape Trial*. New York: Oxford University Press.

Mellinkoff, David. 1953. "How to make contracts illegible." *Stanford Law Review* 5, 418–432.

Mellinkoff, David. 1963. *The Language of the Law*. Boston: Little, Brown and Company.

Merriam-Webster's Collegiate Dictionary. 2003 Eleventh Edition. Springfield MA: Merriam-Webster, Incorporated.

Miller, Norman and Donald Campbell. 1959. "Recency and primacy in persuasion of the timing of speakers and measurements." *The Journal of Abnormal Psychology*" 59(1), 1–9.

Mills, C. W. 1956. C.W. *The Power Elite*. New York: Oxford University Press.

Mumby. D. K. and R. P. Clair. 1997. "Organizational discourse." In *Discourse as Social Interaction Discourse Studies: A Multidisciplinary Introduction*, Teun van Dijk (ed.), Vol. 2, 181–205. London: Sage.

Nieland, Robert. 1979. *Pattern Jury Instructions: A Critical Look at a Modern Movement to Improve the Jury System*. Chicago: American Judicature Society.

Ng, Sik Hung and James J. Bradac. 1993. *Power in Language*. Newbury Park, CA: Sage.

O'Barr, William. 1982. *Linguistic Evidence: Language, Power, and Strategy in the Courtroom*. New York: Academic Press.

Pavlenko, Aneta. 2008. "I'm very not about the law part: non-native speakers and the Miranda Warnings." *TESOL Quarterly* 42(1), 1–30.

Philips, Susan U. 1998. *Ideology in the Language of Judges*. New York: Oxford University Press.

Picornell, I. 2013. "Analyzing deception in written witness statements." *Linguistic Evidence in Security, Law and Intelligence* 1(1), 41–50.

Polsky, Ned. 1969. *Hustlers, Beats, and Others*. New York: Doubleday.

Rabon, Don. 1994. *Investigative Discourse Analysis*. Durham, NC: Carolina Academic Press.

Rabon, Don. 1992. *Interviewing and Interrogation*. Durham, NC: Carolina Academic Press.

Reynolds, E. and J. Rendle-Short. 2010. "Cues to deception in context: Response latency/gaps in denials and blame shifting." *British Journal of Social Psychology*. 50(3), 431–449.

Roach, J. 2010. "Home is where the heart lies? A study of false address giving to the police." *Legal and Criminological Psychology* 15, 209–220.

Robinson, W. Peter. 1996. *Deceit, Delusion, and Detection*. Thousand Oaks, CA: Sage.

Rock, Frances. 2007. *Communicating Rights*. Houndmills: Palgrave Macmillan.

Rock, Frances. 2014. "Every link in the chain." In *Legal-Lay Communication*, 78–103. New York: Oxford University Press.

Roy, Cynthia. 2000. *Interpreting as a Discourse Phenomenon*. New York: Oxford University Press.

Rudacille, Wendell C. 1994. *Identifying Lies in Disguise*. Dubuque, IA: Kendall Hunt Publishing.

Sacks, Harvey, Emanuel Schedgloff, and Gail Jefferson. 1974. "A simplest systematics for the organization of turn-taking in conversation. *Language* 50, 696–735.

Sadock, Jerry and Arnold Zwicky. 1975. "Ambiguity tests and how to fail them." In *Syntax and Semantics*, Gregory Kimball (ed.), Vol. 4, 1 1–36). New York: Academic Press.

Schauer, Frederick. (2015). "On the relationship between legal and ordinary language." In *Speaking of Language and Law*, Lawrence Solan, Janet Ainsworth, and Roger Shuy (eds.). New York: Oxford University Press.

Scheflin, Alan W. 1998. *Memory, Trauma, Treatment and the Law*. Boston: Brown and Company.

Schiffrin, Deborah. 1987. *Discourse Markers*. Cambridge: Cambridge University Press.

Schober, M. and P. Glick. 2011. "Self-deceptive speech: A psycholinguistic view." In *Personality and Psychopathy: Critical Dialogues with David Shapiro*, I. C. Piers, (ed.). New York: Springer.

Schwarzer, William. 1981. "Communicating with juries: problems and remedies." *California Law Review* 69, 731–843.

Searle, John. 1969. *Speech Acts*. New York: Cambridge University Press.

Searle, John. 1975. "A taxonomy of illocutionary acts." In *Language, Mind and Knowledge*, K. Gunderson (ed.). Minneapolis: University of Minnesota Press.

Searle, John. 1979. *Expression and Meaning*. New York: Cambridge University Press.

Searle, John, Ferene Kiefer, and Manfred Bierwisch. 1980. *Speech Act Theory and Pragmatics*. Dordrech Holland: D. Reidel Publishing Company.

Searle, John. 1983. *Intentionality*. New York: Cambridge University Press.

Severance, Laurence and Elizabeth Loftus. 1982. "Improving the ability of jurors to comprehend and apply criminal jury instructions." *Law and Society Review* 17, 153–230.

Shane, Sanford. 2006. *Language and the Law*. New York: Continuum.

Sherzer, Joel. 1974. "Namakke, Sunmakke, Kormakke: Three types of Cuna speech event." In *Explorations in the Ethnography of Speaking*, Richard Bauman and Joel Sherzer (eds.), 263–282. London: Cambridge University Press.

Shuy, Roger W. 1982. "Topic as the unit of analysis in a criminal law case." In *Analyzing Discourse: Text and Talk*, Deborah Tannen (ed.), 113–126. Washington, DC: Georgetown University Press.

Shuy, Roger W. 1990. "Evidence of cooperation in conversation: topic-type in a solicitation to murder case." In *The Language Scientist as Expert in the Legal Setting*, Robert Reiber and William A. Stewart (eds.), vol. 606, 85–105. New York: Annals of the New York Academy of Sciences.

Shuy, Roger W. 1993. "Language evidence in distinguishing pilot error from product liability." *International Journal of the Sociology of Language* 100/101, 101–114.

Shuy, Roger W. 1997. "Ten unanswered questions about Miranda. *Forensic Linguistics* 4(2), 175–196.

Shuy, Roger W. 1998. *The Language of Confession, Interrogation, and Deception.* Thousand Oaks, CA: Sage.

Shuy, Roger W. 2005. *Creating Language Crimes*. New York: Oxford University Press.

Shuy, Roger W. 2008. *Fighting Over Words.* New York: Oxford University Press.

Shuy, Roger W. 2010. *The Language of Defamation Cases.* New York: Oxford University Press.

Shuy, Roger W. 2011. *The Language of Perjury Cases.* New York: Oxford University Press.

Shuy, Roger W. 2012. *The Language of Sexual Misconduct Cases.* New York: Oxford University Press.

Shuy, Roger W. 2013. *The Language of Bribery Cases.* New York: Oxford University Press.

Shuy, Roger W. 2014. *The Language of Murder Cases.* New York: Oxford University Press.

Shuy, Roger W. 2015. *The Language of Fraud Cases.* New York: Oxford University Press.

Sip, K. E., D. Carmel, J. L. Marchant, J. Le, P. Petrovic, A. Roepstorff, W. B. McGregor, and C. D. Frith. 2013. "When Pinocchio's nose does not grow: belief regarding lie-detectability modulates production of deception." *Frontiers in Neuroscience* 7, 16.

Slobogin, Christopher. 1996. "Police perjury and what to do about it." *University of Colorado Law Review* 67, 1037–1060.

Solan, Lawrence M. 1993. *The Language of Judges.* Chicago: University of Chicago Press.

Solan, Lawrence. 2001. "The written contract as safe harbor for dishonest conduct." *Chicago Kent Law Review* 77(1), 87–120.

Solan, Lawrence. 2004. "Pernicious ambiguity in contracts and statutes." *Chicago Kent Law Review* 79(3), 859–888.

Solan, Lawrence. 2009. "Blame, praise, and the structure of legal rules." *Brooklyn Law Review* 75(2), 517–543.

Solan, Lawrence. 2010. *The Language of Statutes: Laws and their Interpretation.* Chicago: University of Chicago Press.

Solan, Lawrence. 2012. "Lawyers as insincere (but truthful) actors." *The Journal of the Legal Professions* 36(Spring), 487–527.

Solan, Lawrence. 2014. "Multilingualism and morality in statutory interpretation." *Language and Law: Linguagem e Diretto* 1(1), 5–17.

Solan, Lawrence and Peter Tiersma. 2005. *Speaking of Crime.* Chicago: University Chicago Press.

Sontag, Lorelei. 1990. *Deciding Death: A Legal and Empirical Analysis of Penalty Phase Jury Instructions and Capital Decision-making.* Ann Arbor, MI: University Microfilms International.

Stanford Encyclopedia of Philosophy. 2014. Stanford, CA: Center for the Study of Language and Information.

Stuntz, W. J. 2001. "Miranda's mistake." *Michigan Law Review* 99, 975–999.

Su, S. P. 1994. *Lexical Ambiguity in Poetry*. London: Longman.

Tannen, Deborah. 1987. "Remarks on discourse and power." In *Power Through Discourse*, Leah Kedar (ed.). Norwood, NJ: Ablex.

Tannen, Deborah. 1994. *Gender and Discourse.* New York: Oxford University Press.

Tannen, Deborah. 1998. *The Argument Culture.* New York: Random House.

Tannen, Deborah. 2005. *Conversational Style.* New York: Oxford University Press.

Therborn, G. 1980. *The Ideology of Power and the Power of Ideology*. London: Verso.

Thomas, G. C. 2004. "History's lesson for the right to counsel." *University of Illinois Law Review*, 545–597.

Thurber, James. 1965. *My World and Welcome to It.* New York: Harcourt Brace Jovanovich.

Tiersma, Peter. 1987. "The language of defamation." *Texas Law Review* 66, 303–350.

Tiersma, Peter. 1990. "The language of perjury: literal truth ambiguity and the false statement." *Southern California Law Review* 63, 373–431.

Tiersma, Peter. 1995a. "Dictionaries and Death: Do Capital Jurors Understand Mitigation?" *Utah Law Review* 1, 1995–2060.

Tiersma, Peter. 1995b. "The ambiguity of interpretation: distinguishing interpretation from construction." *Washington Law Quarterly* 73, 1095–1101.

Tiersma, Peter. 1999. *Legal Language.* Chicago: University of Chicago Press.

Tiersma, Peter. 2001. "The rocky road to legal reform: improving the language of jury instructions." *Brooklyn Law Review* 66, 1079–1118.

Tiersma, Peter. 2006. "Some myths about legal language." *Journal of Law, Culture and Humanities* 2, 9–50.

Tiersma, Peter. 2007. "The language of consent in rape law." In *The Language of Sexual Crime,* Janet Cotterill (ed.), 83–103. Houndmills: Palgrave.

Tiersma, Peter. 2009. "Asking jurors to do the impossible." *Tennessee Journal of Law and Policy* 5, 105–147.

Tiersma, Peter. 2010. *Parchment, Paper, Pixels.* Chicago: University of Chicago Press.

Uviller, R. H. 1996. *Virtual Justice: The Flawed Prosecution of Crime in America.* New Haven, CT: Yale University Press.

Van Dijk, Teun. 1977. "Sentence topic and discourse topic." *Papers in Slavic Philology* 1, 49–61.

van Dijk, Teun. 1985. *Handbook of Discourse.* Vol. 1, *Disciplines of Discourse.* London: Academic Press.

van Dijk, Teun. 2001. "A plea for diversity." In *Methods of Critical Discourse Analysis*, Ruth Wodak and Michael Meyer (eds.). London: Sage.

van Dijk, Teun. 2008. *Discourse Power.* Houndmills, Basingstoke: Palgrave Macmillan.

Villar, G., J. Arciulia, and H. Paterson. 2013. "Vocal pitch production during lying: beliefs about deception matter. *Psychiatry, Psychology and Law* 20(1), 123–132.

Vrij, A. and P. A. Granhag. 2012. "Eliciting cues to deception and truth: what matters are the questions asked." *Journal of Applied Research in Memory and Cognition* 1, 110–117.

Vrij, A. and S. Mann. 2001. "Who killed my relative? Police officer's ability to detect real-life, high stake lies." *Psychology, Crime and Law* 7(2), 119–132.

Walker, Anne Graffam. 1990. "Bilingual court proceedings: the role of the court interpreter." In *Language in the Judicial Process*, Judith Levi and Anne G. Walker (eds.), 203–244. New York: Plenum.

Walters, Stan B. 1996. *Principles of Kinesic Interview and Interrogation.* Boca Raton, FL: CRC Press.

Wascher, James D. 2005. "The long march toward Plain English jury instructions." *Chicago Bar Association Record*, Feb./Mar., 50–54.

Weber, M. 1947. *The Theory of Social Power and Economic Organization* (T. Parsons, trans.). London: Allen & Unwin.

White, D. M. 1976. *The Concept of Power.* Morristown, NJ: General Learning Press.

White, W. S. 1979. "Police trickery in inducing confessions." *University of Pennsylvania Law Review* 127, 581–629.

White, J. B. 1982. "Miranda's failure to restrain pernicious interrogation practices." *Michigan Law Review* 99, 1211–1247.

Wigmore, John H. 1904. *Evidence in Trials at Common Law* (4th ed.). Boston: Little Brown.

Wolfram, Walt and Ralph Fasold. 1974. *The Study of Social Dialects in American English.* Englewood Cliffs, NJ: Prentice Hall.

Wrong, D. H. 1979. *Power: Its Forms, Bases, and Uses.* Oxford: Blackwell.

Zukerman. M., DePaulo, B., and Rosenthal, R. 1981. "Verbal and non-verbal communication of deception. In *Advances in Experimental Psychology*, L. Berkowitz (ed.), 141–159. New York: Academic Press.

Zwicky, Arnold and Jerry Sadock. 1975. "Ambiguity tests and how to fail them." In *Syntax and Semantics*, Gregory Kimball (ed.), Vol. 4, 1–36. New York: Academic Press.

INDEX

Adams, Susan, 16
agendas, 9, 24–25, 77, 82–83, 89–90, 113, 119, 129–130, 135, 143, 151, 158–159, 166, 174, 188–189, 201–205, 227–228
Ainsworth, Janet, 46, 50, 69
Ajirotutu, Cheryl, 30
ambiguity, 4–10, 13–14, 48
  camouflaged, 34
  discourse, 17–19
  interpreting, 7
  language, 13, 15–17
  by police, 8–10, 67–72
  power of, 37–41
  research on, 61–66
  seen by law, 49–51
  seen by linguists, 52–55
  spoken, 11–12
  written, 10–11
American Heritage Dictionary of the English Language, 57
Arciula, J., 61
Ariel, Mira, 52
Atkinson, J. M., 43
Austin, J. L., 20, 29
authority, 38–39, 44–47, 51, 69, 80, 86–87, 96, 105, 144, 146, 235–238

Bailin, Alan, 51
Bakhtin, M., 18
Bartlett, Frederick, 20, 22, 70
Batistella, Edwin, 30
Baugh, John, 241
Bell, R. A., 3, 14
Berk-Seligson, Susan, 45, 69
Black's Law Dictionary, 7, 56, 58
blocking, 9, 13, 30, 44, 65, 71, 83, 84, 91, 107–108, 114, 120, 131, 153, 159, 167, 190, 210–214, 225–233, 236, 238
Bogach, Bryna, 34, 41, 43, 45, 239
Bok, Sissela, 3, 58
Boyne City, G&A. R Co. v. Anderson, 123
Bradac, James, 43
Briere, Eugene, 69
Bronson v. United States, 60
Brown, R., 26–29
Buller, D. B., 4, 15, 61
Burbules, Nicholas, 39
Burgoon, J. K., 4, 15, 61

camouflage, 4, 5, 8, 10, 13, 34, 40–43, 47–48, 55, 62–63, 66, 148, 163, 193, 196–198, 200–218, 221, 226, 234, 236–237
Carter, E., 16
Carter, Michael, 80–85
causals, 99, 216
Chafe, Wallace, 20, 25, 52
Charrow, Robert, 11, 50
Charrow, Veda, 11, 50
Chomsky, Noam, 18
Clair, R. P., 39
Cloud, Morgan, 6
coercion, 4, 6, 45, 62, 70, 71, 78, 233
Cohen, Yochanan, 153–160
Cole, Peter, 29
Coleman, Linda, 3, 14, 58
complainants, 10, 17, 19, 35, 41, 147, 170, 176–177, 179, 182, 187–191, 193, 197, 201–202, 205, 209, 214, 218–219, 224, 226, 228, 230, 232, 234–235, 238, 246–247
compliance, 3, 14, 62, 80
confirmation call, 176, 179
Conley, John, 37, 38, 46
context, 2, 7, 8, 9, 11–23, 25, 26, 29, 33, 38–43, 48–55, 59, 60, 65, 67, 73, 78–79, 81, 87, 92, 93, 99, 105, 108–109, 114, 132, 144–145, 150–152, 175, 179, 182, 186, 189, 200, 206, 215–219, 221–225, 227, 229–231, 233, 235, 237–239, 246–247
control, 12, 38–39, 41–44, 65, 71, 85, 106, 108, 120, 195, 201–203, 227, 235–236
conversational strategies, 9, 30–31, 78, 83–84, 107–108, 114, 120, 131, 137, 153, 159, 167, 175, 181, 190, 209–214, 230–232
cooperating witness, 10, 19, 41, 111, 132, 133, 147–149, 151, 153 161, 165, 167, 169, 170, 188, 193, 196–197, 199, 200–205, 208, 213–214, 218, 224, 226, 230, 232, 234–235, 238, 245–247
cooperative principle, 4, 5, 15, 30, 54
Cotterill, Janet, 38, 44, 69
Coupland, Nicholas, 244
Cruse, D. A., 54

Danet, Brenda, 43, 45
Davis, T. Cullen, 149–153
deception, 3–6, 14–19, 33–35, 47–48, 55–66, 67, 70–72, 74, 76, 78, 80, 120, 135, 150, 180, 196, 197, 207, 210, 221, 227, 228, 230, 238, 239
deceptive ambiguity, 73
  by cooperating witnesses, 147–168
  by complainants, 169–192
  effects of, 221–240
  frequency of, 233–235
  by police interviewers, 61–100
  by prosecutors, 101–122
  socio-cultural differences, 241–247
  by undercover agents, 123–146
DeLorean, John Z., 132–139
DePaulo, B. M., 61
Dickson, Paul, 56
discourse, 8, 10, 13, 18–20, 24–25, 30
  ambiguity, 52
  context, 9, 10, 17, 33, 38, 93, 197, 114, 152, 215, 218–219, 223–235
  elements, 9, 18, 24, 29, 31–32, 222, 239
  macro, 42
  markers, 26, 29
  micro, 42
  power, 37–38, 40, 41, 227, 237
domination, 20, 38–39, 40, 42, 44, 46–47, 236
Drew, Paul, 21, 43, 61
Dumas, Bethany, 11, 50, 51

Eades, Diana, 46, 69
Ehrlich, Susan, 38
Ekman, Paul, 16, 61
El-Hindi, Marwan, 160–168
External cooperating witness, 147–149, 153, 160

Fairclough, Norman, 37, 39, 237
Farnsworth, Ward, 50
Fasold, Ralph, 241
FBI operations, 17, 124–128, 130–135, 139, 154–161, 165, 171–173, 204, 212, 222, 244
felicity conditions, 30, 206
Felsenfeld, Carl, 11
Fillmore, Charles, 20, 22
Foreign Corrupt Practices Act, 154
Fowler, Roger, 38
Frank, M., 16
Friesen, W. V., 16, 61

Galasinski, Dariusz, 3, 14, 61
Galbraith, J. K., 38
Garner's Modern English Usage, 57
Gazdar, Gerald, 29
Gentry, Larry, 109–115
Gibbons, John, 45, 69
Giles, Howard, 244
Glick, P., 61
Goffman, Erving, 20, 22
Grafstein, Ann, 51
Granhag, P. A., 17
Green, Georgia, 29
Greene, Robert, 148
Grice, H. P., 4–5, 8, 15, 25, 30, 54
Gudjonsson, Gisli, 46
Gumperz, John, 20, 27, 70
Gundel, Jeanette, 50
Guzior, Dustin, 50

Hall, Harold, 16
Handel, M., 3, 14
Hansel, Mark, 30
Haworth, Kate, 46
Hedberg, Nancy, 50
Heffer, Chris, 38, 50
Heritage, J., 21, 61
Hess, John, 16
Heydon, Georgina, 61, 69
Heymann, Philip, 17
hidden, 1, 37, 43, 47, 63, 153, 183, 194, 202. 213, 220, 221, 237
hit and run, 30, 44, 65, 91, 108, 137, 159, 210, 211, 225, 231, 237
Hockett, Charles, 25
Hopper, R., 3, 14
Hymes, Dell, 20, 21, 21, 27
hypotheticals, 7, 54, 91, 96, 97, 99, 215

illocutionary acts, 6, 29, 30, 45, 64
inequality, 37–38, 40, 42, 47, 235
inference, 7, 21, 53, 57, 64, 74, 78, 84, 164, 166, 227, 245
intentionality, 3–4, 9, 10, 23–27, 32–34, 173, 193, 219, 221–230
internal cooperating witness, 147, 149
interpretation, 2, 4, 7, 9, 13–16, 19, 22–23, 31, 38–39, 45–49, 50–58, 60, 62, 65, 67, 70, 91, 96, 99–101, 104, 107, 110, 113–114, 116, 118, 120, 126, 131, 136, 139, 151, 162–163, 167, 171, 174–175, 179, 181–185, 190–191, 200, 206–209, 212, 214, 216–219, 222–224, 228–229, 245–246
intonation, 29, 45, 108, 218
inverted pyramid, 31–34, 104, 139, 187, 193–220, 221–222, 232–235, 238, 241

Jarvis, John, 16
Jefferson, Gail, 20
Jokic, Dragon, 85–100

Kates, Carol, 20, 25, 26
Kay, Paul, 3, 14, 58

Kecskes, Istvan, 8, 22, 33, 241
Keenan-Ochs, Elinor, 20, 25
King et al. v. Burwell, 8
Klass, Gregory, 58
Kreedens, Krzysztof, 7

Labov, William, 241
Leal, S., 61
Leo, Richard, 46, 60
Leonard, Robert, 35, 118
Levi, Judith, 11
Levinson, Stephen, 29, 52
lexicon and grammar, 31, 79–80, 84–85, 91–100, 108, 115, 120–121, 132, 138–139, 144–146, 153, 160, 176, 182, 190, 215–219, 223–225
Loftus, Elizabeth, 11, 169

MacDonald, J. M., 16
macro-level, 25, 27, 37, 38, 41, 42, 58, 238
Malani, Anup, 50
Mann, S., 16
Marder, Nancy, 50
Matoesian, Gregory, 38, 44, 50
McNown, John, 170–176
Mellinkoff, 11, 49, 59
Merriam-Webster's Collegiate Dictionary, 57
Michaud, D. L., 16
micro-level, 25, 38, 42, 58, 238, 239
Mills, C. W., 38
Miranda, 50, 68, 69, 79, 215, 243
Mumby, D. K., 39
Muscarrello v. United States, 51

Nieland, Robert, 11
Ng, Sik Hung, 43

O'Barr, William, 37, 38, 44, 46
Oldhorn, Clifford, 1–3, 9
ordinary person, 51
Organized Crime Control Act, 123
O'Sullivan, M., 16, 61
outsider cooperating witness, 154, 161

Patterson, H., 61
Pavlenko, Aneta, 69
persuasion, 9, 38, 40, 42, 47, 58–60, 83, 232, 235
Philips, Susan, 43
Picornell, I., 61
Poli, John, 170–176
police interview, 3, 5, 7, 8, 10, 12, 15, 16, 17, 21, 31, 34, 43, 51, 59–61, 63, 65, 67–72, 76, 77, 81–86, 89, 91, 100–101, 112, 194, 198–199, 201–202, 206, 210–212, 215, 219, 220, 222–223, 226–228, 234–237, 239, 242
Polsky, Ned, 148
power, 12, 37–38, 221
  erosion of, 41–42
  hidden, 47–48
  language, 12, 221
  perceptions of, 40–41
  role of, 235–236
  shifting, 42–43
  transparent, 43–46
  unrecognized, 237–239
predisposition, 9, 22–25, 32–34, 40, 48, 63, 135–136, 142–143, 152–155, 161, 171, 185, 179, 184, 193, 197–202, 204, 219, 221–230, 233–236, 244
Pritchard, David, 16
prosecutors, 1–10, 12, 14–17, 19, 23, 25, 31, 33, 34, 38–41, 43, 54, 56, 58–60, 62, 64–66, 70, 72–78, 83–89, 92, 93–99, 101–121, 124, 130–132, 136, 144, 148, 150–153, 155, 159–160, 164–166, 168, 170–172, 174–175, 179, 181, 184–185, 190–191, 193–195, 198–200, 202–203, 207–219, 221–224, 226–229, 231–238, 242–243, 245

Rabon, Don, 16
reasonable person, 7
recovered memory, 169
referencing, 18, 44, 50, 52, 54, 61, 65, 71, 91, 97, 105, 170, 176, 215, 216, 217
Reid Technique, 16
reinterpretation, 38–39, 42, 47, 235, 242
Rendel-Short, J., 61
Reynolds, E., 61
Roach, J., 16
Robinson, W. Peter, 3, 14, 58
Rock, Francis, 37, 38, 69
Rogers, Kevin, 72–80
Roy, Cynthia, 69
Rudacille, Wendell, 16

Sacks, Harvey, 20, 29
Sadock, Jerry, 54
Scheflin, Alan, 169
Schegloff, Emanuel, 20
Schemas, 8, 9, 11, 13, 18, 20, 22–23, 24, 25, 29, 30, 32–36, 38, 42, 52, 53, 55, 62, 64, 65, 70–71, 76, 82, 87, 88, 100–101, 105–107, 112–113, 118–119, 129, 130, 135, 143, 146, 152, 155, 158, 165, 173–174, 179, 188, 191, 193, 194, 197–201, 203, 215, 222, 225–226, 234, 238–239, 241
Schieffelin, Bambi, 20, 25
Schober, M., 61
Schwarzer, William, 11
Scientific Content Analysis, 16
scripting, 9, 31, 127, 130, 144, 146, 212–213, 236, 232

Searle, John, 3, 20, 29, 30, 54, 64, 131
secrecy, 4, 14, 61, 62
Severance, Laurance, 11
Shane, Sanford, 50
Sherzer, Joel, 21
Shuy, Roger W., 9, 10, 11, 16, 17, 20, 21, 25, 27, 30, 33, 44, 45, 46, 60, 63, 69, 70, 71, 81, 109, 125, 127, 132, 145, 149, 153, 159, 170, 210, 222, 227, 230
Sica, Joseph, 115–121
Siegal, Alan, 11
sincerity, 5–6, 58
Sip, K. E., 61
Sligh, Vaughn, 139–146
Slobogin, Christopher, 6, 58
smoking guns, 7, 9, 33, 133, 136. 139, 150, 152, 163, 180, 215, 218, 222–225, 232
Solan, Lawrence, 5, 11, 19, 43, 52, 57, 60, 69
Sontag, Lorelei, 11
Sorells v. United States, 222
speech acts, 6, 8, 9, 10, 11, 13, 18, 20, 23, 29–30, 32–33, 34, 38, 42, 44, 52, 54, 62, 64–66, 68, 71, 77–79, 83, 87, 90, 100, 107, 113, 119, 130, 132, 136, 143, 146, 152, 155, 159, 166, 175, 180, 189, 193, 206–209, 215, 219, 221–222, 225, 227–230, 234–235, 238, 239
speech events, 8–13, 18, 20–25, 27, 29, 31–34, 38, 42, 44, 52–54, 59, 62–63, 65–68, 70–71, 76, 81–82, 87–88, 100, 104–106, 108, 112, 116, 118–120, 127–129, 132, 134–135, 142–143, 146, 151–152, 153–155, 157–158, 165, 170, 173, 179, 187–188, 193–197, 199, 200, 215, 219, 221–222, 225–227, 234–239
statement analysis, 16
Stewart, Potter, 54
Su, S. P., 53
Suyat, Stephen, 102–109

Tannen, Deborah, 20, 42
Therborn, G., 38
Thurber, James, 37
Tiersma, Peter, 7, 11, 49, 50, 52, 60, 69
topic analysis, 8, 9, 11, 13, 20, 23–24, 25–29, 31, 32, 44, 45, 47, 52, 62–72, 77, 81, 95, 104, 106, 113, 126, 129, 130, 135, 137–138, 143, 150, 151, 152, 155, 158, 159, 166, 167, 170, 174, 176, 179, 180, 181, 182–186, 188, 201–202, 203, 204, 205, 206, 214, 218, 227, 229, 230, 236, 246
transparent, 7–8, 10, 13, 16, 34–37, 41, 43, 46, 47, 55, 62, 66–67, 85, 123, 148, 193–195, 198, 200–203, 210–211, 215–216, 221, 234–239

undercover agents, 3, 4, 5, 6, 9, 10, 12, 14, 17, 19, 31, 33, 39, 41, 43, 47, 48, 56, 58, 60, 63, 64, 65, 114, 123–124, 131–132, 139, 141, 144, 146, 164–165, 168, 188, 191, 193, 196, 203, 207, 212, 217, 223–224, 227–229, 233–239, 243
United States v. Poehlman, 223

van Dijk, Teun, 19, 20, 24, 37, 38, 39, 42, 44, 70, 238
Villar, R. H., 61
voluntariness, 9, 32–34, 165, 193, 219, 221–224, 225–234
Vrij, A., 16, 17, 61

Walker, Anne G., 11, 45, 46
Wascher, James D., 50
Weber, M., 39
White, D. M., 38
White, W. S., 60
Williams, Harrison A., 124–132
Wrong, D. H., 38

Yule, George, 26–29

Zacharski, Ron, 50
Zuckerman, M., 3, 14
Zwicky, Arnold, 54